W9-CHP-907

PRAISE FOR
Cleveland Golfer's Bible

"Looking for something new and challenging in the world of golf? Look no further than the *Cleveland Golfer's Bible*" – **Sun Newspapers**

"An informative and superbly written guide for those on the quest for the 'one good one.'" – **Scene**

"For golfers looking to broaden their experiences in course-laden northeast Ohio, the *Cleveland Golfer's Bible* is a worthwhile investment. – **The Plain Dealer**

"A comprehensive guide to all things golf in Northern Ohio." – **Northern Ohio Live**

"If you're an avid golfer, this book is bound to become the most useful thing you own next to your pitching wedge." – **West Life**

"Tidyman holds back no punches." – **The Bulletin**

Also by John H. Tidyman:

Golf Getaways from Cleveland

Cleveland Golfer's Bible 5th EDITION

John H. Tidyman

GRAY & COMPANY, PUBLISHERS
CLEVELAND

For Yoshiro Takaoka, M.D., PH.D.,
a man of grace

Copyright © 2002 by John H. Tidyman
Maps copyright © 2002 by Gray & Company, Publishers

All rights reserved. No part of this book may be
reproduced or transmitted in any form or manner
without written permission from the publisher, except
in the case of brief quotations embodied in critical
articles and reviews.

Gray & Company, Publishers
1588 E. 40th St.
Cleveland, OH 44103-2302
www.grayco.com

Library of Congress
Cataloging-in-Publication Data
Tidyman, John H.–
Cleveland golfer's bible / John H. Tidyman.—5th ed.
Includes index.
1. Golf courses—Ohio—Cleveland Metropolitan
Area—Directories. I. Title.
GV983.C57T53 1997b   796.352'06'877132—dc21
99-6235

ISBN 1-886228-56-6
Printed in the United States of America

Contents

Introduction

This book was researched and written to guide players to the incredible wealth of golf that makes Greater Cleveland a duffer's paradise. There is no instruction between the covers. That's for the professionals. What is presented here is an armchair tour, a smorgasbord of golf.

We live in a region that offers a wealth of opportunity to pursue our favorite pastime. We have golf courses in quantity, and in quality, too. We play in valleys, on plains, and over hills—golfing terrain that was created when the glaciers slid across North America, scooping out water hazards such as the Great Lakes.

Players familiar with these courses will compare notes and perhaps take issue with the author.

Many of us, though, do ourselves a regular disservice by sticking with just a few courses where we are already comfortable. It can take a long time to find out through trial and error which courses we like best, so it's natural to want to spend our playing time on layouts we *know* we're going to enjoy.

This book should help you discover some new places to enjoy.

The data and descriptions are meant to give the inside scoop on courses that can mean the difference between a wasted trip and a pleasant round. No more trips to courses that are pushovers or too difficult; too crowded or too expensive. Anyone who's spent time and money getting to a course where a golf disaster awaited knows how valuable such information can be.

No advertising or sponsorship was solicited for this guide, nobody paid to be in it, and no restraints were placed on the author. Still, it is a bit subjective.

The author thanks all those who called or wrote with suggestions on the first four editions and hopes this fifth edition will inspire additional comment.

Cleveland
Golfer's
Bible
5TH EDITION

Maps

Areas Covered in this Book:

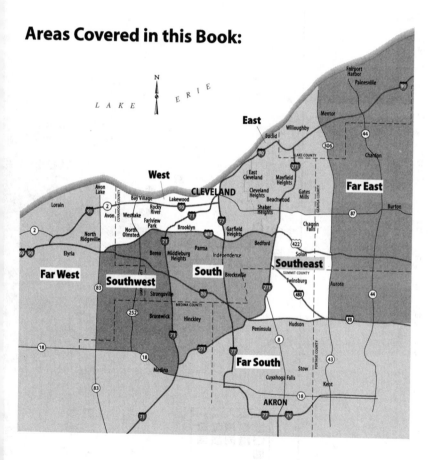

Public Golf Course

Private Golf Course

LAKE ERIE

CLEVELAND

Avon Lake

Lakewood

Lorain

Westlake

Berea

Elyria

Strongsville

Parma

Brunswick

MEDINA COUNTY

Medina

Not shown on map:
4 8 32 61 63
76 90 122 137 139
140

Areas
E . . . East
FE . . . Far East
FrE . . Farther East
W . . . West
FW . . Far West
FrW . . Farther West

S . . . South
FS . . Far South
FrS . . Farther South
SW . . Southwest
SE . . . Southeast

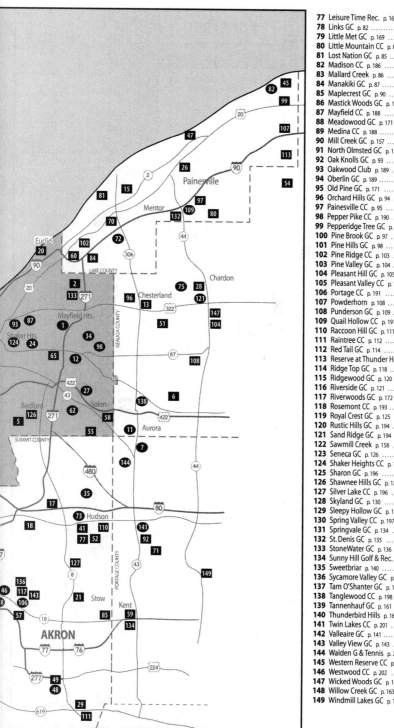

MAPS

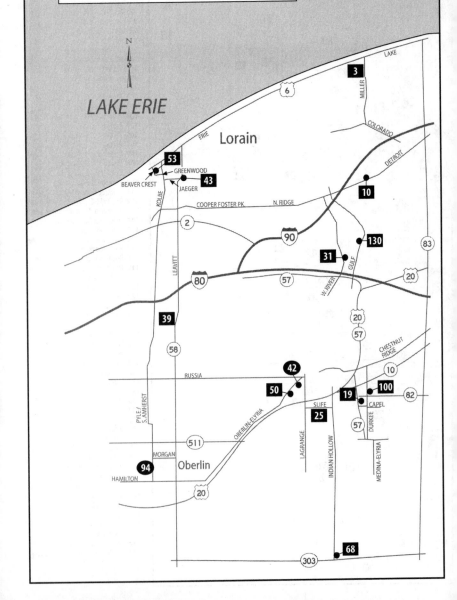

Far West

3	Aqua Marine CC p. 165	**43**	Emerald Valley GC p. 166
10	Avondale GC p. 28	**50**	Forest Hills GC p. 61
19	Brentwood GC p. 40	**53**	FoxCreek GC p. 66
25	Carlisle GC p. 47	**68**	Indian Hollow Lake GC p. 79
31	Cherry Ridge GC p. 166	**94**	Oberlin GC p. 189
39	Deer Track GC p. 52	**100**	Pine Brook GC p. 97
42	Elyria CC p. 181	**130**	Spring Valley CC p. 197

LAKE ERIE

Lorain

Oberlin

MAPS

West

9	Avon Oaks CC p. 174	86	Mastick Woods GC p. 170
14	Big Met Public GC p. 32	88	Meadowood GC p. 171
16	Bob-O-Link GC p. 35	91	North Olmsted GC p. 171
66	Hilliard Lakes GC p. 77	112	Red Tail GC p. 114
74	Lakewood CC p. 185	131	Springvale GC p. 134
78	Links GC p. 82	135	Sweetbriar p. 140
79	Little Met GC p. 169	146	Westwood CC p. 202

N

LAKE ERIE

135 JAYCOX

LORAIN COUNTY BRADLEY CROCKER / BASSETT

2 252 146

LEAR NAGLE

9 HILLIARD

DETROIT CLAGUE 90

20

14

74

CUYAHOGA COUNTY CENTER RIDGE

Westlake OLD LORAIN PURITAS

16

66 88 DOVER CENTER 10 MASTICK 79 86

83

112 71 42

480

BUTTERNUT RIDGE VALLEY PWKY

CANTERBURY

91 131

FITCH JOHN 78

80 Berea

East

1	Acacia CC p. 173	**81**	Lost Nation GC p. 85
2	Airport Greens GC p. 23	**84**	Manakiki GC p. 87
12	Beechmont CC p. 175	**87**	Mayfield CC p. 188
20	Briardale Greens GC p. 42	**93**	Oakwood Club p. 189
24	Canterbury GC p. 177	**96**	Orchard Hills GC p. 94
34	Country Club, The p. 178	**98**	Pepper Pike CC p. 190
60	Green Ridge GC p. 168	**102**	Pine Ridge CC p. 103
65	Highland Park GC p. 75	**124**	Shaker Heights CC p. 195
70	Johnny Cake Ridge GC p. 168	**133**	StoneWater GC p. 136
72	Kirtland CC p. 184		

N

LAKE ERIE

Euclid

HODGSON

LOST NATION **81**

PELTON

70

KIRTLAND

72

91   2

BRIARDALE **20**

BABBITT

60   RIDGE   **102**

MAPLE GROVE

306

90

20

BISHOP

EDDY

WHITE

84

LAKE COUNTY

2

ABERDEEN

133

WILSON MILLS

96

CAVES

CUYAHOGA COUNTY   GEAUGA COUNTY

271

MAYFIELD

322

MAYFIELD

93

87 **1**   Mayfield Hts.

CEDAR

FAIRMOUNT

34

24

98

S. WOODLAND

COURTLAND

CHAGRIN

91

124

65

12

87

77

WARRENSVILLE CTR.

GREEN

RICHMOND

LANDER

SOM CENTER

271

MAPS

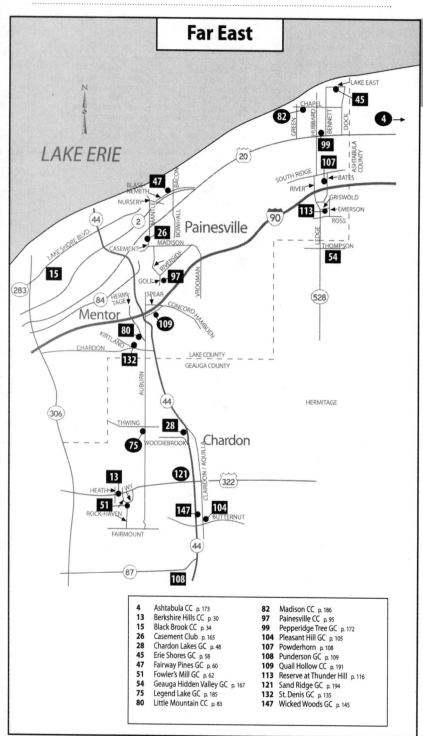

Far East

4	Ashtabula CC p. 173	**82**	Madison CC p. 186
13	Berkshire Hills CC p. 30	**97**	Painesville CC p. 95
15	Black Brook CC p. 34	**99**	Pepperidge Tree GC p. 172
26	Casement Club p. 165	**104**	Pleasant Hill GC p. 105
28	Chardon Lakes GC p. 48	**107**	Powderhorn p. 108
45	Erie Shores GC p. 58	**108**	Punderson GC p. 109
47	Fairway Pines GC p. 60	**109**	Quail Hollow CC p. 191
51	Fowler's Mill GC p. 62	**113**	Reserve at Thunder Hill p. 116
54	Geauga Hidden Valley GC p. 167	**121**	Sand Ridge GC p. 194
75	Legend Lake GC p. 185	**132**	St. Denis GC p. 135
80	Little Mountain CC p. 83	**147**	Wicked Woods GC p. 145

MAPS

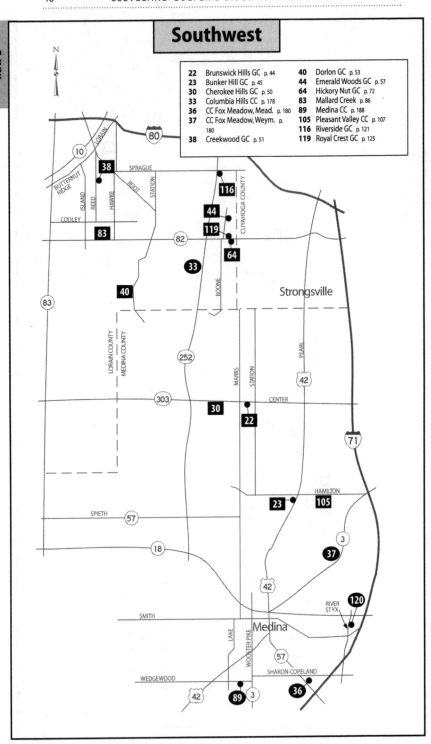

Southwest

22	Brunswick Hills GC p. 44	40	Dorlon GC p. 53
23	Bunker Hill GC p. 45	44	Emerald Woods GC p. 57
30	Cherokee Hills GC p. 50	64	Hickory Nut GC p. 72
33	Columbia Hills CC p. 178	83	Mallard Creek p. 86
36	CC Fox Meadow, Mead. p. 180	89	Medina CC p. 188
37	CC Fox Meadow, Weym. p. 180	105	Pleasant Valley CC p. 107
38	Creekwood GC p. 51	116	Riverside GC p. 121
		119	Royal Crest GC p. 125

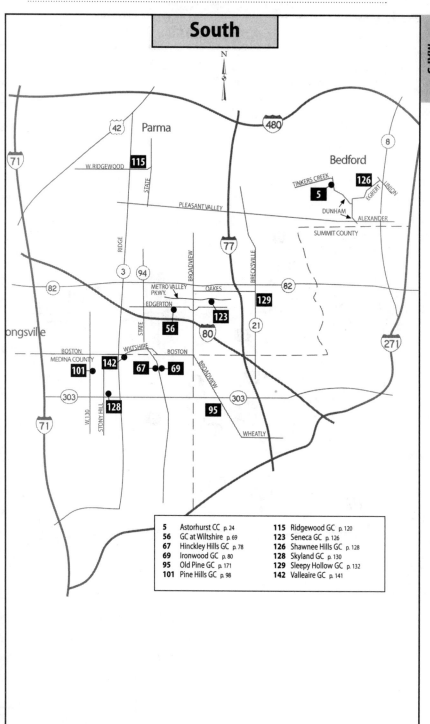

South

N

Parma

Bedford

MAPS

5 Astorhurst CC p. 24
56 GC at Wiltshire p. 69
67 Hinckley Hills GC p. 78
69 Ironwood GC p. 80
95 Old Pine GC p. 171
101 Pine Hills GC p. 98

115 Ridgewood GC p. 120
123 Seneca GC p. 126
126 Shawnee Hills GC p. 128
128 Skyland GC p. 130
129 Sleepy Hollow GC p. 132
142 Valleaire GC p. 141

MAPS

Southeast

6	Auburn Springs CC p. 27	**55**	Gleneagles GC p. 67
7	Aurora G&CC p. 174	**58**	Grantwood p. 70
11	Barrington GC p. 175	**62**	Hawthorne Valley CC p. 183
17	Boston Hills CC p. 37	**138**	Tanglewood CC p. 198
27	Chagrin Valley CC p. 177	**144**	Walden G & Tennis p. 201
35	CC of Hudson p. 179		

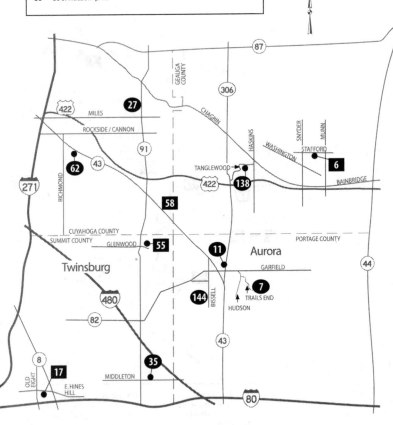

MAPS

Far South

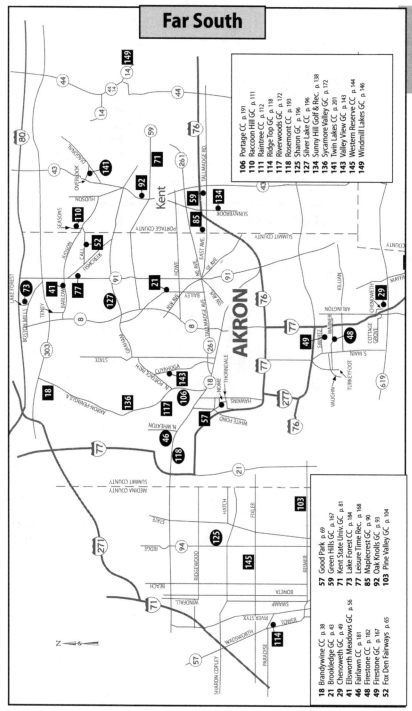

106 Portage CC p.191
110 Raccoon Hill GC p.111
111 Raintree CC p.112
114 Ridge Top GC p.118
117 Riverwoods GC p.172
118 Rosemont CC p.193
125 Sharon GC p.196
127 Silver Lake CC p.196
134 Sunny Hill Golf & Rec. p.138
136 Sycamore Valley GC p.172
141 Twin Lakes CC p.201
143 Valley View GC p.143
145 Western Reserve CC p.144
149 Windmill Lakes GC p.146

57 Good Park p.69
59 Green Hills GC p.167
71 Kent State Univ. GC p.81
73 Lake Forest CC p.184
77 Leisure Time Rec. p.168
85 Maplecrest GC p.90
92 Oak Knolls GC p.93
103 Pine Valley GC p.104

18 Brandywine CC p.38
21 Brookledge GC p.43
29 Chenoweth GC p.49
41 Ellsworth Meadows GC p.56
46 Fairlawn CC p.181
48 Firestone CC p.182
49 Firestone GC p.167
52 Fox Den Fairways p.65

Key to Golf Information

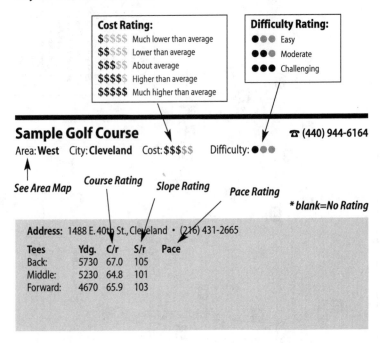

Cost Rating:
$$$$$ Much lower than average
$$$$$ Lower than average
$$$$$ About average
$$$$$ Higher than average
$$$$$ Much higher than average

Difficulty Rating:
●●● Easy
●●● Moderate
●●● Challenging

Sample Golf Course   ☎ (440) 944-6164
Area: **West**   City: **Cleveland**   Cost: **$$$$$**   Difficulty: ●●●

See Area Map   *Course Rating*   *Slope Rating*   *Pace Rating*

* blank=No Rating

Address: 1488 E. 40th St., Cleveland · (216) 431-2665

Tees	Ydg.	C/r	S/r	Pace
Back:	5730	67.0	105	
Middle:	5230	64.8	101	
Forward:	4670	65.9	103	

Note: Changes Prices, hours, and season of operation, and other factual information were carefully verified before this book went to press. However, this kind of information is always subject to change without notice. Golfers should **always call ahead** to confirm important details before heading out to play.

Public Courses
18 HOLES OR MORE

Airport Greens Golf Course ☎ (440) 944-6164
Area: **East**   City: **Willoughby Hills**   Cost: $$$$$ Difficulty: ●●●

Address: 28980 White Rd., Willoughby Hills

Tees	Ydg.	C/r	S/r	Pace
Back:	5730	67.0	105	
Middle:	5230	64.8	101	
Forward:	4670	65.9	103	

Specials: Senior & Ladies cart special weekdays

Season: Year-round **Hours:** 6 a.m.–10 p.m. **Tee times:** Recommended
Leagues: Weekdays 3:30–6:30 p.m. **Ranger:** Most days **Practice facil:** Range,
Putting Green, Chipping Green, Lighted range **Clubhouse:** Food, Beer, Liquor,
Dining room **Outings:** Available (catered) **Lessons:** Available

Directions: I-90 to Exit 187 for Bishop Rd. in Willoughby Hills;
south on Bishop; left (east) on White Rd.; on right.

Description Though there are no federal marshals checking bags here, playing without caution can cost more than stroke and distance. It can send players to federal prison. While signs on most golf courses are limited to directing cart traffic, at Airport Greens one reads, "Warning. This facility is used in FAA air traffic control. Loss of human life can occur from service interruption. Any person who interferes with air traffic control, or damages or trespasses on this property will be prosecuted under federal law." One more distraction while lining up a putt.

This is what happens when a golf course is built on an airport. Dick LaConte, PGA, who designed the course on Cuyahoga County Airport turf, has mixed golf and aviation before. On the clubhouse wall is a copy of a 30-year-old newspaper story about LaConte crashing his light plane into a tree while photographing the 13th hole at the now-defunct Mayfield Heights Golf Club.

Of the layout, LaConte said, "It's a combination of Scottish links in the open areas because we had the restrictions of the airport. The airport demands that we put nothing through the landing light system area. We can't plant trees there because we have a height restriction and we were restricted in the areas adjacent to the course. It's a unique piece of property."

No one is going to argue with that, though anyone who is reminded of Scottish links after walking this course will likely see the White Cliffs of Dover in the Terminal Tower.

This is a wonderful little track for new players—not much trouble and an easy walk. A wonderful course for beginners, mixed foursomes, and women groups.

Highlights The opening hole, a 295-yard par 4, is pretty typical of the holes here. The fairway is wide and bends softly to the right. Mounds on either side help define the hole. The fairway dips and rolls before arriving at a green elevated about 10 feet.

No. 2, a 215-yard par 3, is an unusual hole for a short course described as "sporty"—a 215-yard par 3 is a pro-length hole. Double bogeys will be posted here far more often than pars. A culvert runs 75 yards in front of the green, which is surrounded by mounds.

No. 6 is a par 3, 170 yards. A hook on this tee will send the ball off the course and across Bishop Road. The green is substantial, and players cross the county line—Cuyahoga/Lake—when walking from one end of the green to the other.

At the No. 7 tee, the sign promising prosecution is attached to the door of a small building used, obviously, for airport business. Landing lights mark the way to the tee. The hole is a 455-yard par 5, the number two handicap on this side.

The last hole before crossing White Road and leaving the airport for a half-dozen holes is No. 10, a short 130 yards from the white tees. Across the road, the course becomes much more attractive. Grass on the fairways will do that. This doesn't alleviate the difficulties of playing with planes in the background (and foreground), however, and players with air combat experience will likely rise to the top.

Nos. 17 and 18 are consecutive par 3s that play around a long and narrow lake. No. 17 is 165 yards with a small lake down its left side. For No. 18, players turn around and play 175 yards back to the clubhouse, water again on the left. Finishing holes like these suggest the designer forgot how much land was available and suddenly realized that two holes had to fit.

Airport Greens has an attractive clubhouse, a good pro shop, and a 60-station practice range.

Astorhurst Country Club   ☎ (440) 439-3636

Area: **South**   City: **Walton Hills**   Cost: $$$$$ Difficulty: ●●◉

PUBLIC 18+

Address: 7000 Dunham Rd., Walton Hills

Tees	Ydg.	C/r	S/r	Pace
Back:	6342	70.3	120	
Middle:	6075	69.1	118	
Forward:	5945	73.7	124	

Specials: Senior specials Mon–Fri before 3 p.m.

Season: Year-round **Hours:** Sunrise–10 p.m. **Tee times:** Taken **Leagues:** Mon–Thu after 3:30 p.m. **Ranger:** Most days **Practice facil:** Putting Green **Clubhouse:** Food, Beer, Dining room **Outings:** Available **Lessons:** Available **Pro:** Douglas Smith, PGA

Directions: I-77 to Exit 153 for Pleasant Valley Rd.; east on Pleasant Valley through Cuyahoga Valley National Recreation Area (becomes Alexander Rd. after Canal Rd.); left (north) on Dunham Rd. to the entrance within CVNRA.

Description One hundred forty-seven acres is not a lot of space for a golf course. But by pushing a few holes against one another, the designers created a reasonable track here. A couple tee shots are off cliffs, so they've provided some drama, too. Leagues fill the course Monday through Thursday afternoons, and Fridays are popular for outings, so call before coming.

The trees have grown large over the years and now add to the difficulty of keeping the ball in play. Most of the holes are already tight. Fairways and rough are well defined. Yardage markers in the fairways and cart paths are helpful. Twelve of the eighteen have doglegs.

Highlights No. 1, a 359-yard par 4, begins the match with a pine tree-lined, sharp dogleg left; there are trees at the corner turn and the right side of the fairway. Drive through the fairway and more trees will be waiting. As opening holes go, it's ugly. It will become clear that design is not the strong suit here.

No. 2 is an awesome 455-yard par 4 that calls for a big drive but offers a wide landing area. The terrain rises and falls as much as 20 feet. Halfway to the green, in the right rough, is an unusual set of sand traps. Not visible from the tee, there are five rectangular traps laid side by side—reminiscent of the famous "church pews" at Oakmont Country Club in Pennsylvania. There is more sand on the left side, but none at the green. On this hole, length is the key.

No. 7 is the only par 5 on the front nine, 590 yards. Its tee looks out over a wide fairway and, off to the right, a practice area. Still, care must be taken in this crowded corner of the course. A pulled tee shot can whistle over the heads of putters on the 5th green or drivers on the 6th tee. The 7th fairway drops from the tee and spreads out for the first few hundred yards. Then it takes a sharp dogleg to the right and rises. The

PUBLIC 18+

flag is not visible for the second shot, and there is the chance of hitting through the fairway.

Cart riders should be extremely cautious while leaving the tee at No. 8. If you get going too fast and lose control, the thrill rides at Cedar Point would be mild in comparison to what you will experience. (It is an 80- to-100-foot drop.)

No. 13, par 3, plays to two different greens. You hit over a ravine for the longer green—a hole for heroes. Lesser beings play the 105-yard front green.

No. 14, par 4, is short at 305 yards, but it features woods and a deep ravine on the left. A line of trees on the right separates the hole from No. 15. A slight dogleg left takes you to a green with a ravine drop-off and trees on both sides.

No. 18, par 5, 498 yards, tees off from the top of a cliff to a landing area 100 feet below. It's a sharp dogleg right with trees right and left of the fairway. Out-of-bounds to the right prevents players from going for the green in two. Out-of-bounds in the middle of the course is another indication of amateur design.

This old course is aging well, and the two cliffside tee boxes make it fun.

Astorhurst Country Club   (photo: Jonathan Wayne)

Auburn Springs Country Club   ☎ (440) 543-4448

Area: **Southeast**   City: **Chagrin Falls**   Cost: $$$$$ Difficulty: ●●●

PUBLIC 18+

Address: 10001 Stafford Rd., Chagrin Falls

Tees	Ydg.	C/r	S/r	Pace
Back:	6835	71.5	117	
Middle:	6488	70.8	112	
Forward:	5588	71.5	113	

Specials: Senior specials Mon–Fri; hot dog & beverage special

Season: Year-round **Hours:** Sunrise–sunset **Tee times:** Taken weekends
Leagues: Mon–Fri 4 p.m.–dark **Ranger:** None **Practice facil:** Putting Green,
Chipping Green **Clubhouse:** Food, Beer, Liquor, Dining room
Outings: Available **Lessons:** Not available

Directions: I-271 to Exit 27 for US 422; east on US 422; north on SR 306; right (east)
on Bainbridge Rd.; left (north) on Snyder Rd.; right (east) on Stafford Rd.; on right.

Description "Men are usually wild," manager Evelyn Weese says, "they go everywhere." She was explaining high scores on this course. And she knows what she's talking about—Weese turns in scores in the mid-80s on a regular basis. "On the front there's a lot of water and in the back a lot of woods. If you hit a straight ball, you're okay." Well, if you hit a straight ball *long* maybe. The front side measures 6,543 from the whites. From the blue tees, it stretches to 6,874, a length familiar to the Senior PGA Tour.

The course was built in the late sixties on farmland. Ernie Mizda is the builder and owner. This golf course is a tough one, a bit rough around the edges as well. To call it rough-hewn is an act of kindness. (And it would be easy to be kind if the lack of conditioning resulted in low greens fees.) The men and women who show up at the cashier's desk are here only to play golf. The club has a "basics-only" pro shop. No driving range here, and no rangers on the course. There isn't a pro on the staff, and no lessons are provided. Mizda has two noteworthy rules on the scorecard: no one under 21 may drive a golf cart, and beginners are not allowed on the course during busy periods.

Highlights No. 1 is a 375-yard par 4 that begins from an elevated tee. The fairway drops down to the left. Plenty of players try to cut the dogleg, because hitting straight can send a ball through the fairway. There are trees down the left side and a small pond, too. Behind the well-maintained green is a second pond.

No. 2, a 490-yard par 5, starts rising and doesn't stop rising until it approaches the green. It plays much longer than the listed 490 yards. A snap hook off this tee will send a ball into a small lake about 100 yards out. The left side here is thick woods. Down the right side, the hole is marked by a big willow and a line of trees.

Three tough par 4s finish the front side—two of them 440-yarders.

No. 17 is a par 5—570 yards that bend constantly to the right. About halfway to the green there is a small lake on the right side. This is a workingman's par 5; it calls for nothing fancy, only three solid, straight shots to cover the yardage and avoid the hazards. Just like Ms. Weese said.

After putting out on No. 18 and heading for the clubhouse, players run into the original Paul Bunyan driver. It is almost 15 feet tall, carved of two large pieces of wood with a black grip, brown shaft, and black hosel. It is handsome and rough-hewn. Just like the course.

Auburn Springs has the charm of a country picnic; it is not a course that stands on ceremony.

Avondale Golf Club   ☎ (440) 835-5836

Area: **Far West**   City: **Avon**   Cost: **$$$**$$ Difficulty: ●●●

Address: 38490 Detroit Rd., Avon

Tees	Ydg.	C/r	S/r	Pace
Back:	6263	69.9	118	
Middle:	5993	68.5	116	
Forward:	5400	70.7	114	

Specials: Senior & Junior specials Mon–Fri before 1 p.m.; Early Bird Special: Mon–Fri before 7:30 a.m.

Season: Apr–Dec **Hours:** 5:30 a.m.–10:00 p.m. **Tee times:** Taken
Leagues: Various times **Ranger:** Daily **Practice facil:** Putting Green
Clubhouse: Food, Beer, Pavilion **Outings:** Available (catered outings: 18 holes & cart, includes lunch or dinner, $48 per guest; seating for 200) **Lessons:** Not available

Directions: I-90 eastbound to Exit 153 for SR 83; left (south) on SR 83; right (west) on Detroit Rd. (SR 254); on right, after Long Rd. OR, I-90 westbound to Exit 148 for SR 254 (Detroit Rd.); east on SR 254; on left, after Moon Rd.

Description George Noll built the front side of Avondale on farmland and opened it for play in 1974. It was his dream to operate the course in his retirement; he had the back nine sketched when he succumbed to a heart attack. His sons built the back nine and today run the operation with their mother, Jane Noll. "It became a family affair," Al Noll said. So if the course looks homemade, it should.

There is some variety in the greens here: a couple are two-tiered, a few are small or unusually shaped (pin placement on the par 3 No. 16 can mean a putt as long as 120 feet), more are big. Many are surrounded by sand and mounds. They are all kept in excellent condition. "That's what we're noted for," Al Noll said. "They're the best greens in the county." A familiar boast of course owners.

Electric lines cut through the course, especially on the front side.

Holes were designed to avoid them, though, and landing near poles is no penalty; a two-club length drop is offered.

Highlights No. 1 is a par 5 of 500 yards. Three mounds in the middle of the fairway confront players on the tee, and more mounds come into play for the second shot. The approach must take into account the lake and the sand to the right of the green. For first-time players, this can be a hectic opening hole.

No. 3, a par 3 of 175 yards, is one of many holes studied carefully by Al Noll. When scoring for outings, he sees more high scores on this hole than on any other. Although it is technically the number 15 handicap, he says it plays the hardest. "It's always playing into the wind and most people are short of the green," he explained. Short of the green there is trouble where mounds protect the front. Off to the right is a small pond, and on the right side of the green, sand.

No. 4 is a 360-yard par 4, a dogleg left. In the corner of the turn is The Pit—a mound with a pit in the middle. The corner can still be cut, but only by big and accurate hitters. Missing it and playing the second shot from The Pit will likely add at least one stroke. There is sand beside the green, behind which sits a sizable pond.

No. 12, a par 4 of 365 yards, has three pot bunkers waiting at 210 yards on the right side of the fairway. The hole also has the toughest green on the course, including a two-tiered putting surface and a pair of sand traps.

The only par 5 on the back side is No. 13, a 470-yard hole that tempts players to reach for the green in two. "It doesn't get eagled very often," Al Noll said. The hole bends to the left, and getting on in two calls for clearing a few 50-foot oaks en route. If that shot leaks to the right it will end up in a pond close to the green.

The finishing hole has water in front of the tee. The drive on this 375-yard par 4—the only uphill hole here—has to carry a large pond. Sand lines both sides of the two-tiered green. The putting surface has plenty of action to it and, for reasons not clear, is faster than others here. "It's a knee-knocker," Noll said.

TIDYMAN'S TIDBITS #1

The Donald Ross Courses in Greater Cleveland:

1) Shaker Country Club (1913)
2) The Oakwood Club (1915)
3) Acacia Country Club (1920)
4) Hawthorne Valley Country Club (1926)
5) Manakiki Golf Course (1928)

Berkshire Hills Country Club   ☎ (440) 729-9516

Area: **Far East**   City: **Chesterland**   Cost: **$$$$**$ Difficulty: ●●●

Address: 9758 Mayfield Rd., Chesterland

Tees	Ydg.	C/r	S/r	Pace
Back:	6607	72.1	129	
Middle:	6346	71.0	127	
Forward:	5512	71.8	122	

Specials: Senior specials

Season: Year-round **Hours:** Sunrise–sunset **Tee times:** Taken weekends until 1p.m., carts required until 1 p.m. **Leagues:** Mon–Fri **Ranger:** Daily **Practice facil:** Range, Putting Green **Clubhouse:** Food, Beer, Soft drinks, Beer avail. on course **Outings:** Available **Lessons:** Not available

Directions: I-271 to Exit 34 for US 322 East (Mayfield Rd.); east on US 322 through Chesterland; on right, after Heath Rd. (2.5 miles east of SR 306, Chillicothe Rd.)

Description A player arguing that Berkshire Hills is the most beautiful course in the area would find plenty of supporting evidence between the first tee and the 18th green. The course is only about 30 years old and was designed by Ben Zink, who also designed the layout for Landerhaven (now defunct). Landerhaven was a prairie without features; Berkshire is a roller coaster without tracks.

The winding and hilly drive from US 322 to the parking lot is much like the course itself: lined with trees and given to following the terrain.

The clubhouse is like an old family album: battered a bit, but treasured. Tee times are taken for weekend and holiday mornings. To play at other times, just show up. Not much of a pro shop here, just the basics, and the driving range prohibits the use of woods.

On the other side of the clubhouse is the dining facility for outings: an old dairy barn. It is a splendid setting for prime rib and cloth napkins. Friday is the day for outings.

Highlights Berkshire is a well-manicured and -maintained course, and few starting holes match the grandeur of its No. 1. This par 5, 537-yard dogleg sweeps down from the tee, then veers up and to the right. In the elbow of the dogleg is a large lake. It is a rare player who tries to clear the lake with a tee shot; the fairway is wide, the rough easily playable. When the sky is clear but for a few clouds, the view here belongs on a picture postcard. The big, round green at No. 1 has a couple of slender traps on either side, traps that wrap around the perimeter. This type of trap will be seen the rest of the round.

No. 4 is another par 5, this one a 505-yard uphill hole that will likely confuse the first-time player. A pond rests in front of the tee, and the drive must be straight. Few players can reach the top of the hill with their drives, making a second, blind shot necessary. As throughout the course, old hardwoods line the fairway and stand ready to slap down errant shots. More than accuracy is called for here; good scores are often posted by long hitters. The fairway rises towards an aiming flag, where it crests and then rolls straight to the green. The green is half-surrounded in the rear by heavy, heavy brush.

No. 7 is the number one handicap hole, a 448-yard par 4 that demands a straight hit from the elevated tee and an approach shot of great accuracy and length. The fairway rises and dips more than once before nearing the green, where the left side of the fairway precipitously drops off.

Some golfers may choose to go from the 9th green directly to the 10th tee rather than stop for refreshment at the clubhouse; for all the beauty and challenge of the front side, the back side is more beautiful and more challenging. Furthermore, a cart patrols the course with a cooler full of cold beer and soft drinks. A nice touch.

No. 10, a 252-yard par 4, goes up. And up. And up. It's not a difficult hole if players stay on the straight and narrow. If the ball strays left, it finds deep woods. Trees protect the front and right of the green, but even players not known for their length off the tee might be able to drive it.

With No. 12 begins what may be the four best consecutive holes in Northern Ohio. No. 12 is a 453-yard par 4 that takes a woodland ride the Headless Horseman wouldn't consider. The tee shot, ideally a soft draw, has to go uphill and slightly left. Deep forest lines the left and plenty of maples and pin oaks line the right. Starting at the 150-yard marker, the fairway descends rapidly, crosses water, and finally comes to the green.

The next tee, No. 13, presents a target only a couple dozen yards wide. The tee shot has to go almost straight uphill; at the crest, trees close in on both sides. This 472-yard par 5 plays down a snug fairway.

No. 14 is a 360-yard par 4, which sounds easy. But this hole calls for careful shotmaking—especially the approach to the green, which is slightly elevated.

No. 15 is a par 5, 509-yard hole that bends right, falls to a creek, then rises sharply up and left to the green. Play outside of the short grass makes this hole especially tough. The walk through the woods to the next tee is a good time to catch one's breath; some interesting golf is played in those last four holes.

The 18th hole looks like it was designed by Andrew Wyeth. It's a par 3, 135 yards from a small, even private, tee box and across a sparkling lake. The green has water on three sides, and to the rear the ground rises dramatically. Players who are walking get to stroll across the wooden footbridge from tee to green. (Carts must use a more substantial bridge.)

Berkshire is long: 6,346 for par 72. The blue tees take the course to 6,607, par 73. The women's tees were not provided as an afterthought; they are well built and maintained, and they provide reasonable advantage. Water fountains and phones for emergency use dot the course.

This is a great course for hosting out-of-town guests unfamiliar with the quality of public golf available here.

PUBLIC 18+

Big Met Public Golf Course   ☎ (440) 331-1070
Area: **West**   City: **Fairview Park**   Cost: $$$$$ Difficulty: ●●●

Address: 4811 Valley Pkwy., Fairview Park

Tees	Ydg.	C/r	S/r	Pace
Back:	6356	69.1	113	4:15
Middle:	6137	68.3	111	
Forward:	5687	71.5	117	

Specials: Golfer's Dozen: 12 rounds for the price of 10; Senior (62+) & Junior specials

Season: Mid-Mar–Dec **Hours:** Sunrise–sunset **Tee times:** Taken
Leagues: Women's League on Tuesday **Ranger:** Daily **Practice facil:** Range, Putting Green **Clubhouse:** Food, Beer **Outings:** Available (for small outings Mon, Wed, Fri.) **Lessons:** Not available **Pro:** David Alexander

Directions: I-480 to Exit 9 for Grayton Rd.; north on Grayton; left (west) on Puritas Rd. into Rocky River Reservation; right (north) on Valley Pkwy.; on right.

Description This Cleveland Metroparks course has been a West Side favorite for a couple of generations. It is attractive and playable, and so conveniently located that getting there for many is a matter of 10 or 15 minutes. It is also the slowest playing course in the history of golf. Rangers should be armed with shotguns and allowed to fire after a single warning. There are days when the parking lot overflows with cars and the wait to tee off can be excruciating. Management is stymied though cognizant of the problem.

It is not a difficult course, though there are tough holes on it. Sitting in the Rocky River Reservation—"The Valley," to West Siders—this essentially flat layout provides great physical beauty to players. Animals like it, too, including a pair of red foxes and dozens of deer. A minor inconvenience is provided by planes leaving and arriving at Hopkins Airport, just south of the course.

Highlights The first hole is a 403-yard par 4 with a generous fairway—often ignored by players who slice their drives into the adjacent No. 2 green. It is a straight hole calling for two long shots. The fairway is lined on the right with small trees, mostly pines. Except for a stand of tall hardwoods, the left side is open. There is sand at the left side of the green. The greens on this course are neither tricky nor fast, but they hold approach shots well and are always in very good shape.

No. 5, the first par 5, measures 452 yards and includes a dogleg left near the green. A small lake was added recently, and it's made a wonderful change in the green at 5 and the next tee box. Again, it's a wide-open fairway. At one time a huge tree stood in the elbow of this dogleg.

Lightning eliminated that hazard, but more trees have been planted there, and as time goes on the hole will narrow. Behind the sloped green is the Rocky River.

No. 14 is certainly the most difficult hole on the course, even though No. 9 is designated the number one handicap. At 424 yards, it's a long par 4. A dogleg right turns around the 150-yard mark. To score well on this hole calls for a pro-length drive and great second shot. If the drive leaves the ball on the right side, trees in the elbow of the dogleg will prevent a clear approach. And the green itself is unfair and tricky; it is egg-shaped and has steep sides. It's not unusual to land a ball on the green only to watch it roll off. Whose brilliant design idea was that?

The final two holes are short par 4s more at home on an executive-length course than here. No. 17 is a straight, 289-yard hole with a plateau in the fairway and plenty of room. Big hitters who are also big slicers, however, can land on the 18th tee. No. 18, 293 yards slightly uphill toward the clubhouse, has a mound in front of the green that makes judging the approach shot difficult.

There are occasional surprises on the course. Sometimes red foxes raise eyebrows as they take their evening walk. Or a heron swooping down to land in a marsh will hush a foursome. But mostly this course is comfortable, familiar, and convenient. Which explains why Big Met does such big business.

Big Met Public Golf Course   (photo: Casey Batule/courtesy of Cleveland Metroparks)

PUBLIC 18+

PUBLIC 18+

Black Brook Country Club

☎ (440) 951-0010

Area: **Far East**   City: **Mentor**   Cost: $$$$$$ Difficulty: ●●●

Address: 8900 Lake Shore Blvd., Mentor

Tees	Ydg.	C/r	S/r	Pace
Back:	6216	69.1	118	
Middle:	5870	68.0	116	
Forward:	5398	70.5	117	

Specials: Senior specials weekdays

Season: Year-round **Hours:** 6 a.m.–10 p.m. summer; 8 a.m.–5 p.m. winter
Tee times: Recommended **Leagues:** 4–6 p.m. **Ranger:** Daily **Practice facil:**
Range, Putting Green **Clubhouse:** Food, Beer, Pavilion **Outings:** Available
(catered for 20–120 guests) **Lessons:** Available **Pro:** Tim Ausperk

Directions: SR 2 to SR 44; north on SR 44 (Heisley Rd.) to exit for Lake Shore Blvd.
(SR 283); west on Lake Shore Blvd.; on left.

Description The tee markers here are carved granite. It is an elegant touch and in keeping with Mary Lou Colbow's affectionate regard for the game. The president and owner of Black Brook comes from a golfing family; her father, Robert Shave, was the pro at Manakiki when it was a private club.

Colbow is also a player of some repute and a student of the game. Black Brook, she said, invests heavily in its junior program. Young players who are taught the game and its etiquette will likely always be grateful. Just as important, they will fill courses with golfers who play fast and well, and who take care of the course as they use it.

The course is open all year, and play is permitted according to the weather. Colbow said, "It's a good course for everybody. It's not super long, but it's not short and it has a lot of challenge in it—the back nine, especially, because it's tight." The greens are consistently fast and the course very well maintained. Tees, greens, and fairways are watered.

Highlights No. 4 is the only par 5 on the front side, and, at 444 yards, it is quite short. There is plenty of room to fit a slice before reaching the white o.b. stakes on the right side. This hole has one of the tougher greens. Plenty of sand around and in front of it, so rolling the ball on it is not possible. The green itself has tough hills. It is easy enough to three-putt here (maybe more).

The back side is slightly longer and more difficult than the front. The terrain changes are marked by shallow and not-so-shallow valleys and much more water. The toughest hole is saved for last.

No. 11, a 185-yard par 3, is a gorgeous hole, calling for a big iron shot over valley and creek to a large green. Sand traps prevent big hits from bouncing into the woods behind the green.

No. 18, the most challenging hole on the course, is equally beautiful.

The tee shot on this 425-yard par 4 is blind; players
hundred yards to see the green. There are only a few tre
but the target area for the drive is not large. A straigh
dropping about 200 yards from the green. On the righ
floor is a lake. The terrain rises quickly to a green with th
deep woods behind it. Separating the woods from the gre
rail fence.

Black Brook is an old, and old-fashioned, layout with holes that can
delight the average player and holes that can confound. It is a little gem,
off the side of the road, where management's commitment to the game
is clearly evident.

Bob-O-Link Golf Course

☎ (440) 835-0676

Area: **West**   City: **Avon**   Cost: $$$$$ Difficulty: ●●●

Address: 4141 Center Rd. (SR 83), Avon

Tees	Red & White				Red & Blue				Blue & White			
	Ydg.	C/r	S/r	Pace	Ydg.	C/r	S/r	Pace	Ydg.	C/r	S/r	Pace
Back:	6263	68.1	108	3:42	6052	68.0	115	3:44	6383	69.6	115	
Middle:	5911	66.7	105		5656	66.3	111		6023	67.9	112	
Forward:	5050	66.6	107		4808	66.7	112		5102	68.4	115	

Specials: Senior & Junior specials Mon–Fri

Season: Mar–Dec **Hours:** 6 a.m.–10 p.m. **Tee times:** Taken weekends **Leagues:** Various times **Ranger:** Most days **Practice facil:** Range, Putting Green, Chipping Green, Sand **Clubhouse:** Food, Beer, Liquor, Pavilion, (3 pavilions, 2 enclosed) **Outings:** Available (also regular course events) **Lessons:** Available **Pro:** Joe Kris

Directions: I-90 to Exit 153 for SR 83 in Avon; south on SR 83 (Center Rd.); on left, after Riegelsberger Rd.

Description Bob-O-Link features 27 holes (all watered), three pavilions
(one totally enclosed), 85 riding carts, a driving range, and a rule that
should appear on all scorecards: Rule No. 9, under Local Rules, reads,
"This is a fun game; play with courtesy."

More than 40 leagues play here, and a great outing business is done
on Wednesdays and Saturdays. The new clubhouse, built in 1986, is
roomy and comfortable and includes the pro shop, which carries the
essentials only. Weather permitting, play continues all year.

Manager Bill Fitch remembers his first foursome. The original owners of the course gave this foursome the keys to the clubhouse. They
were always out playing before the owners showed up. They even made
coffee for the owners. The foursome played together steadily from 1969.
Two members are dead now, both killed by heart attacks. "One was on
the 14th hole and one was on the 16th," Fitch said. "The coincidence of
that happening . . ." The survivors continue to play.

PUBLIC 18+

The nines are designated by colors: Red, White, and Blue. The 150-yard markers are 4 x 4s with yellow numerals. The greens are not lightning fast but not slow either. Except for the occasional gully or mound, the course is built on flat terrain.

Highlights No. 3 is a pro-length, 440-yard par 4, and it's the number one handicap hole on this nine. (Each of the three nines has handicaps 1 through 9.) Nothing fancy, just straightaway and long. All down the left side, however, are dense underbrush and tall trees, which hide an 8-foot-deep gully. Water courses through the gully, and balls hit into this jungle often stay there, waiting for the sharp-eyed hawker.

Then it's a short walk over a covered bridge to the next tee, shared by a hole from the Red nine. Look before you hit to make sure you don't switch nines by accident. When standing on the tee, it's difficult to see where No. 4 goes. The par 4 is 395 yards, and halfway out begins a serious dogleg right. A large sand trap marks the elbow of the dogleg, and more sand is on the right of the green. To the left, for players who skipped breakfast for an early tee time, stands a pear tree. At the right time of year the branches are filled with fruit.

No. 9, a 515-yard par 5, opens straight then turns sharply left near the approach. There, the Bob-O-Link version of the Eisenhower tree sits, a huge cottonwood on the right side of the fairway. In addition, mounds line the right side. On both sides, pines guide to the hole. There is a spot of sand directly in front of the green and a small pond there, as well. The pond cannot be seen until players get close.

The first two nines are fun to play but have no real signature holes. The third nine, the newer Blue Links, is not the longest of the three but is the most interesting. Only 3,086 yards, none of the par 4s on this nine is longer than 375 yards. The two par 5s make up the yardage, measuring 520 and 573. This nine calls for greater golf skills.

No. 1, for instance, is only 320 yards long and could be reached with two mid-iron shots. But no one is likely to pull a mid-iron from their bag on the tee. The hole narrows as it nears the green. Tall hardwoods line the left side of the fairway. Forty yards in front of the green a creek crosses the fairway. With more hardwoods leaning in on the right side, the tee shot and approach shot have to fly true. The greens here are much different from those on the Red and White Links; they are faster and have a great deal of shape to them. Double-break putts are common. If bets are made on this nine, it would pay to bet on the player with the best short game.

No. 5, a 520-yard par 5, heads out and to the right over a creek that won't be much trouble, to a small lake that will be. The lake is 150 yards across; once past it, the fairway narrows and cuts right through the forest. The green here is unusual. Narrow and fast, it is almost 50 paces long.

Bob-O-Link is a good layout for the average golfer, but one that takes a little getting used to. That isn't a fault of the course so much as it is a fact of the terrain. And one of the best things about Bob-O-Link is the number of teenagers playing the course. A course with a future.

Boston Hills Country Club   ☎ (330) 656-2438

Area: **Southeast**   City: **Boston Heights**   Cost: **$$$$$**   Difficulty: ●●●

PUBLIC 18+

Address: 105 East Hines Hill, Boston Heights

Tees	Ydg.	C/r	S/r	Pace
Back:	6167	69.	114	4:12
Middle:	5865	67.8	112	
Forward:	4987	68.2	108	

Specials: Senior specials Mon–Fri before 3 p.m.

Season: Year-round **Hours:** 6 a.m.–7 p.m. **Tee times:** Taken **Leagues:** Mon–Thu afternoons **Ranger:** Most days **Practice facil:** Range, Putting Green, Chipping Green, Sand, Covered heated practice tees (across street from club at The Range at Boston Hills, see separate entry). **Clubhouse:** Food, Beer, Liquor, Dining room, Pavilion, 1,400 sq. foot outing facility **Outings:** Available (for up to 250 people) **Lessons:** Available **Pro:** Ron Burke, PGA

Directions: I-271 to Exit 18 for SR 8; south on SR 8; right (west) on E. Hines Hill Rd.; on right. OR, Ohio Turnpike (I-80) to exit 12, to exit 12 (SR 8), 1/4 mile north on SR 8; left (east) on E. Hines Hill; on right.

Description There is lots of activity at this old course, built in 1924 by Wink Chadwick (perhaps the quintessential yuppie name). Much of it has to do with marketing golf and golf services. A driving range with heated units for year-round practice and partnership with a golf store are good examples.

The entire course tilts down to Route 8, and holes play uphill, downhill, and sidehill. The elevation is gentle, never steep, and this is a good course to walk and carry. Most of the holes have generous landing areas, and the greens are medium speed. A dress code is strictly enforced.

Highlights It is a wide-open and comfortable layout, often without features. No. 3, a 449-yard par 5, is an example of one of its better holes. An aiming flag guides players to the optimum landing area from the tee. Though it is a decided dogleg right with a huge old maple tree in the elbow of the bend, it's not a particularly challenging par 5 but a beautiful one. On both sides of the broad fairway are hardwoods. The shallow green is egg-shaped and set at an angle. The approach shot here may be the most challenging.

The first par 3, No. 5, is under 100 yards. Many players would score better if they just threw the ball. Between the tee and the green is a tiny lake. The green has old hardwoods on the right and left sides. Bunkers are on both sides, too, and the rear of the green falls steeply away. Only

98 yards, it is an unfair hole, jammed in only because the number of holes called for is 18 and not 17.

No. 11, a 411-yard par 4, is the number one handicap. It used to be a ar 5. A blind tee shot leads to a wide fairway that bends sharply to the left. Trees define the hole and prevent cutting the dogleg. The approach is generally a long one to a small green in a forest of hardwoods.

PUBLIC 18+

Brandywine Country Club   ☎ (330) 657-2525

Area: **Far South**   City: **Peninsula**   Cost: $$$$$ Difficulty: ●●●

Address: 5555 Akron-Peninsula Rd., Peninsula

| | | | | | Par 3 Course | | | |
Tees	Ydg.	C/r	S/r	Pace	Ydg.	C/r	S/r	Pace
Back:	6470	70.2	120					
Middle:	6088	68.4	116		1003	27.0		
Forward:	5625	70.5	119					

Specials: Senior specials: 18 hole special Mon–Fri before 12 p.m.; 9 hole special Mon–Fri before 2 p.m.

Season: Year-round, weather permitting **Hours:** Sunrise–sunset **Tee times:** Taken, up to 2 weeks in advance **Leagues:** Mon–Thu 3:45–6 p.m. May–Aug **Ranger:** Weekends **Practice facil:** Putting Green **Clubhouse:** Food, Beer, Liquor, Pavilion **Outings:** Available **Lessons:** Available **Pro:** Jim Bricker

Directions: I-271 to Exit 12 for SR 303 (Streetsboro Rd.); east on SR 303; right (south) on Akron-Peninsula Rd. (also called S. Locust St.); on left.

Description In the parking lot on a summer day, license plates give an indication of this course's drawing power: Cuyahoga, Ashtabula, Stark, Summit, Trumbull, Portage, Huron, and Wayne counties are all there.

The front side offers a rolling, tree-lined, and well-maintained nine holes; the back side is legendary for its unusual holes that claw up and down hillsides, drop over cliffs, and steal balls from all but the most accurate players. In the pro shop is a shirt emblazoned with "I Survived the Back Nine at Brandywine."

If the Z-hole here—the 545-yard par 5 that is impossible to eagle—is legendary, it's also, like other holes on the back side, a novelty. The tee shot is a short iron, and the green is hidden and unreachable for the second shot. Approaches from sidehill/uphill lies are not uncommon on the back nine.

Peninsula is a pretty little town off the beaten path. And Brandywine's drama is attractive.

Highlights For players taken with the sensual beauty of courses, get the first tee time on a weekday. The gorgeous, deep-green front nine, sparkling with dew and framed on one side by tall, tree-covered hills, is awe inspiring. The game begins with a straightaway 376-yard par 4. The fairway rises past a century oak on the right side. Even though it should not come into play, it may stay in players' memories: it is a magnificent old tree. The fairway is generously wide on this hole, and the green slopes slightly forward. Sand marks the right edge.

The front nine is lovely, but the heroic shots and bragging rights come from the back nine. It opens with a 347-yard par 4. From a slightly elevated tee the fairway is straight, though narrow as it nears the green. Woods on either side and an equipment barn on the right emphasize the importance of staying in the fairway. Water comes into play in the last 100 yards, where a creek runs parallel to the fairway. There is sand at the right side of the green.

No. 12 is short, a 277-yard par 4. Cottonwood and poplars provide shade on the tee; hickories and oaks fill the woods on either side. To the left rear of the green, and not visible from the tee, is a lake. The ground behind the green falls away to the water. It's at this hole players realize the game is moving deeper into the hills that previously only lined the fairways.

At No. 13, the fairway dips in front of the tee, then shoots up and veers right. It's a 350-yard dogleg to the right and not one that tempts drivers to clear the elbow. The first couple hundred yards are all up—at about a 45-degree angle. On both sides of the fairway, tee to green, mature hardwoods begin where rough ends. Leaving the narrow fairway at any point can add a substantial number of strokes.

No. 15 is only 148 yards, but it can be reached with a well-hit short iron; the tee box is virtually the edge of a cliff, and the green is 150 feet below. Maintenance and conditioning are problematic on the back nine and this tee is a good example, with its rubber mats. This is one of the signature holes here and is pictured on the scorecard.

Between the 13th tee and the 16th green is the Ohio version of the Khyber Pass. The famous Z-hole—No. 16, a 545-yard par 5 (and number two handicap)—is played on a valley floor. Its fairway goes out straight about 200 yards, takes a sharp right to the 150-yard marker, then an equally sharp left toward a green with sand on the left side. The fairway on this hole is narrow and seems more so because the valley walls rise on both sides. Walking off this green with a 5 is wholly satisfactory.

On the other side of the road is a par 3 course recently created by the Yesberger family on what had previously been a practice area.

Brandywine has a juniors program that should be copied and instituted at every course. Lee Yesberger and her corps of teachers and rangers give kids the opportunity to learn well and play fairly the greatest game in history. She runs tournaments, holds parties, and keeps records for her junior players at the log-cabin clubhouse built in front of the practice green. Lots of golfers, years from now, are going to think warm thoughts about the grandmotherly Mrs. Yesberger, the woman who introduced them to golf.

PUBLIC 18+

PUBLIC 18+

Brentwood Golf Club   ☎ (440) 322-9254
Area: **Far West**   City: **Grafton**   Cost: **$$$$$**   Difficulty: ●●●

Address: 12415 SR 57, Grafton

Tees	Ydg.	C/r	S/r	Pace
Back:	5148			
Middle:	4695			
Forward:	4223			

Specials: Senior & Junior specials Mon–Fri before 3 p.m.

Season: Mar–Oct **Hours:** Sunrise–sunset **Tee times:** Taken weekends
Leagues: Various times **Ranger:** Weekends **Practice facil:** Range, Putting Green,
Chipping Green **Clubhouse:** Food, Beer, Pavilion **Outings:** Available
Lessons: Available **Pro:** Andrew Bobrock

Directions: I-480 to SR 10 (I-480 ends here); west on SR 10 to SR 57;
south on SR 57 (Medina-Elyria Rd.); on left.

Description The Brothers Jalowiec—Bernard, Henry, and Walter—caddied as kids at Spring Valley Country Club, just north of Elyria. While rearing their own families in the late sixties, they built Brentwood during vacations, on weekends, and at night. The property was originally farmland.

Brentwood has a comfortable clubhouse and a super driving range. The course is mostly flat and easy to play.

It is a course popular with older golfers. "We have a lot of senior citizens, being that the course is a little shorter," Mr. Jalowiec said. "We give them a special rate, they don't abuse the course. They enjoy themselves." Some mornings the clubhouse looks like God's Waiting Room.

The course has no sand, but water comes into play.

Highlights Greenskeeper Joe Yourkiewicz likes No. 4 on the front side, normally a 180-yard par 3 with a sizable green. It can play as short as 130 or as long as 245, he said. On the back nine, he selected No. 15 as the signature hole. It's a 370-yard par 4 with a narrow landing area. This dogleg left has a tricky green, he added.

The layout gets a bit crowded on the back nine, but it's a nice walk in the woods. The owners are notably gracious. The back of the scorecard says it well: "A Family-Owned Golf Club for Friendly Golfers."

TIDYMAN'S TIDBITS #2
Most Handsome Clubhouses:
1) Painesville
2) The Country Club
3) Manakiki

Boulder Creek

Getting off the turnpike at the Streetsboro exit, I noticed a golf course under construction. "What's the name of the new course?" I asked the toll booth worker. "I don't know," she said. "Everybody asks me." Not one to ask a state employee to do anything that was beyond a job description, I made a note to call around.

Before I could get around to it, the call came from Tim Weiman, a local player who studies golf course architecture here and around the world the way lawyers study accident reports.

Weiman was impressed with the course, with the routing and the design, but especially with the guy building it, Joe Salemi.

Weiman said Boulder Creek is being built without the services of a designer, an architect, a construction company, environmental consultants, or the bane of civilization, lawyers.

The first nine holes will open in June, the second nine in July. Even a cursory ride around the almost-finished course is impressive. And the word is out. Though not even open, it's been honored for its practice range by *Golf Range Times*, and *Golf Digest* accepted its nomination in the Best New Courses 2002 survey. At this rate, Boulder Creek Golf Club, the brand-new course in Streetsboro, will have to build a trophy room.

It's certainly a worthy candidate, this wonderfully routed, meticulously crafted, high-quality addition to upscale golf. But that's not the story. The story is the guy who created the course, Joe Salemi. Salemi's business, before he became a golf course designer/architect/builder/owner, was commercial and residential development.

When Salemi bought the first of the two 100-acre parcels that now make up the course, it was destined for a housing development—until the second 100-acre adjoining tract became available. It was at that point that Salemi wondered aloud, "Could I build a golf course here?"

The land already had three ingredients for a great course: water, changes in elevation, and hardwood trees.

Now it was a matter of learning how to build a great course on a great property. The 1977 Ohio State University graduate took up golf after college and played to a 12 handicap. When playing, he often stared from the tee box and silently announced, "I could build a better hole than this."

Now he had gotten his chance to put up or shut up.

Salemi buried his nose in books written by the great designers, Tillinghast, Ross, and McKenzie among them. He learned what makes a good hole, what makes a great hole, and what makes lots of holes eminently forgettable.

With a basic understanding of design, he went to work clearing the land. He brought in specialists for the tee boxes and greens. He created a true island green. The great hardwoods, including many black walnut and ash, were preserved to help define holes. He sunk wells deep enough to outlast an entire summer of drought, and he built a course that will impress and amaze the golf world. In addition to investing a great deal of money on this bet, he put in sweat equity that might be measured in 55-gallon drums, uncounted hours of manual labor, and a steadfast faith in his own abilities.

PUBLIC 18+

Briardale Greens Golf Course   ☎ (216) 289-8574

Area: **East**   City: **Euclid**   Cost: $$$$$$ Difficulty: ●●●

Address: 24131 Briardale Ave., Euclid

Tees	Ydg.	C/r	S/r	Pace
Back:	6050	70.5	122	
Middle:	5723	68.4	119	
Forward:	4932	68.4	108	

Specials: Senior specials Mon–Fri

Season: Mar–Nov **Hours:** Sunrise–sunset **Tee times:** Required **Leagues:** Mon–Fri 8–10 a.m., 3:30–6 p.m. **Ranger:** Daily **Practice facil:** Range, Putting Green, Chipping Green **Clubhouse:** Food, Beer **Outings:** Available **Lessons:** Available **Pro:** Tom Sloat

Directions: I-90 to exit for Babbitt Rd.; north on Babbitt Rd.; right on Briardale Ave.

Description The first sign golfers read as they drive into Briardale Greens says, "You play at your own risk here." In the parking lot, the sign reads, "You park at your own risk here." Is there something we should know? On the property is one of the Euclid senior citizen activity buildings, and lots of older players tee it up here. The flat course, opened in 1977, is not distinguished, but it is inexpensive and accessible. Situated in the middle of this densely populated East Side suburb, it is a very busy course. Tee times are taken for weekday as well as weekend play. A half dozen or more leagues line up for play on weeknights. The small clubhouse seats only a handful before strangers rub elbows; the pro shop is similarly small. For outings, however, the pavilion seats more than a hundred and still has room for grills.

Highlights No. 1 is a no-frills par 4, 337 yards long. It is representative of what is going to follow. The fairway is defined by a few small stands of trees on both sides and a few bushes. Behind the green is a little lake.

No. 3 is a 350-yard dogleg right around a lake, which is inexplicably marked o.b. Cattails fill the bank on the green side of the water, and there is sand on the left side of the green. The sand slows some balls from bouncing to the chain-link fence that marks the edge of the course and the beginning of a residential area.

The number one handicap hole is No. 7, a par 5 of 495 yards, two lakes, tall trees, and a well-bunkered green. There are backyards all along the left side and a few trees on the right. About 170 yards from the green, a small lake appears on the right and a second lake behind it. If the lakes don't grab balls sliced from the fairway, tall sycamores on the right side will knock them down. The green has a large trap in front and a smaller trap in the rear.

No. 8 is a 170-yard par 3. Behind the tee is Babbitt Road, from which drivers of cars sometimes critique drivers of golf balls. The second body of water on the previous hole shows up on the right side here. Mallards raise families at water's edge. A brace of sand traps rests on the right side of the green.

Briardale is successful for a short list of reasons. It is not pretentious. It's a muny course for muny players, men and women from the neighborhood who enjoy the game. It is fun and inexpensive.

PUBLIC 18+

Brookledge Golf Club   ☎ (330) 971-8416
Area: **Far South**   City: **Cuyahoga Falls**   Cost: **$$$$$**   Difficulty: ●●●

Address: 1621 Bailey Rd., Cuyahoga Falls

Tees	Ydg.	C/r	S/r	Pace
Back:	6297	68.9	116	
Middle:	5733	66.4	111	
Forward:	5334	66.2	107	

Specials: Senior specials Mon–Fri

Season: Mar 1–Nov 30 **Hours:** 6:30 a.m.–sunset **Tee times:** Recommended, Taken up to 2 weeks in advance **Leagues:** Mon–Fri evenings **Ranger:** Daily **Practice facil:** Range, Putting Green, Chipping Green, Sand, 2 ranges (mat & grass tees) **Clubhouse:** Food, Beer, Pavilion **Outings:** Available **Lessons:** Available **Pro:** Steve Black

Directions: I-271 to Exit 18 for SR 8; south on SR 8; left (east) on Howe Ave.; "soft" left (north) on Bailey Rd. at six-point intersection; right (east) on Kennedy Blvd. to entrance.

Description Up until the late 1980s, this course had only nine holes. Management asked Arthur Hills to stretch it out to 18, and when he did he made a very playable course. There is only one par 5 on the back side, but it is the par 3s that are the holes of note, especially No. 12, which measures 165 yards from the whites, 188 from the blues. The ball has to carry a ravine while slipping through a tree-lined passageway. Hills does not overdo anything. He wants courses to be playable for all levels. When a sand bunker is put in on one side of the green, the other side will have a grass bunker or mound.

Three teaching pros here stay busy at the range, a first-rate facility open year round. During the wintertime, heated stalls are open. During the warm weather, grass tees are moved every day. On either end are chipping and putting greens, and there is a new teaching tee. There are also five target greens.

PUBLIC 18+

Brunswick Hills Golf Course   ☎ (330) 225-7370

Area: **Southwest**   City: **Brunswick**   Cost: **$$**$$$ Difficulty: ●●●

Address: 4900 Center Rd. (SR 303), Brunswick

Tees	Ydg.	C/r	S/r	Pace
Back:	6538	70.8	119	
Middle:	6198	69.1	113	
Forward:	5096	69.1	110	

Specials: Senior (60+) & Junior (under 17) specials Mon–Fri before 3 p.m.; season memberships available

Season: Year-round **Hours:** 5:30 a.m.–10 p.m. (peak season, weather permitting)
Tee times: Taken **Leagues:** Mon–Fri, various times **Ranger:** Most days
Practice facil: Putting Green **Clubhouse:** Food, Beer, Liquor **Outings:** Available
(seating for 120 people) **Lessons:** Available **Pro:** Perry Savetski

Directions: I-71 to Exit 226 for SR 303; west on SR 303 (Center Rd.) to entrance on left.

Description In the late sixties, a group of golfers pooled their loot, bought this farmland, and had the first nine holes of Brunswick Hills built. They got an easy nine, with generous fairways and level ground. The stockholders built most of the second nine themselves. What a difference. It's a hilly, beautiful romp through woods of hawthorn, ash, maple, cottonwood, and pines. Many of the holes on the back side, though, while beautiful and often fun to play, lack good design and are penal—a style of design replaced by strategic design long ago, and with good reason. Brunswick Hills is one of the longer courses in the area. It stays open year round. League play is scheduled every day of the week but is not heavy. The front nine here is especially nice for mixed twosomes playing twilight golf.

Highlights Play begins on a 355-yard par 4 across a valley to a wide and trouble-free fairway. The valley, which cuts across the fairway, has a stream coursing through it and will affect play on holes 5, 7, and 9, too. On the back side, the stream will influence play on more than half the holes. The first green is slightly elevated but has no sand.

The front nine is fun, wide open, and not difficult. The back nine is fun, tight, and tough. Players lulled by the front side are brought up short with No. 10, a big dogleg to the left of 355 yards. Attempts to cut the corner are thwarted by a stand of tall trees. Along the right side, the course property ends and o.b. begins. And the sloped green is not easy to hold.

No. 12, a 399-yard par 4, is a beautiful hole. What appears to be a tree farm bounds the right side, and a couple of stands of trees on the left make this fairway narrow. It is not only narrow, but fast headed downhill, where it crosses a creek then rises to a lovely green balanced on the side of a hill.

No. 14, a 325-yard par 4, continues the roller-coaster ride. Missing the fairway can prove costly, but even being on the fairway, with its uneven lies, calls for concentration. This is clearly a side that favors experience.

No. 15, a long, 568-yard par 5, has all the virtues and beauty of the previous three holes—in spades. Not only does the creek have to be cleared, it has be watched, too. After crossing the fairway, it sneaks up the right side. The fairway narrows in the last 200 yards. It ends at a small green; three very good shots are needed to reach it in regulation.

The designers of this back nine just followed Mother Nature and let her have her way. There is nothing forced or artificial about the holes; each takes advantage of the terrain. So there are holes that are both aesthetically pleasing and very challenging.

PUBLIC 18+

Bunker Hill Golf Course   ☎ (888) 749-5827

Area: **Southwest**   City: **Medina**   Cost: $$$$$ Difficulty: ●●◉

Address: 3060 Pearl Rd., Medina

Tees	Ydg.	C/r	S/r	Pace
Back:	6711	71.3	124	
Middle:	6156	69.2	119	
Forward:	5026	68.5	114	

Specials: Senior & Junior specials Mon–Fri until noon and weekends after 3 p.m.

Season: Mar–Nov **Hours:** Sunrise–sunset Sat, Sun; 7 a.m.–10 p.m. Mon–Fri
Tee times: Taken **Leagues:** Mon–Fri evenings; some mornings
Ranger: Daily **Practice facil:** Putting Green **Clubhouse:** Food, Beer, Liquor, Dining room, Pavilion **Outings:** Available (large pavilion for special events)
Lessons: Not available **Pro:** Todd Ingraham

Directions: I-71 to Exit 222 for SR 3; right off the highway; right (west) on Hamilton Rd.; left (south) on US 42 (Pearl Rd.); on right.

Description The ad says it all: if you haven't played Bunker Hill lately, you haven't played it. The newest old course in the area, which was farmland until its transformation to a 9-hole golf course in the 1920s, and an 18-hole course in the 1940s, has undergone another transformation.

The original clubhouse was a small part of a restaurant, well known at the time as the Bunker Hill Inn. A fire destroyed the building in 1959; it was rebuilt as a clubhouse only in 1960. The Ingraham family, which purchased the property in the 1940s and was responsible for adding the second nine holes, still runs the operation. Arnold Ingraham is at the helm.

Bunker Hill might once have been regarded as a second- or third-tier track, but the improvements have not only stretched the course out—they've given it some personality, too.

PUBLIC 18+

The major changes start with the switching of the nines. The former No. 17, now No. 8, remains a par 3 but now features tees built back into the hillside and a rebuilt, larger green. New tees have been added to No. 9. No. 12 and No. 13 are completely new, built around a seven-acre lake. The former Nos. 3 and 4 were combined to make No. 14. No. 15 has been shortened from a par 5 to a par 4, but it still has a severe dogleg left to contend with. For No. 18, holes 8 and 9 were combined to create a par 5. The old No. 8 green was taken out, and the hill behind it was leveled.

The clubhouse and snack bar have also been remodeled. The sausage sandwich here is worthy fare, and, for the sophisticates among us, cappuccino is served. You can't get this much change out of a parking meter.

The pavilion area is private, with its own parking, and will accommodate 140–150 people. The club is adding two floors on top of the clubhouse for a pool room, seven golf simulators, dart boards, a kitchen, and a few televisions. It will make the long, cold Sunday afternoons much easier to bear.

Changes in the future will not be as dramatic but will be important. Superintendent Scott Brickley's work is cut out for him: rebuild and enlarge the greens and add some new tees.

One thing that hasn't changed is Bunker Hill's laudable support of Junior Golf, which provides instruction and playing opportunities for more than 100 kids.

Highlights Soft spikes are mandatory. You will first see a new practice putting green. Remember the old No. 1 tee? That's it. Ten holes feature doglegs of various degrees. If you like carts, the paths here make riding in wet or otherwise inclement weather possible. Paths are marked at 200, 150, and 100 yards. (On par 5s, 250 yards is marked, too.) There are now four sets of tees and monument-type tee markers that add a touch of class.

No. 1 is a big and hilly par 5 of 525 yards. You need a good drive to get over the first hill to reach a flat area in the ravine. Another big hill awaits your next shot. After the second shot, don't forget to ring the bell letting the golfers behind know you cleared the area.

No. 3, par 3, 188 yards. A good-sized tree in front of the green will be the target of a lightning strike if the Great God of Golf hears our prayers.

No. 8, par 3, 130 yards. The changes have made this hole an interesting one; the tees are moved back in to the hill, and three sand traps on the hill lead up to an elevated green that is two-tiered and double-width.

No. 9, par 4, 396 yards, is the signature hole (though No. 18 is also a legitimate candidate). Woods and water on the right; trees on the left. Then the first of two creeks crossing the fairway. And as if you needed any more challenge, the green is steeply elevated. Am I the only guy who questions the design of this hole and its Evil Twin, No. 18? A good drive leaves a downhill lie . . . to a very elevated green. Somehow it doesn't work.

No. 12 is a short yet demanding par 5 of only 484 yards. The seven-acre lake on the right runs the length of the hole. A smaller lake on the left shouldn't be overlooked either. Hitting into a narrow green adds to the challenge.

No. 15, a par 4 of 367 yards, was a longer hole—and a par 5—in a previous life. Shortening it and lowering par didn't do away with the sharp dogleg left, though. Thick woods on the left go all the way to the corner turn. A small green is surrounded by trees.

Bunker Hill is a beautiful and scenic course, with natural terrain that has been enhanced. Right now, it could be the best-kept secret on the west side of town. It won't be for long.

PUBLIC 18+

Carlisle Golf Course   ☎ (440) 458-8011

Area: **Far West**   City: **Grafton**   Cost: **$$**$$$ Difficulty: ●●●

Address: 39709 Slife Rd., Grafton

Tees	Ydg.	C/r	S/r	Pace
Middle:	5860	71.2		

Specials: Senior and Junior specials available Mon–Fri before 3 p.m. (except holidays)

Season: Year-round **Hours:** Dawn–sunset **Tee times:** Not taken **Leagues:** Various times **Ranger:** Daily **Practice facil:** Putting Green **Clubhouse:** Food, Beer, Liquor, Dining room, Pavilion **Outings:** Available **Lessons:** Available

Directions: I-480 to SR 10 (I-480 ends here); west on SR 10; merges with US 20 and SR 301 (LaGrange Rd.); continue on SR 301 south 1/4 mile; right (west) at Slife Rd.; on right.

Description Few things smell as good as Carlisle Golf Course in late autumn. At this rough-hewn course, leaves are raked and burned, wafting an olfactory reminder that summer has passed. After the round, there is a fire to be found in the clubhouse, too. Additions to the wooden clubhouse, a two-story affair, have become annual projects.

Getting to Carlisle is a pleasant trip, because State Route 301 glides past scenic farms; one does not have to go far from the city to enjoy rural delights. A local celebration at the course is Boog Smith Day. Mr. Smith loved golf, and he loved a pitcher of beer. One day after having both, he keeled over and introduced himself to his Maker. Owner Jim Mullins said ol' Boog wanted to go that way. In Boog's honor, players gather to drink beer and play golf.

Highlights Nothing fancy here. It is a homemade, neighborhood course for locals. The front side opens with a straight and unassuming par 4 of 365 yards. The first green is nearly two-tiered, and tricky. Fairways tend to brush up against one another here, and it takes a couple rounds to get comfortable with club selection.

There are riding carts available, but only the aged and infirm should be using them. This is a course made for walking.

The back side is more interesting than the front. The four holes before Norton's Knoll take advantage of the century oaks and a couple manmade lakes. The physical beauty of the course peaks from Nos. 12 through 15.

It is not a long course, at 2,785 out, 3,075 in, par 71. And it is not an especially challenging course. But it can be a fun place to chase the ball. And golfing dreams can come true here—just ask about Boog Smith.

Chardon Lakes Golf Course   ☎ (440) 285-4653

Area: **Far East**   City: **Chardon**   Cost: **$$$**$$ Difficulty: ●●●

Address: 470 South St., Chardon

Tees	Ydg.	C/r	S/r	Pace
Back:	6799	73.1	135	
Middle:	6224	70.2	129	
Forward:	5685	73.0	130	

Specials: Season pass available; Senior specials Mon–Fri

Season: Apr 1–Nov 15 **Hours:** 7 a.m.–9 p.m. weekdays; 6 a.m.–9 p.m. weekends **Tee times:** Taken **Leagues:** Mon–Thu 4–6:15 p.m.; Thu a.m. (Ladies League) **Ranger:** Daily **Practice facil:** Range, Putting Green, Sand **Clubhouse:** Food, Beer, Liquor, Lockers, Showers, Pavilion **Outings:** Available **Lessons:** Available **Pro:** Michael Tirpak

Directions: I-90 to Exit 200 for SR 44; south on SR 44 (becomes South St. in Chardon); on right.

Description This tough and pretty course opened in 1931. It has a wonderful history graced by great names: Tom Weiskopf, Jack Nicklaus, and Arnold Palmer have gone around here more than once. Weiskopf's parents were members throughout the sixties. And Nicklaus holds the course record, a 67 shot during an American Cancer Society benefit in 1974.

Par is 72 over 6,174 yards. Out-of-bounds appears on the first five holes and again on the back side. Aprons in front of the greens add a country-club touch to the course. Another such touch is yardage marked on sprinkler heads. The 150-yard markers are Norway spruces.

Highlights No. 1 is a 348-yard par 4 that begins at a tee with a sign reading: "No Mulligans," No hitting 'til you're happy here.

No. 2 is the only par 5 on the front side and is a short 473 yards. A lake on the right side of the tee should not come into play. Pines are on both sides of the fairway, and on the right is a housing development. A big slice can put the ball into a sunroom. The straight fairway rises gradually to a green with sand on the right front.

No. 4 is a long 205-yard par 3 uphill all the way. On the right, o.b. leads into a field with a sign promising "You'll Be Prosecuted to the Fullest Extent of the Law" for trespassing. Sounds like looking for a ball is a felony. A rude touch to a game marked by civility.

At No. 6, a beautiful hole, stone steps lead up to the blue tees. The hole leaves straight from the tee, then turns sharply left toward the green. This 384-yard par 4 has plenty of creek defining the right side. For the last stretch into the green, pines mark the left side, and water marks the right. It's a very narrow fairway coming in, only 18 yards across. Little wonder this is the number one handicap hole.

No. 17 is a 518-yard par 5 with a creek cutting across the fairway about 100 yards from the green. On the right near the green is a pond that has swallowed thousands of sliced balls. Getting to the green should be a simple matter. It's a wide fairway here with a few stands of trees on either side. But the water combines with an elevated green, a large trap on the right, and a small one on the left to make the hole difficult.

No pushover, this little course is in good hands. Shooting for a record held by Nicklaus (from the blues, slope 135) adds glamour.

PUBLIC 18+

Chenoweth Golf Course   ☎ (330) 644-0058

Area: **Far South**   City: **Akron**   Cost: $$$$$ Difficulty: ●●●

Address: 3087 Chenoweth Rd., Akron

Tees	Ydg.	C/r	S/r	Pace
Back:	6109	68.5	120	
Middle:	5613	66.3	115	
Forward:	4750	67.0	112	

Specials: Senior specials Mon–Fri before 11 a.m.

Season: Year-round **Hours:** Sunrise–sunset **Tee times:** Taken
Leagues: Mon–Fri evenings **Ranger:** Daily **Practice facil:** Range, Putting Green
Clubhouse: Food, Beer, Liquor, Pavilion **Outings:** Available **Lessons:** Not available

Directions: I-77 to Exit 120 for Arlington Rd.; north on Arlington Rd.; right (east) on Chenoweth Rd.

Description This young course was started in 1991; the second nine was added two years later. Although a short course, it's certainly not executive length; the two best holes are longer than 500 yards. Fairways are tight here, and the rolling terrain has plenty of trees. There's only a bit of water, and bunkering is light. No. 5 is worthy of note. This dogleg par 5 is 532 yards long, and the water that runs down the right side from the tee crosses the fairway at the elbow. The home hole is another challenge. It's 502 yards, and a dogleg shows up for the second shot. Water in front of the green. Eagles are rare, indeed.

Cherokee Hills Golf Club

☎ (330) 225-6122

Area: **Southwest**   City: **Valley City**   Cost: $$$$$$ Difficulty: ●●●

Address: 5740 Center Rd. (SR 303), Valley City

Tees	Ydg.	C/r	S/r	Pace
Back:	6210	68.3	109.2	3:45
Middle:	5880	67.0	109.2	
Forward:	5420	70.3	116.2	

Specials: Cart special Mon–Fri before 3 p.m., Sat–Sun after 3 p.m. (tee times required); Senior & Junior specials Mon–Fri before 2 p.m.

Season: Year-round **Hours:** Sunrise–sunset **Tee times:** Taken
Leagues: Various times **Ranger:** Most days **Practice facil:** Putting Green, Chipping Green **Clubhouse:** Food, Beer, Liquor, Dining room, Private rooms
Outings: Available (a specialty) **Lessons:** Not available **Pro:** Chad Gibson

Directions: I-71 to Exit 226 for SR 303 (Center Rd.); west on Center Rd. for 5 miles; on left.

Description A handsome red barn has served as clubhouse at Cherokee Hills for many years. Ed Haddad owns this 30-year-old course and keeps it open as much as Ol' Man Winter allows. They play the game at a quick pace here; at the third tee, for example, a sign reads: "If it has taken you more than 25 minutes to get here, you are playing too slowly." Though this is not a particularly long course (only one par 5 on each side), it offers some tough holes.

Highlights The opener, a 340-yard par 4, starts at an elevated tee. It's a lovely view, one of the higher spots on the course. It is lined on both sides with trees. Closer to the green, a creek shows up on the left side in the rough, and a huge old willow stands at the left side of the green.

No. 6, or The Hole from Another Planet, is a 510-yard par 5 played on ground high and low, wide and very narrow. A huge sycamore stands in the middle of the fairway. From the tee, the hole begins innocently enough by stretching straight out for 250 yards. A lake appears on the right side but should not come into play. The surprise is on the left, where the fairway falls over and down a steep hill and then shoots off to the right. In the middle of this low ground is the sycamore. Behind it a hundred yards or so is the green, stuck in the base of a hill. Making matters more interesting is a creek down the left side of the last part of the fairway that then cuts across in front of the green. This hole can likely be played a dozen different ways, and scoring well on it has to be a matter of experience with the hole as well as excellent shotmaking.

No. 10 is a 410-yard par 4, a hole with generous fairway and water at the green. It finishes at the low point on the course, and getting back out and up to the next tee can wind players not used to hauling their own clubs over hill and dale.

PUBLIC 18+

A stepladder on the tee is a good indication that the shot will be blind. So it is at No. 13, where a 390-yard par 4 rolls and rises to the 150-yard marker before heading downhill. Sand is on both sides of the green and, more dangerous, a good-sized lake rests on the left.

Creekwood Golf Club   ☎ (440) 748-3188

Area: **Southwest**   City: **Columbia Station**   Cost: $$$$$ Difficulty: ●●●

PUBLIC 18+

Address: 9691 N. Reed Rd., Columbia Station

Tees	Ydg.	C/r	S/r	Pace
Middle:	6117	68.8	116	
Forward:	4775	69.1	112	

Specials: Call for specials

Season: Year-round **Hours:** Sunrise–sunset **Tee times:** Required weekends
Leagues: Various times **Ranger:** Daily **Practice facil:** Range, Putting Green
Clubhouse: Food, Beer, Pavilion, Patio **Outings:** Available **Lessons:** Not available

Directions: I-480 to Exit 1B for Lorain Rd.; west on Lorain Rd. to Root Rd.; left (south) on Root Rd.; bear right onto N. Reed Rd.; on left.

Description David Sandvick, who built this course, was a bricklayer who loved the game. Sandvick needed three years to build the front nine, which opened in 1960. Six years later, the back side was completed. Sandvick died in 1967, and succeeding management of the course was not what it should have been.

But the Sandvick family has been rebuilding this course for over a dozen years, and it looks like it. The course is in good shape: the drainage problem of years ago grows smaller every year. Fairways, tees, and greens are watered.

Highlights The first hole is wide open and long, a 430-yard par 4. Like a number of holes here, it is not well defined. Water is on the right near the green but should not be a problem. Sand is used judiciously here and seems to be of a finer grain than that of other clubs. This is a good warm-up hole with a green that is easily chipped to.

Several of the greens here have steep sides to them; missing the green and hitting the side can send a ball 30 or 40 yards, a design feature that is penal—and on this course, with these league players, penal design doesn't help.

While No. 10 appears wide open, the 365-yard dogleg to the left calls for some accuracy off the tee. The elbow of the dogleg, which veers to the left, is filled with tall hardwoods and sits on the edge of a creek running across the fairway. It is here that the women's tee is placed, one of the few women's tees on this course that looks like it was not designed as an afterthought. Going down the right side of the fairway is o.b. A rail

PUBLIC 18+

fence marks the end of the course property, and the farm there—fields, silo, barn—is beautiful.

Holes 13, 14, and 15 constitute Amen Corner as designed by Bizarro. No. 13 is a 330-yard par 4. Only 150 out and then 150 to the left, it is a suspiciously short 330 yards. The trouble is the corner of the dogleg; it holds the next tee, and players trying to cut the corner run the risk of killing someone teeing off on No. 14. White stakes make the area o.b.

No. 15 is a 455-yard par 5 that is straight until the final 50 yards, at which point the fairway lurches to the right. In the elbow of the tight dogleg is a stand of tall hardwoods. To get on in two calls for a shot not found in most bags: a high, long fade that drops suddenly. And while chipping the last shot to the green, one runs the risk of getting clobbered by players on the 13th tee. A very crowded corner. The final holes play on more open territory, though.

Deer Track Golf Club   ☎ (440) 986-5881

Area: **Far West**   City: **Elyria**   Cost: **$$$**$$ Difficulty: ●●●

Address: 9488 Leavitt Rd., Elyria

Tees	Ydg.	C/r	S/r	Pace
Back:	6410	70.3	124	4:10
Middle:	6159	69.1	122	
Forward:	5350	68.7	115	

Specials: Senior specials Mon–Fri before 1 p.m.

Season: Year-round **Hours:** 6 a.m.–10 p.m. Apr–Oct; 8 a.m.–4 p.m. Nov–Mar
Tee times: Taken **Leagues:** Various times **Ranger:** Some days
Practice facil: Range, Putting Green, Chipping Green, Sand, 5 target greens
Clubhouse: Food, Beer, Liquor, Pavilion **Outings:** Available (also regular course events) **Lessons:** Available **Pro:** Tony Dulio, PGA

Directions: SR 2 to SR 58 (Amherst/Oberlin); south on SR 58 (Leavitt Rd.); on right.

Description Deer Track is a course that grew up. It started as a par 3 and driving range in 1958. In 1970, it was turned into an executive-length, nine-hole layout. In 1972, Tony Dulio and his late father, Jim, bought the place and remodeled it, making it a regulation par 36. The second nine opened in July of 1989. The course name was originally Midway; it was renamed when the back nine was built. The name comes from the construction period, when the owners would walk the course early in the day and find deer tracks. On the back side lives a fox family; its breadwinner often steals balls from the greens and takes them home. Why? The fox mistakes them for eggs, it is theorized. Someplace on the edge of the course is a fox den filled with Titleists, Slazengers, and Pinnacles.

Tony Dulio continues to invest in his course. New are tees on 2, 9, 11, 17, and 19. No. 17 is an island green that plays 175 yards from the blues,

150 from the whites, 120 from the golds, and 100 from the reds. Deer Track now has four tee boxes on every hole.

Highlights The greens here are well cared for and challenging. The use of manmade lakes and mounds adds a great deal to an otherwise flat layout.

No. 8 is the number one handicap hole, a very difficult dogleg left. It calls for a minor tee shot but an approach of heroic proportions. It is 398 yards, and depending on location of the tee, the drive can be anywhere from 180 to 230 yards. There is a long and narrow lake along the left side of the fairway from the tee. After less than 200 yards, the fairway abruptly turns left. From the tee, players look down a fairway with tall trees on both sides. These narrow the fairway considerably. So it's a tough—some might call it confusing—tee shot. The second shot has to be a long iron or fairway wood down a narrow fairway. Behind the green is plenty of water.

Holes 1, 9, 10, and 18 are parallel and close together. Sharing fairways on these straight and hazard-free holes is common.

PUBLIC 18+

Dorlon Golf Club ☎ (440) 236-8234

Area: **Southwest**   City: **Columbia Station**   Cost: **$$**$$$ Difficulty: ●●●

Address: 18000 Station Rd., Columbia Station

Tees	Ydg.	C/r	S/r	Pace	Women's tees Ydg.	C/r	S/r	Pace
Back:	7154	73.1	125	4:15				
Middle:	6475	70.3	118		5251	70.1	115	
Forward:	5691	66.3	107					

Specials: Call about: Senior specials; specials Apr–Oct weekdays; winter rates; frequent golfer card; winter scrambles

Season: Year-round **Hours:** Sunrise–sunset **Tee times:** Taken **Leagues:** Yes **Ranger:** Daily **Practice facil:** Range, Putting Green, Chipping Green, Sand **Clubhouse:** Food, Beer, Dining room, Pavilion **Outings:** Available **Lessons:** Available **Pro:** Jeri Reid

Directions: I-71 to Exit 231 for SR 82 (Royalton Rd.); west on Royalton Rd. for 6.8 miles; left (south) on Station Rd. for 1.5 miles; on right.

Description A new sign and new landscaping greet golfers at the entrance of Dorlon Golf Club, formerly known as Dorlon Park Golf Course. There's a new owner, too: Deborah Lontor-Bonham has taken over for her late father. Along with pro Jeri Reid, this is one of the rare female owner/head pro combinations in golf. Other things are changing here, including the clubhouse, which has been renovated. The course is also receiving attention—notably the reconstruction of sand traps and major improvements on the driving range. Other recent improvements include continuous cart paths, improved irrigation, and tee reconstruction.

Like your golf courses long? Pack a lunch and tee it up on the blues here. They measure 7,154 yards, par 72.

Highlights This is a flat course, but not without natural beauty or challenge. In some instances, the water hazards have an artificial look about them, but they should: they're man made. The course opens with a par 5, though an easy one. It is 472 yards and has a small lake on the right side about 50 yards from the tee. Water shows up again a couple hundred yards out, also on the right side and reachable. Getting on this green in regulation is often dramatic. There is a big trap on the left front and the green itself is slightly elevated. It falls off steeply in the rear. The greens here are not slow by any means.

No. 7 is a 518-yard par 5 that begins with a long and narrow lake right in front of the tee box. The water is almost a hundred yards long, 20 yards across, and in the shape of a C. Beyond the water, a generous fairway bends a bit to the left. The back and sides of this green fall away sharply. All the greens here call for a steady hand, a sharp eye, and patience.

No. 14 is a 364-yard par 4 from an especially beautiful tee box. Surrounded by oaks more than 100 feet tall and far from the clubhouse, this part of the course seems to encourage players to be quiet. This is a sharp dogleg to the right, and no chance of shooting over the corner here unless one of the 14 clubs is a mortar. Both sides of the fairway lead to deep woods. Grass bunkers show up close to the green.

The greens here tend to be hilly and fast, and many are protected by sand traps. They can teach caution to rash players. It is a long and challenging 18 holes, a course for men and women who have no need for pro shops or lessons.

TIDYMAN'S TIDBITS #3
Stuff every public course should offer:

1) Complimentary tees
2) Scorecards and pencils on the second tee
3) Complimentary handicapping service
4) Refreshment cart
5) Starters who have some idea of what it is to serve as starter
6) On-course toilet facilities

PUBLIC 18+

MacSmith Golf

Bando Boys is how I refer to them behind their backs. Makes them sound like the power behind the power on Murray Hill, doesn't it?

But the Bando Boys aren't power brokers; they're artisans, craftsmen, magicians with golf clubs. They are the stewards of MacSmith Golf Club Company, which, for nearly a half century, has been taking in the bent, the broken, the nicked and battered, the scarred and shattered. After a couple weeks with the Bando Boys, clubs are ready again to do battle, always looking and feeling better than when they were new. There are two Bando Boys, father Vic and son Bob. The third musketeer is Steve Kogovsek.

Bob Bando says, "Lots of times, players will pick up woods we've refinished and stare at them like they never saw them before. Finally, the guy will say, 'I can't hit this. It's too perfect.' As far as compliments go, that's about as good as it gets."

The shop, at 4177 Mayfield Road in South Euclid, isn't much to look at. The one-story cinder block building is a shop, though, not a showroom. It is filled with all the power machines, work tables, hand tools, and supplies needed to care properly for golf clubs.

The Bando Boys create custom clubs, refinish used clubs, and adjust clubs brought in by hundreds of area players as well as customers from across the country. Customers here, whether country club golf professionals or club members or daily fee players, share one trait: each wants his or her clubs to be cared for by the best.

"When we first took over the shop," Bob says, "we had a customer bring in his irons for some work. And my dad noticed the guy talked about his clubs the way most of us talk about our kids. My dad said, 'If that's the way he feels about his clubs, then that's the way we should treat his clubs. We should treat everybody's clubs that way.'"

MacSmith is named in honor of MacDonald Smith and was started by Ken Paxton, who later sold it to Joe Fontana. Fontana hired a young auto mechanic from the neighborhood, Bob Bando, and began the long process of teaching him all he knew.

"It appealed to me because Joe insisted on such high quality. He used to tell me not to compare our work with any other golf shop because no other golf shop cared about quality like we did."

The virtues of the Bando shop are legion, but speed ain't one of them. "If you want it done fast," Bob says, "then you don't want me to do it. When we refinish a club, we go through steps that just can't be hurried."

If price is what you pay and value is what you get, MacSmith's is one of the last great values in golf. Not only is the work done as well as it can be done, there is a pot of coffee brewing and a small indoor range.

Customers and friends drop in for a cup of coffee, some golf talk, and maybe to hit a few balls. "I notice customers talk louder in the summer," Bob says. "And when they pick up their clubs, they don't hang around."

PUBLIC 18+

Ellsworth Meadows Golf Club   ☎ (330) 656-2103
Area: **Far South**   City: **Hudson**   Cost: **$$**$$$ Difficulty: ●●◐

Address: 1101 Barlow Rd., Hudson

Tees	Ydg.	C/r	S/r	Pace
Back:	6503	70.4	125	
Middle:	6125	68.7	119	
Forward:	5233	69.6	116	

Specials: Senior specials Mon–Fri until 3 p.m.; Senior cart special Mon–Fri before noon. Discount for Hudson residents.

Season: Year round weather permitting **Hours:** Mon–Fri 7:30–sunset; Sat, Sun 6:30–sunset **Tee times:** Required **Leagues:** Available **Ranger:** Daily **Practice facil:** Putting Green, Chipping Green **Clubhouse:** Food, Beer, Liquor **Outings:** Available **Lessons:** Available **Pro:** Denny Smith, PGA

Directions: I-271 to Exit 18 for SR 8; south on SR 8; left (east) on SR 303; right (south) on Terex Rd.; left on Barlow Rd.; on left, after Nicholson Dr.

Description Ellsworth Meadows Golf Club is now city owned, and that's a good thing here. Before the purchase in 1997, the course was known as Big Springs, and playing conditions were less than optimal. That was then. This is now. Denny Smith, PGA, is the pro and manager, so the course and club are in excellent hands.

The Ellsworth name is a prominent one in Hudson. James W. Ellsworth was born here and left much of his fortune here—in Hudson Academy, the clock tower, the underground utility system . . . you get the idea.

Players who avoided Big Spring in recent years might want to play again. Almost three quarters of a million dollars is being invested in the course, including clubhouse renovation, the beginning of cart paths, drainage on the west side of the course where rainwater was problematic, a new pump house, and a watering system. Smith brags about the greens being handled as they are, "Each one has been aerated, seeded, top-dressed with loving care. And the results are showing already."

Highlights This has always been a shotmaker's course, with demanding landing areas and narrow fairways. The trees here define many of the holes and the par 5s are all risk/reward holes. You can leave your driver in the bag for lots of tee shots here; accuracy rules.

No. 7, a par 3, is all water and a 160-yard carry.

Among other changes, the nines have been reversed. Good. With the old layout, the home hole was a 330-yard par 4. With the new layout, players charge down a 500-yard par 5 to the clubhouse.

Always a joy to see a course saved; a toast is in order. To Hudson!

Emerald Woods Golf Courses   ☎ (440) 236-8940

Area: **Southwest**   City: **Columbia Station**   Cost: $$$$$ Difficulty: ●●●

Address: 12501 N. Boone Rd., Columbia Station

Tees	Audrey's-Heatherstone				Pine Valley-St. Andrew's			
	Ydg.	C/r	S/r	Pace	Ydg.	C/r	S/r	Pace
Back:	6673	71.7			6629	72.1		
Middle:	6165	69.1			6058	69.1		
Forward:	5295	69.2			5080	69.4		

Specials: Mon–Fri before noon free cart w/ 18 holes (2 players)

Season: Year-round **Hours:** 7 a.m.–sunset weekdays; 6 a.m.–sunset weekends
Tee times: Taken weekends **Leagues:** Mon–Fri 4:30–6 p.m. (one 9-hole layout always available for public) **Ranger:** Most days **Practice facil:** Putting Green
Clubhouse: Food, Beer, Pavilion **Outings:** Available (Large groups welcome; incentives for weekday outings; 3 pavilions.) **Lessons:** Available **Pro:** Dan Banks

Directions: I-71 to Exit 231 for SR 82 (Royalton Rd.); west on Royalton Rd.; right (north) on N. Boone Rd.; on right.

Description In this neck of the woods—farmland for most of its settled history—there are lots of golf holes. Within five minutes of each other are Dorlon, Royal Crest, Hickory Nut, Mallard Creek, and this 5-nine course. The first nine opened in 1965, and that was Audrey's. Heatherstone opened in 1967, Pine Valley opened in 1969, and St. Andrew's in 1977. A fifth nine, called A Walk in the Park, is the latest (and is actually a separate executive-length layout).

Highlights While none of the nines is championship caliber, who cares? These nines are for people who enjoy the camaraderie of golf, who would love to play better but don't have the time or talent. Except for one nine, all are playable and pleasurable.

Audrey's is listed as the No. 1 course. Its No. 2 is a 382-yard par 4, a dogleg left that begins with a pine-lined fairway then gives way to hardwoods. In the last 130 yards to the green, the fairway is made more narrow by Lake Deborah on the right side. There is sand at this green, as well. It is a representative hole here, with woods, water, and sand getting between players and birdies.

No. 4, a soft dogleg left, is a 400-yard par 4. It is the longest par 4 on this nine and for that reason alone the number two handicap. No. 6, a 355-yard par 4 is open, but Lake Deborah guards the left side of the green, and sand sits on the right. No. 8, a 385-yard par 4, has Lake Celestine on its left.

The scorecard matches Heatherstone with Audrey's to make a round.

No. 13 is a long par 3; at 194 yards, more golfers will miss than hit the green. A hook can send the ball into an adjacent backyard, despite a wooden fence erected to prevent such shots. A sign on the fence reads:

"Please, do not enter yard for your ball. Pick up good ball at pro shop counter. Thanks." On the left side of the green stands a handsome locust tree, one of many that dot the course.

The number one handicap on the Audrey-Heatherstone layout is No. 15, a par 4 of 445 yards. It calls for a huge drive to get in position for the approach shot. It is a soft dogleg left, and trees on both sides can slow progress to the egg-shaped green.

No. 17 is another long par 4,417 straight yards with just a few trees giving pause to big hitters. This green has a big, smiling sand trap with a four-foot lip separating sand from green.

The next nine is Pine Valley, known to some players as The Nine Holes From Hell. Jungle combat experience provides the best training for this nine, which begins with the number one handicap hole, a par 4 of 353 yards. The terrain here is hilly and best covered by jeep. The woods get thick enough at times for inexperienced players to need directions to the next tee. Many pack sandwiches and leave a trail of crumbs. It has some unusual holes.

Emerald Woods has some very tough holes, but that doesn't mean great holes.

Erie Shores Golf Course   ☎ (440) 428-3164; (800) 225-3742

Area: **Far East**   City: **Madison**   Cost: $$$$$$ Difficulty: ●●●

Address: 7298 Lake Rd. East, Madison

Tees	Ydg.	C/r	S/r	Pace
Back:	6000	68.2	116	
Middle:	5823	67.2	114	
Forward:	5053	67.0	108	

Specials: Season pass available; winter rates Nov–Apr; call for cart & Senior specials

Season: Year-round **Hours:** Sunrise–sunset **Tee times:** Required weekends, Taken daily **Leagues:** Daily, various times **Ranger:** Daily **Practice facil:** Range, Putting Green, Chipping Green, Sand **Clubhouse:** Food, Beer, Lockers, Pavilion, Indoor patio **Outings:** Available (up to one year in advance) **Lessons:** Available **Pro:** Roger Kreuter, PGA

Directions: I-90 to Exit 212 for SR 528; north on SR 528; right (east) on US 20; left (north) on Bennett Rd. for 3 miles; right (east) on Lake Rd. East; on right.

Description Erie Shores' management completed a $1-million renovation in 1993 that changed and improved this course owned and operated by Lake County Metroparks. Players will be pleased. So will other animals.

"We're certified by the state as a backyard wildlife habitat," Tom Weiss PGA, said. "To qualify, we planted flowers and ferns. Thirty-three species of flowers are laid out strategically to accommodate the life cycles of hummingbirds and butterflies. We have purple martin houses and bat houses and squirrel houses, as well."

They also have golf. This short course was buit in 1957 on two farms; the chicken barn from one was turned into the first clubhouse.

After the park board assumed title, it hit the ground running and has not stopped. At present, Erie Shores (you can reach Lake Erie with a driver and a 6-iron) is a pretty course, well maintained, and staffed with friendly, helpful employees. The courtyard in front of the clubhouse is brick and decorated with flowers. Every tee also has a flower bed, most of them in wooden barrel halves. When not playing, Sherri Davis serves as gardener for the course.

New practice areas have been built, including a 28-station driving range, and the cart paths have been redone.

Calling for tee times is an especially good idea here, as the course schedule is filled with league play, including women, juniors, seniors, mixed couples, and, every Sunday morning, a weekend league of stalwarts. The Sunday morning league, 50 strong, is out before 7:30 a.m. And that is more than "rain or shine." It is year round. When the greens are covered with snow, the players take shovels along with clubs. At least once a month, Weiss puts on some sort of tournament. Night-light tourneys, the nine-hole matches played after dark, are well attended.

Few courses treat "family golf" as warmly as this one.

PUBLIC 18+

Erie Shores Golf Course   (photo courtesy of Lake Metroparks)

Highlights The terrain at Erie Shores is flat, but the course offers some very pretty holes. The greens here are not very fast, but they are healthy. Around most of them, groundskeepers maintain an apron of short grass about seven feet wide.

The course plays easy, and it's a pleasure to walk. It's a pleasure to look at, as well, thanks to the care taken with the flora. At No. 3, a soft dogleg left, the tee looks out over two small lakes in front, and there is a home for purple martins. The 355-yard par 4 has a wide fairway. On some days, a ball hawker sits in the left rough and offers used balls to players.

The No. 8 tee is often completely in shadow. This par 4 of 379 yards bends softly to the left. Bird houses for chickadees and bluebirds show up here.

Erie Shores steadily improves. It's a wonderful course for family golf, where skill levels can differ greatly, but the pleasures of the course can be enjoyed equally.

Fairway Pines Golf Course ☎ (440) 357-7800

Area: **Far East**   City: **Painesville**   Cost: **$$$**$$ Difficulty: ●●●

Address: 1777 Blase-Nemeth Rd., Painesville

Tees	Ydg.	C/r	S/r	Pace
Back:	6619	70.9	112	
Middle:	5910	67.3	107	
Forward:	5081	68.1	106	

Specials: Senior specials Mon–Fri

Season: Mar 15–Nov 15 **Hours:** 8 a.m.–sunset Mon–Fri; 7 a.m.–sunset Sat, Sun
Tee times: Taken weekends, holidays **Leagues:** Mon–Thu evenings (one nine only)
Ranger: Daily **Practice facil:** Range, Putting Green **Clubhouse:** Food, Beer,
Lockers, Showers, Banquet room **Outings:** Available (air-conditioned clubhouse
accommodates 20–200) **Lessons:** Available **Pro:** Milt Johnson, PGA

Directions: SR 2 to exit for SR 535 (Fairport/Nursery Rd.); left off exit across freeway;
right on Blase-Nemeth Rd.; on left past Greenside Rd.

Description While still a young course, Fairway Pines looks and plays as if it has been around much longer than a decade. Fast greens with aprons in front, much water, judicious use of sand traps, and a very challenging layout are among its virtues; yet this course will not intimidate average players. The front side has only one par 5, and that is shorter, at 435 yards, than many par 4s in the area. The course can be dramatically lengthened, though, by playing the blue tees.

"Slow play will not be tolerated," the scorecard reads, and one of the local rules calls for playing o.b. shots stroke only, the ball to be dropped at the point of entry. While disrespectful of the USGA, it will speed play.

Highlights A grove of sycamores and willows leads to the first tee. There, next to an old-fashioned and comfortable park bench, are twin garbage cans; players are asked to separate their trash for recycling.

No. 8, a 372-yard par 4, looks open from the tee but tightens with trees in the last 100 yards. This is one of many tee boxes here that are especially handsome by public course standards. It is 42 yards long and only 8 yards wide. The course can play much longer and with much more challenge using the back of the box. A creek cuts across the fairway before the green, which is surrounded on three sides by tall trees.

The back side begins with a straight par 4 of 353 yards. As on many holes here, stands of trees on both sides add to the physical beauty of the course and insist on play in the fairway. Trees surround a big green, including a stand of white birch on the left side.

No. 15 is only 338 yards from the white tees but no easy par. It's a dogleg left, and blocking players who want to try cutting the corner is a stand of tall trees. An accurate tee shot is vital because the approach must clear a sizable lake waiting in front of the green. The water continues on the right side of the green.

Fairway Pines was designed and built with the modern public player in mind. Neither a pushover nor a U.S. Open layout, these 18 holes offer players plenty of opportunities for par.

PUBLIC 18+

Forest Hills Golf Course

☎ (440) 323-2632

Area: **Far West**　City: **Elyria**　Cost: **$$$**$$　Difficulty: ●●●

Address: 41971 Oberlin Rd. (US 20), Elyria

Tees	Ydg.	C/r	S/r	Pace
Back:	6280	69.7	117	
Middle:	6035	68.6	115	
Forward:	4825	67.6	104	

Specials: Senior specials available; two for one special before 8 a.m.

Season: Mar 14–Dec 30, weather permitting　**Hours:** 7 a.m.–sunset
Tee times: Taken weekends　**Leagues:** Various times　**Ranger:** Weekends
Practice facil: Range, Putting Green　**Clubhouse:** Food, Beer, Liquor, Pavilion
Outings: Available　**Lessons:** Available　**Pro:** Thomas Porter, PGA

Directions: I-480 to SR 10 (I-480 ends here); west on SR 10; merges with US 20 and SR 301 to exit for Lagrange Rd.; right (north) on Lagrange; left (west) on Butternut Ridge Rd.; right (north) on Oberlin Rd.; on right.

Description Forest Hills is owned by Lorain County and leased to Tom Porter, PGA, who started playing here as a youngster and worked on the maintenance crews during high-school summers.

The course has the Black River running through it and a wealth of trees, including cottonwood, walnut, buckeye, and ash.

PUBLIC 18+

Players should take care on arrival to pull into the Forest Hills drive-way and not the drive next door, which belongs to the Elyria Country Club. At Forest Hills, play can be had for around $20; next door, the initiation is more than 20 grand.

Highlights This is a fun course with opportunities for birdies and pars. The first hole is a par 5 of 565 yards. It is a wide-open hole and straight. There is an apron in front of the green, and an apron, when cared for, always provides a country-club look to a hole. There is sand on the left side of the green, which slopes to the rear. The greens here are very well maintained and often fast.

No. 2 shares a tee with No. 16. This 330-yard par 4 sweeps into a valley from an elevated tee. The green is off to the right and is eerily beautiful: in front is a moat-like water hazard and behind, a stand of trees. No. 4 and No. 6 also share a tee, and both holes (like many others on the course) play alongside the Black River.

No. 7 can confound and delight. The tee shot here is crucial. It must go far enough to leave a clear approach to the small elevated green, but not so far that it tumbles into the boomerang-shaped lake that is straight out from the tee. At that point, the fairway turns left and rises. Pines guide the hole to the green.

No. 11, a gorgeous par 3, is only 135 yards. The tee is elevated, the green at the bottom of a valley. Both sides of the hole are wooded, and there is a small pond to the right of the green.

Fowler's Mill Golf Course   ☎ (440) 729-7569

Area: **Far East**   City: **Chesterland**   Cost: **$$$$$**   Difficulty: ●●●

Address: 13095 Rock Haven Rd., Chesterland

Tees	Lake/River				Lake/Maple				River/Maple		
	Ydg.	C/r	S/r	Pace	Ydg.	C/r	S/r	Pace	Ydg.	C/r	S/r
Back:	7002	74.7	136	4:01	6595	72.1	128		6385	70.7	125
Middle:	6623	72.8	133		6375	70.6	126		6226	69.5	122
Forward:	5950	73.9	122		5913	73.6	123		5797	73.0	123

Specials: Mon–Fri specials before 8 a.m. and after 3 p.m.; Senior specials Mon–Thu before 10 a.m.

Season: Mar–Nov **Hours:** Sunrise–sunset **Tee times:** Taken, credit card guarantee for Fri, Sat, Sun, hol. **Leagues:** Mon–Fri 4–6 p.m. on Maple nine only **Ranger:** Daily **Practice facil:** Range, Putting Green **Clubhouse:** Food, Beer, Liquor, Dining room, Lockers, Pavilion **Outings:** Available (Indoor banquet space for 200+ guests) **Lessons:** Available

Directions: I-271 to Exit 34 for US 322 (Mayfield Rd.); east on US 322 for 10 miles, through Chesterland; right (south) on Rock Haven Rd., right at fork in road, on left.

Description What do you think about a public course that has a rough-renovation program? Fowler's Mill, the course designed for TRW in 1970, often looks more like a private club, and that renovation project is a good example of the management's commitment to a great course. TRW operated the course exclusively for employees. When American Golf Corporation bought it in 1986, Fowler's Mill was opened to the public. The course was designed by Pete Dye, and the signature par 4 is the 438-yard No. 4, a hole for heroes. There are just a couple of ways to succeed on that hole but a hundred ways to get in trouble. It is only one of a number of rewarding holes here.

Fowler's Mill is not a course for beginners or for those with short tempers. Lessons are available on the grass driving range and sizable practice green. Even with such help, the average score here hovers around 101. The greens here are maintained as well as any in this area. Conditioning is exemplary. A new clubhouse opened in 1998; the guest of honor was Mr. Dye himself.

PUBLIC 18+

Fowler's Mill Golf Course   *(photo © D² Productions, Murphy/Scully)*

Highlights The infamous No. 4 fairway is narrow and dangerous. It runs along the side of a large lake on the right. An inadvertent slice, however slight, can be the beginning of disaster. But bailing out to the left means lengthening the hole and making par a more difficult score. From the tee, players must stay straight. Even a great drive is just a beginning. The approach shot, a long iron, has to be equally great. About 200 yards out, the fairway takes a 90-degree right turn and continues to hug the lake. The green is protected by plenty of sand and fortified with Dye's trademark railroad ties. It would be interesting if management measured the average score on this one.

No. 5, the only par 5 under 500 yards, is a 483-yarder with a fairway that bends first to the left and then back to the right. It's hilly, and there's plenty of sand at the green. This hole is representative of the course in that it can't be played well by first-timers. The pleasures of playing here grow with subsequent visits, but the first round can be confounding.

No. 9 is the first hole since No. 4 to have water, and unusual water it is. A wide creek cuts diagonally across the fairway, creating two landing areas. This 366-yard par 4 calls for an accurate tee shot. The approach shot also calls for judgment. The water and sand are hazards on the left.

A number of area courses are distinguished by having one side far more difficult than the other. Not so here. Both sides are hard. The front nine is called the Lake Nine, the back nine is called the River Nine. There is a third nine, the Maple Nine, which is treated by most players as an oddity. It will be covered below.

The River Nine has holes numbered and handicapped one through nine. The fact that it is almost always played as the back nine is not considered on the scorecard.

A real premium is placed on the tee shot on No. 6, a 405-yard par 4 and the number one handicap on this nine. Trees guide the hole down the left side and a few tall hardwoods stand on the right. Also down the right are sand traps. The fairway is narrow, and it slopes left to right. Unusual lies are not unusual here.

No. 9 is a hard one to win matches on. It's a long and tough par 5 that sees few birdies. It is 544 yards long and almost impossible to reach in two. From the tee, it looks wide open, and it is, but this dogleg left has sand on the right and left sides of the fairway as well as around the green. The sand continues down the left side and the green is elevated. A par here is a great way to finish a round.

Many players here are ardent fans of Pete Dye's layout but know little or nothing about the third (Maple) nine. That's a shame—it's gorgeous.

Across Rock Haven Road, the Maple No. 1 is wide and comfortable (though occasional car traffic behind the tee can be noisy). This par 4, 351 yards, is a dogleg left with deep woods down the right side and a few trees on the left. In the last 100 yards the fairway narrows, turns sharply left, and rises 15 or 20 feet to the green.

After leaving the road behind, this nine is much quieter, most of the noise supplied by crickets.

No. 3, a magnificent par 5, is 516 yards. The fairway rises slowly and crests about 220 yards from the green. It slips gradually down to the green and narrows. Trees stand up in the left rough and create a place for Canada geese to mill about. Sand is on the left side of the green and an old hardwood grows next to it. The hole is magnificent not for the degree of difficulty but for the physical beauty of its surroundings.

What a delightful difference between the Maple Nine and the other two on the other side of the road. But it shouldn't be hard to believe the same designer dreamed up all three. The aim of golf design, after all, is to create both challenging and playable courses. That was certainly done here at Fowler's Mill.

PUBLIC 18+

Fox Den Fairways   ☎ (888) 231-4693
Area: **Far South**   City: **Stow**   Cost: **$$$$**$ Difficulty: ●●●

Address: 2770 Call Rd., Stow

Tees	Ydg.	C/r	S/r	Pace
Back:	6447	70.6	125	3:40
Middle:	6136	69.1	121	
Forward:	5273	71.0	114	

Specials: Special prices Mon–Thurs before 3 p.m., all day Friday; Senior specials Mon–Thu before 3 p.m.

Season: Mar 25–Dec 1 **Hours:** Sunrise–sunset **Tee times:** Required weekends, suggested weekdays **Leagues:** Tue–Thu 8–9:45 a.m; Mon–Thu 4:30–6:30 p.m. **Ranger:** Most days **Practice facil:** Range, Putting Green, Chipping Green, Sand **Clubhouse:** Food, Beer, Pavilion, Picnic area **Outings:** Available (Limited to 32 or fewer) **Lessons:** Available **Pro:** Tom McKinney

Directions: I-271 to Exit 18 for SR 8; south on SR 8 to exit for Hudson/SR 303; east on SR 303 (E. Streetsboro Rd.) into Hudson; then right (south) on SR 91 (Main St.) into Stow; left on Fishcreek Rd.; left on Call Rd.; on right.

Description Fox Den has a comfortable clubhouse, a very good juniors program, and a solid layout. It was built in 1966 and is today an important part of the Stow/Akron community. It is home to the Memorial Four-Person Scramble to benefit Edwin Shaw Hospital, the Junior Championship, a couple of pro-ams, and the Akron Amputee Open.

The sand here seems to be of particularly high quality, clean, light and fluffy. A number of holes are too close to each other. Three tees have been relocated: 2, 12, and 13. This will stretch the blue tee course to nearly 6,500 yards and the regular tees to 6,136.

Highlights The first tee box is notable for its gorgeous flower garden. Throughout the course, well-tended and colorful flower boxes show up

PUBLIC 18+

at tees. There are no white tees here. Instead, yellow marks the middle tees. Blue is the championship length, red for forward markers.

The course gets prettier with each hole. The tee box at No. 3 backs into tall hardwoods. On No. 4, the number two handicap hole, the Arbor Committee tends to locusts, willows, oaks, and firs.

No. 5 is an unfair par 5 that goes out only 165 yards before turning right and chugging uphill. It is unfair because there is no chance for players to get on in two, and the drive—only 165 yards—is not important.

For players using the blue tees, the difference really comes into play on No. 8. It's a 320-yard downhill par 4 from the yellow tees. But from the blues, it suddenly stretches to 414 and calls for a Trevino fade.

On the back side, players again march uphill. But the pleasant surprises there are worth the walk. At No. 12 is a flower box 4 ½ feet deep, 30 feet long, and 10 feet wide. With that kind of investment, you know it will be well tended, and it is.

FoxCreek Golf and Racquet Club ☎ (440) 282-9106
Area: **Far West**   City: **Lorain**   Cost: **$$$**$$ Difficulty: ●●●

Address: 5445 Beavercrest Dr., Lorain

Tees	Ydg.	C/r	S/r	Pace
Back:	6407	71.5	131	
Middle:	6004	69.8	127	

Specials: Limited membership available; Senior specials available (limited times)

Season: Apr–Nov **Hours:** Sunrise–sunset **Tee times:** Required **Leagues:** Mon–Fri, one side 5 p.m.–close **Ranger:** Daily **Practice facil:** Putting Green **Clubhouse:** Food, Beer, Liquor, Dining room, Lockers, Showers, Tennis, Racquetball, Health club **Outings:** Available **Lessons:** Available **Pro:** Mike Masterson

Directions: SR 2 to exit for SR 58 (Leavitt Rd.); north on SR 58; left (west) on Jaeger Rd.; right (north) on Kolbe Rd.; left (west) on Beavercrest Dr.; on left.

Description FoxCreek is a semi-private value rarely matched among the best golf courses in Northern Ohio. Lorain CC was started in 1958 when Curley DeBracey designed the front nine. The next year the back nine was designed by local builder Frank Nardini. Both men took advantage of Beaver Creek, which does more twisting and squirming than a member of Congress. It provides water hazards on 13 holes.

The course record is held by PGA Pro Mike Masterson with a 62.

Highlights No. 1 quickly introduces players to the course's virtues. The view from the elevated tee is magnificent and inspiring. Inspiration helps, because the drive on this 492-yard par 5 really has to get out there. It's a dogleg left, and the approach is made more challenging by huge willows on the left side and Beaver Creek ambling across the fairway in front of the green. All that is necessary to par this opening hole is a big and accurate drive, a very accurate second shot (move the ball to the right side of the fairway, but keep it out of Beaver Creek), and a wedge to the green. Oh, and good putting, too.

No. 3, the number one handicap hole, is a 420-yard par 4 that bends around to the left. About 90 yards from the green, the fairway suddenly rises. Course management is very important.

The back nine, said to be tougher than the front, starts with a 355-yard par 4 from an elevated tee. It's another tough tee shot, and the pro here says the rough on the right is better than the fairway on the left.

There is more water on this nine, and accuracy is more valuable. There are no holes for coasting here.

The two finishing holes are short, but each calls for control. No. 17 is only 306 yards, but with water to the right and a very narrow landing area before hitting to an elevated green, it is demanding just when player fatigue becomes a factor. No. 18 is a par 3 of only 117 yards, and with the clubhouse in the background, novices tend to hit short.

Don't expect liveried doormen here or formal dining. But to play a challenging course with players of like mind, it's well worth the trip and the expense.

PUBLIC 18+

Gleneagles Golf Club   ☎ (330) 425-3334
Area: **Southeast**   City: **Twinsburg**   Cost: $$$$$$ Difficulty: ●●●

Address: 2615 Glenwood Dr., Twinsburg

Tees	Ydg.	C/r	S/r	Pace
Back:	6545	72.2	121	
Middle:	5918	69.6	118	
Forward:	5147	69.4	115	

Specials: Senior specials Mon–Fri before noon

Season: Apr–Dec **Hours:** Sunrise–sunset **Tee times:** Required, two weeks in advance **Leagues:** Mon–Fri 4–6 p.m. **Ranger:** Daily **Practice facil:** Range, Putting Green **Clubhouse:** Food, Beer, Pavilion, Covered porch **Outings:** Available (for corporate or group outings–provide own caterer, cookouts, buffets; party tent for up to 200 people) **Lessons:** Available **Pro:** Michael Brown, PGA

Directions: I-480 to Exit 37 for SR 91 (Darrow Rd.); north on SR 91; right (east) on Glenwood Dr.; on left.

Description The patron saint here is Lazarus, who knows a thing or two about coming back from the dead. Gleneagles, named after the course at the Gleneagles Hotel in Perthshire, England, struggled its first few years. Maintenance and conditioning were not high on the to-do list, and enjoying the wonderful design of Ted McAnlis was difficult. The driving range was more suited to goat farming than golf practice.

PUBLIC 18+

When the city fathers decided to buy the young course a few years ago, Gleneagles was on its way to becoming a very good municipal course. But, for some reason, the nines have been reversed.

One excuse was that the first tee was too far from the clubhouse to keep an eye on it; the fear was that players would sneak on. This is a reason for disregarding the designer's design? Another excuse was that the first tee was too far from the driving range. Say what? In McAnlis's original design, the opening hole was a wide-open, lazy par 5 of only 460 yards—a great hole to warm up with. And the home hole was a dandy: a par 4 that hung on the edge of a lake and virtually insisted on a dramatic finish. Such disregard for the designer's wishes is shameful— some would call it a capital crime. Now instead of the course being played as it was meant to be played, which in this case means building to a climax, it is just two very nice nines.

Highlights The front side starts off like a roller coaster and hints at the excitement that will follow. The first tee looks out on a fairway racing steadily downhill and sloping right. Such downhill/sidehill lies can challenge the most experienced player in any foursome. Only 371 yards, this hole has trouble spots enough to upset a good round. A creek crosses 40 yards in front of the green.

The elevated tee at No. 3, a par 4 of 393 yards, encourages thought and concentration. It faces a steep drop to a valley bottom and water, after which the fairway veers sharply left and up. The large green is surrounded by tall trees. This hole calls for consecutive good shots and offers little margin for error.

No. 9 is dramatic. It begins easily enough, a straight shot from the tee, but suddenly the fairway drops steeply off to the left, and the remainder narrows like a corset-cinched waist. The big lake on the left reaches up the left side of the green, and suddenly the approach shot takes on another dimension.

The back side starts with a big, lazy par 5 and ends with a big, lazy par 4. With the original design, the course was exciting, even memorable, but with the nines switched, the magic isn't there.

Golf Club at Wiltshire   ☎ (440) 237-5271

Area: **South**   City: **Broadview Hts.**   Cost: **$$$$**$ Difficulty: ●●○

Address: 2737 Edgerton Rd., Broadview Hts.

Tees	Ydg.	C/r	S/r	Pace
Back:	6526	72	121	
Middle:	6079	69.6	115	
Forward:	5241	70.2	114	

Specials: Senior specials Mon–Fri before 11 a.m.

Season: Opens in Mar **Hours:** 7 a.m.–sunset **Tee times:** Taken
Leagues: Mon–Fri **Ranger:** Daily **Practice facil:** Range, Putting Green
Clubhouse: Food, Beer, Liquor, Lockers, Showers, Banquet rooms
Outings: Available **Lessons:** Available **Pro:** Dave Moskal

Directions: I-71 to Exit 231 for Royalton Rd. (SR 82); east on SR 82; right (south) on State Rd., left on Edgerton Rd.

Description What used to be Briarwood is changing to Wiltshire golf community, and in the process, the three nines there will be reworked to 18 holes. Luxury housing will surround the course, and a new clubhouse, four brand new holes, improved cart paths, and other improvements will make the new, semi-private course a better place to play. More expensive, too. Stay tuned.

Good Park Municipal Golf Course   ☎ (330) 864-0020

Area: **Far South**   City: **Akron**   Cost: **$$$**$$ Difficulty: ●●●

Address: 530 Nome Ave., Akron

Tees	Ydg.	C/r	S/r	Pace
Back:	6663	72.0	123	3:50
Middle:	6270	70.3	119	
Forward:	5094	69.1	115	

Specials: Senior & Junior specials Mon–Fri before 11 a.m.

Season: Apr–Nov **Hours:** Sunrise–sunset **Tee times:** Taken weekends **Leagues:** Mon–Fri 4–6 p.m. **Ranger:** Most days **Practice facil:** Putting Green, Chipping Green
Clubhouse: Food, Beer, Lockers, Showers **Outings:** Available **Lessons:** Not available

Directions: I-77 to Exit 132; north on White Pond Dr.; right (east) on Mull Ave.; right (south) on Hawkins Ave.; right (west) on Sunsetview Dr.; left on Nome Ave.; on right.

Description J. E. Good Park is sneaky tough. It is tight and green and softly rolling. It's beautiful for the strong hardwoods that frame the holes and the care provided for the flora. It is a snug course and hemmed in on all sides by avenues and drives . . . and one major interstate. But thanks to the efficacious use of trees, it never feels crowded or tight.

Soft doglegs and straightaways make up this course, which is a great track for golfers who walk and carry their bags. The rough is hardly a bother. If you can't control your tee shots, you won't lose many balls here. But you won't get honors, either.

PUBLIC 18+

Grantwood Recreation Park   ☎ (440) 248-4646

Area: **Southeast**   City: **Solon**   Cost: $$$$$ Difficulty: ●●●

Address: 38855 Aurora Rd., Solon

Tees	Ydg.	C/r	S/r	Pace
Back:	6374	70.7	124	
Middle:	6063	69.7	122	
Forward:	5607	69.1	119	

Specials: Senior specials Mon–Fri before 3 p.m.

Season: Apr–Nov **Hours:** Sunrise–sunset **Tee times:** Required **Leagues:** Mon–Fri 3:30–6:30 p.m. **Ranger:** Daily **Practice facil:** Putting Green, Chipping Green **Clubhouse:** Food, Beer, Pavilion, Banquet room **Outings:** Available **Lessons:** Available **Pro:** Scott Pollack

Directions: I-271 to Exit 27 for US 422; east on US 422 to Solon; south on SR 91; left (south) on SR 43 (becomes Aurora Rd.); near intersection of Aurora and Pettibone Rds.

Description In the mid-1980s, the city of Solon purchased 18 holes on Aurora Road from private owners and created Grantwood Recreation Park. The course, originally built as a nine-hole layout in the twenties, used an old barn for its clubhouse.

In 1981, a new clubhouse and banquet facility went up; a party was held to celebrate the opening. Among the honored guests were members of the Solon Fire Department. And a highlight of the party was the burning down of the old clubhouse.

Though it is owned by the city, Grantwood is not subsidized by taxpayers. Operating funds come only from greens fees, services of the banquet facilities, and pro shop receipts.

Since the town bought it, the course has undergone substantial change. The change continues. New red tees were installed because the original tees were not fair. Other work included planting 200 trees, expanding some greens, and installing more sand traps. It is a busy course, and most of the work was done not to make play more difficult, but to make it safer.

Tee times are strongly recommended here. More than 35,000 rounds are played every year, and leagues account for a good part of that; industrial, seniors', women's, and traveling leagues all enjoy Grantwood.

The clubhouse does a good banquet business, and golf outings and fundraisers are often held here. The facilities, the location, and the excellent parking make it useful year round.

The rough is allowed to grow to about three inches and water comes into play on eleven holes. The course is bisected by a railroad line, which players cross under via an old tunnel. One golfer tells of landing a drive in a slow-moving coal car headed east—his longest drive ever. It must be pointed out, though, that eventually that drive went out of bounds. And out of state. The railroad line is no longer in use, but the tunnel under it still adds a bit of charm to the layout.

Highlights No. 1 is wide open with a trap about 140 yards out. It plays 390 yards, a good warm-up hole. It's difficult to lose a ball on this hole, though the second shot is blind because of the rolling fairway. Better here to ignore the checkered aiming flag and instead shoot for the birdhouse, designed for those great mosquito-eaters: purple martins. Traps protect both sides of the green.

After the first five holes, it's through the tunnel, where traffic to many holes converges. The holes run parallel on this side, but there is enough space between fairways to minimize shooting into (and from) adjacent fairways. This side of the course is carved out of rich farmland and the thick growth and old hardwoods around its edges give it a stadium-like feel. Much more impressive than the other, open side of the tracks.

The two par 5s on the front nine are consecutive. No. 6 is almost 100 yards longer than No. 7, which plays 465 yards. It is No. 7 that is the more interesting, however, because it tempts big hitters to send the second shot to the green, and that shot is blind. The fairway rises gently, dips and bends softly left, and narrows all the way to the green. A bell at this green would make putters feel a bit more secure and, for players approaching, eliminate the need to run up and check for a cleared green.

No. 17, a par 3, tempts adventurous players to hit from the blues even if they are playing the whites. The blue tee is 250 yards—all over water—from the green. The white tees are 100 yards shorter but still over part of the lake.

Grantwood is an amiable course and shows what muny government can do when it puts its mind to running a golf course.

TIDYMAN'S TIDBITS #4
Where the best-dressed players play:
1) Windmill Lakes
2) Little Mountain
3) Fowlers Mill

PUBLIC 18+

PUBLIC 18+

Hickory Nut Golf Club   ☎ (440) 236-8008

Area: **Southwest**   City: **Columbia Station**   Cost: $$$$$ Difficulty: ●●●

Address: 23601 Royalton Rd., Columbia Station

Tees	Ydg.	C/r	S/r	Pace
Middle:	6424		114	

Specials: Senior specials available

Season: Apr 1–Oct 31 **Hours:** Sunrise–sunset **Tee times:** Taken
Leagues: Mon–Fri 4–6 p.m. **Ranger:** Weekends **Practice facil:** Range, Putting Green
Clubhouse: Food, Beer, Pavilion **Outings:** Available **Lessons:** Available

Directions: I-71 to Exit 231 for SR 82 (Royalton Rd.); west on Royalton Rd.;
on left past Marks Rd.

Description The course is flat and easy to walk. The arbor committee did well (trees planted when the course was built in 1961 have grown to thick woods), and the greens are especially well conditioned. New ownership is in place and Hickory's reputation for being the screwiest place to play is changing.

Highlights The first two holes are a good indication that the course is long: the opener is a 440-yard par 4 with an elevated green; No. 2 is a 545-yard par 5.

No. 8 is another long par 5, this one 530 yards. Watch out for a large tree on the right side of the fairway, only a few yards from thick woods. If you aim left, there are more trees to combat. As you work your way down the fairway you will notice the approach to the green narrowed by a tree on the left with overhanging limbs and sand traps on the right. Both the tree and traps are about 20–30 yards from the green. The approach is almost like trying to split the uprights on a 40-yard field goal attempt.

Country Clubs

Slices...

Despite feeling a bit out of place every time I'm at a country club, I have a high regard for them for a number of reasons.

First and foremost: private clubs might be the last business that provides excellent service. Day in and day out, the employees know they are employed to do one thing: provide service to members.

Ah, service. Remember service? When the salesperson or counterman smiled and said, "Can I help you?" When the clerk said, "Right away, sir." And meant it?

It could be that as a society we don't have time for service, that we don't think service is worthwhile. What a shame. Service is the foundation for an atmosphere marked by comfort and ease. Service is the key to relaxing. Service is one of the teachers of good manners.

At private clubs, bag boys, caddies, waiters and waitresses, golf professionals, locker room attendants, and parking valets personify service.

(I shudder to think what sort of profits Burger King could make if the burgers and fries were sold by staff dedicated to service.)

Back to private clubs, though, and their many virtues. There is service and then there is golf. Courses here were designed by some of the great names in golf: Tillinghast, Strong, Dye, Fazio, Ross, Hurdzan & Fry, Von Hagge, and Weiskopf. Each course is maintained and conditioned to delight the senses and make the game more enjoyable.

At the better clubs, caddies vie for the privilege of carrying your bags, keeping your ball clean, finding it when it goes astray, replacing divots, repairing ball marks, providing accurate yardages, tending the flag, smoothing the traps.

There is this wonderful exclusivity at private clubs that allows you to play whenever you want with whomever you want. At private clubs, you're not paired up at the first tee with some moron wearing a muscle shirt and high top tennies and sporting a tattoo that reads, "Born to Lose," smiling a toothless grin as he reaches for a can of beer from his bag.

On private club courses there is a halfway house with fresh lemonade, sandwiches for those who can't make it 18 holes without eating, and restrooms with toilets that flush and basins that run hot water. At private clubs, your clubs are cleaned after a round and safely stored, waiting for the next time you play. No hauling them in and out of the trunk of the car.

Locker rooms have unlimited supplies of hot water, clean towels, and attendants whose job it is to make hygiene a pleasure. Nothing like a round of golf, a quick shower and change, and into the dining room for supper.

The chefs and the kitchen and dining room staff are dedicated to meeting the expectations of the members. Does a bond develop between great chefs in country club kitchens and some of the members who appreciate excellent food? I don't know, but it wouldn't surprise me.

Of course, there's a price for those many pleasures. Initiation fees in this area run between $12,000 and $40,000, though some are lower. Monthly dues, to be spent in the dining room or grill, are another few hundred every month.

Assessments can be expensive surprises, but if the clubhouse roof is about to fall, it has to be repaired.

Money is not the only criterion. At clubs like Pepper Pike CC and The Country Club, membership is limited to the landed gentry, old money, and corporate executives. At others, like the less expensive Tanglewood CC and Avon Oaks CC, entry has more to do with money than breeding. At new clubs with luxury housing, such as Red Tail CC in Avon and Little Mountain in Chesterland, membership is not required with home ownership, but very desirable.

With all the good, there is some not-so-good, of course. The behavior of members, while a few notches above that seen on public tracks, is not perfect by any means. A few years ago a member was suspended from his West Side club for urinating in the middle of a fairway.

A new generation of club members has already slid in the side door of many clubs. They are the nouveau riche, men and women who didn't grow up enjoying club life and often have no idea what sort of behavior is expected. Referred to as "nouveau imbeciles" at some courses, they are the suddenly-rich who think they have to be overbearing and obnoxious to make themselves heard.

They are direct descendants of the moron in the muscle shirt with the tattoo and toothless grin reaching for a beer, and they are an embarrassment to other members.

Club life, after all, is not marked by boorishness; it is marked by class. Members are treated well by the staff, but the staff is treated well by the members, too.

TIDYMAN'S TIDBITS #5

Most Beautiful/Toughest/ Beautiful & Tough

1) *Par Three:* No. 18 at Berkshire Hills/No. 2 at Sleepy Hollow/No. 17 at Hinckley Hills

2) *Par Four:* No. 10 at Dales Course/ No. 3 at FoxCreek/No. 10 at Manakiki

3) *Par Five:* No. 3 at Skyland/No. 17 at Hinckley Hills/No. 12 at Orchard Hills

4) *Opening Hole:* Pine Valley/ Powderhorn/Windmill Lakes

5) *Home Hole:* Fowlers Mill/ Orchard Hills/Berkshire Hills

6) *Front Nine:* Boulder Creek/ Sleepy Hollow/Lakewood CC

7) *Back Nine:* Gleneagles/ Painesville/Little Mountain

Highland Park Golf Course   ☎ (216) 348-7273

Area: **East**   City: **Highland Hills**   Cost: $$$$$ Difficulty: ●●●

Address: 3550 Green Rd., Highland Hills

| | Red Course | | | | Blue Course | | | |
Tees	Ydg.	C/r	S/r	Pace	Ydg.	C/r	S/r	Pace
Middle:	6341	69.7	113	3:40	6709	71.7	119	3:42
Forward:	5945	73.1	119		6289	75.7	125	

Specials: Senior & Junior specials Mon–Fri before 3 p.m. and Sat–Sun after 3 p.m.

Season: Mar 1–Dec 31 **Hours:** Sunrise–sunset **Tee times:** Taken weekends
Leagues: Various times **Ranger:** Daily **Practice facil:** Putting Green, Chipping Green
Clubhouse: Food, Beer, Lockers, Showers **Outings:** Available **Lessons:** Not available

Directions: I-271 to Exit 29 for US 422 (Chagrin Blvd.); west on Chagrin Blvd.;
left (south) on Green Rd.; on right.

PUBLIC 18+

Description Highland, where it once appeared no capital improvements had been made since the sand wedge was invented, is now undergoing important changes. Fairway irrigation has been completed, and a new clubhouse is open.

Highland was built in 1912 and opened for play in 1913. It's really a fine layout; in the mid-sixties, the Cleveland Open was played here and won by "Champagne" Tony Lema. There is a Blue course and a Red course. The Red is almost 400 yards shorter than the Blue, but neither is short.

Highlights The Blue course does not turn at the clubhouse and so does not lend itself to nine-hole play. It opens with a 393-yard par 4 from an elevated tee that looks down on a fairway lined with trees. The terrain continues down until, at about the 150-yard mark, a creek cuts across. On the other side, the ground rises suddenly to a green with sand around the right side and rear.

The number one handicap, No. 3, is a par 4 of 454 yards. The fairway rolls a bit on this and many holes at Highland, but the only drama here is provided by length. The fairway is generous and straight to the green, which has a grass bunker in front and seven white oaks like sentinels behind.

The 18th hole on the Blue course is only the number four handicap hole, but it is a true match-decider hole. A long and dangerous par 4 of 449 yards, it begins with a tee shot into a valley that has a creek running diagonally across the fairway. On the other side of the creek, the fairway leans to the left and rises to an elevated green. A finishing hole of U.S. Open proportions. The strength of the Blue course is definitely the length of many of its holes.

The Red course is decidedly different. The hilly terrain comes into play more than it does on the Blue. Both nines finish at the clubhouse.

And the Red course winds up with a pair of par 4s totaling only 729 yards.

No. 1 is a blind tee shot. A par 4, it is 388 yards over an up-and-down fairway. It rises from the tee and crests at about 200 yards, then falls steadily until 50 yards from the green, where it rises again. This hole could use a bell to ring to let players on the tee know when it is safe to hit. A ranger could fill the same need, but neither is provided.

The 4th tee is reached after a short walk through the woods. This par 5 is 480 yards and straight as the crow flies. For golfers, however, the wide fairway drops suddenly at the 150-yard marker. All the way down the right side are deep woods; a line of trees marks the left side. Forty yards from the green, a long and narrow trap runs down the right rough and continues past the green.

No. 8 begins with a tee box obviously used for tank maneuvers. It is yet another blind tee shot with thick woods down the left side and an open area on the right. A 402-yard par 4, it's the number one handicap hole on the Red course. It is number one because it has a blind tee shot, a hilly fairway, and a green that cannot be safely reached except by air. About 40 yards in front of the green, the left side of the fairway suddenly drops, cliff-like, about a dozen feet. Bouncing the ball onto the green is out of the question. And the green, sitting in a shallow valley, is the toughest at Highland. The right side is two or three feet higher than the left. At the left rear, the ground suddenly rises, and on the right is a stand of trees. A tough pin placement can easily add three or four strokes to a score. A par on No. 8 is something to talk about.

All in all, Highland could again become one of the area's best public courses. Lots of well-designed holes and a convenient East Side location are two of its many virtues. But it needs a commitment to golf on the part of the owners. The players are ready and waiting.

TIDYMAN'S TIDBITS #6

Big names in local course design:

1) Avalon and Fowlers Mill by Pete Dye
2) Quail Hollow by
   Jay Parrish and Tom Weiskopf
3) Sawmill Creek and
   Sand Ridge by Tom Fazio
4) Little Mountain and
   Stonewater by Hurdzan-Fry
5) Quail Hollow and RedTail
   by Robert Von Hagge

Hilliard Lakes Golf Course   ☎ (440) 871-9578
Area: **West**   City: **Westlake**   Cost: **$$$$**$ Difficulty: ●●●

PUBLIC 18+

Address: 31665 Hilliard Blvd., Westlake

Tees	Ydg.	C/r	S/r	Pace
Back:	6785	70	124	
Middle:	6386	69.5	121	
Forward:	5611	74	118	

Specials: Senior specials Mon–Fri 10 a.m.–3 p.m.

Season: Mar–Dec **Hours:** Sunrise–sunset **Tee times:** Taken
Leagues: Mon–Thur 4:30–6 p.m. **Ranger:** Daily **Practice facil:** Range,
Putting Green **Clubhouse:** Food, Beer, Liquor, Dining room
Outings: Not available **Lessons:** Available **Pro:** Sandy Davis

Directions: I-90 to Exit 156 for Crocker-Bassett Rds.; south on Crocker Rd.;
right (west) on Hilliard Blvd. to dead end at Lincoln Rd.

Description On a flat piece of land with a little water going through it,
Matthew Zaleski built this course in 1967. His son Ron manages it. Part
of the land was once officially listed as Avon Airport. The 18th hole was
the runway, and in World War II military pilots trained here.

No outings here. "Just room for golfing only," Zaleski says. No tee
times, either. Just show up and get in line.

The blue tees are 6,665 yards and the whites are 6,183 yards. The forward tees are 5,611 yards, long by most standards for forward tees.

Highlights "The whole back nine is different," Zaleski says. No. 11 used
to be a par 5, now it's a long par 4 at 426 yards. No. 12 is a par 5, 548
yards—the combination of a former par 4 and par 3; number 15 is a
new par 3. Tees are being moved back on some of the holes on the front
side. It will make them longer, of course. All in all, Hilliard Lakes is a
wonderful, playable, accessible, well-maintained, well-conditioned,
well-run golf club.

PUBLIC 18+

Hinckley Hills Golf Course

☎ (330) 278-4861

Area: **South**   City: **Hinckley**   Cost: **$$$$**$ Difficulty: ●●●

Address: 300 State Rd., Hinckley

Tees	Ydg.	C/r	S/r	Pace
Back:	6846	71.6	125	3:55
Middle:	6253	69.2	120	
Forward:	5478	70.9	118	

Specials: 2 players & cart specials daily and holidays after 2 p.m.

Season: Apr 1–Nov 15 **Hours:** Sunrise–sunset **Tee times:** Taken
Leagues: Daily **Ranger:** Daily **Practice facil:** Putting Green, Chipping Green, Driving net **Clubhouse:** Food, Beer, Liquor, Pavilion, Party room
Outings: Available **Lessons:** Available **Pro:** Michael Smith

Directions: I-71 to Exit 226 for SR 303; east on SR 303 (Center Rd.); left (north) on State Rd.; 2 miles, on left.

Description This challenging and hilly course is a tough one to walk. Designed by the late Harold Paddock, Sr., and opened in 1963, it plays 6,248 yards, most of them uphill, downhill, or sidehill. Those numbers are from the white tees. From the blue tees, it plays 6,846 yards, par 73 (there is a second par 5 on the back). It's a powerful course from the white and blue tees, and women golfers have no pushover in front of them: the ladies' tees play 5,478 yards, par 72. Unless groups have lots of good players, outings will have a hard time on this course. The pro shop/clubhouse has been expanded and improved in recent years and combines with a nearby pavilion to provide services, including outings, that are first rate. The course is filled with hills, water, big greens, sand, and, on two holes, natural gas wells. Free drops from the wells.

Hinckley Hills Golf Course   *(photo: Jonathan Wayne)*

Highlights The course wastes no time in showing off its virtues. No. 1 is a 510-yard par 5 from an elevated tee. The wide fairway sweeps up and down, then up and down again as it makes its way to an elevated green. Trees fill both sides of the last 100 yards. While neither short nor easy, Hinckley does play wide open. Length here is slightly more valuable than accuracy. With twenty-four yards of turf, the difference between the white tees and the blue tees is substantial yardage if the hole is a par 3 or par 4, but on the legendary par-5 No. 9, it's not much. Hitting from the white tees begins a journey of 592 yards. Hitting from the blues, it's 630 yards. Regardless of starting point, the hole is tough. Not just because of the length, but because the fairway, which rises and falls steeply, provides players with difficult uphill and downhill lies. It is a straight hole, o.b. all the way down the left side. To make it more scenic, a three-acre lake bed was excavated and allowed to fill with springwater and runoff. Hinckley Hills is one of five public courses in tiny Hinckley, Ohio.

PUBLIC 18+

Indian Hollow Lake Golf Club   ☎ (440) 355-5344

Area: **Far West**   City: **Grafton**   Cost: $$$$$ Difficulty:

Address: 16525 Indian Hollow Rd., Grafton

Tees	Ydg.	C/r	S/r	Pace
Middle:	5910			
Forward:	4865			

Specials: Special prices Mon–Thu until 1 p.m. & anytime Fri

Season: Year-round **Hours:** Sunrise–sunset **Tee times:** Taken weekends **Leagues:** Various times **Ranger:** Most days **Practice facil:** Putting Green, Chipping Green **Clubhouse:** Food, Beer, Liquor, Snack bar **Outings:** Available **Lessons:** Available

Directions: I-71 to Exit 226 for SR 303; west on SR 303 past SR 83 and across the Black River; right (north) on Indian Hollow Rd.; on right.

Description The Black River graces the back nine of this very playable layout put together by Don Gardner, golf fanatic and mechanic by trade, in 1968. It remains a family-run operation.

No. 13, a par 4 of 340 yards, is a dogleg left with the Black River on the right. The tee shot doesn't have much landing room, and the approach has to take into account a grove of black walnut trees. The course has specials every weekday until 1 p.m. On Fridays, the special goes on all day. A third nine is being constructed.

Ironwood Golf Course   ☎ (330) 278-7171
Area: **South**   City: **Hinckley**   Cost: **$$$$$**   Difficulty: ●●●

Address: 445 State Rd., Hinckley

Tees	Ydg.	C/r	S/r	Pace
Back:	6360	69.7	118	
Middle:	6042	68.3	115	
Forward:	5785	72.8	124	

Specials: Senior specials Mon–Fri before 3 p.m.

Season: Apr–Oct **Hours:** Sunrise–sunset **Tee times:** Taken **Leagues:** Mon–Fri 3–6 p.m. **Ranger:** Daily **Practice facil:** Putting Green, Chipping Green **Clubhouse:** Food, Beer **Outings:** Available (for golf only) **Lessons:** Not available **Pro:** Mark Bell

Directions: I-71 to Exit 226 for SR 303 (Center Rd.); east on Center Rd. to SR 94 (State Rd.); left (north) on State Rd.; on right, after Eastwood Rd.

Description Ironwood was laid out by the late Harold Paddock, a designer who also helped create Hinckley Hills and other courses. He was in a wheelchair by the time he worked on Ironwood. The first nine holes opened in 1967; the back nine opened a year later. Even unable to play, he laid out a track with a lot of personality. In addition to the usual golf skills, stamina, and endurance help here.

More than 20,000 rounds are played here each year. There is plenty of league play, including traveling leagues on the weekends. Tee times are taken for weekend play but are unnecessary weekdays. The pro shop is in one end of a clubhouse that seats more than 80.

From the white tees, it plays 6,042, par 71. If that sounds short, players should know that three of the par 4s on the front side stretch more than 420 yards. And Ironwood takes advantage of its many hills. Walking this course is a joy. If you have a pack mule to handle your bag.

Highlights No. 1 is one of the long par 4s—431 yards, all downhill, to a green that falls away on the sides. The entire right side of the hole is o.b., and trees mark the left side. The view of the valley from the first tee is magnificent. The first green is sizable.

Behind the first green is the tee for No. 2, a par 3 of more than 200 yards, again downhill. On both sides of the steep fairway are woods. So the tee calls for more than a big hit—it also has to be accurate. This green is also substantial. But it is sloped steeply, and getting a tee shot to stick here is no guarantee of par. The sides of the green, especially in the back, fall away.

To play the second nine, it's back into the valley. No. 10 is a 368-yard par 4, all downhill. No. 11, still downhill, is a par 3 of 171 yards. The penalties for a poor tee shot are severe: the green is protected by a pond in front; on both sides are hardwoods and thick brush.

Players may not usually brag about getting on a 359-yard par 4 in regulation, but No. 14 might be an exception. The tee shot on this 359-yard par 4 must avoid water in front of the tee and more water on the right side of the narrow landing area. The approach shot has to reach a much-elevated green. To make the shot more interesting, at the bottom of the green on the left is a sizable pond. The fairway narrows to 30 yards. At the green, woods line the rear and right side. No sand here, but that adds small comfort.

Ironwood opens April 1 and closes November 15. Outings are no longer held here ("They're a hassle"), though Bob Brown welcomes small golf parties. He has enough to worry about. Maintaining the course, with its hills and valleys and ponds, is job enough. The ponds supply water for the course, so it suffers much less during drought periods than courses with only municipal water.

PUBLIC 18+

Kent State University Golf Course   ☎ (330) 673-4000
Area: **Far South**   City: **Franklin Township**   Cost: **$$**$$ Difficulty: ●●●

Address: 2346 SR 59, Franklin Township

Tees	Ydg.	C/r	S/r	Pace
Middle:	5327	64.9	107	
Forward:	4524	64.2	109	

Specials: KSU faculty & staff specials Mon–Fri before 1 p.m.; KSU students specials weekdays; KSU Alumni specials; Senior specials Mon–Fri

Season: Mar 1–Dec 24 (weather permitting)   **Hours:** Sunrise–sunset
Tee times: Recommended   **Leagues:** Various times   **Ranger:** Weekends
Practice facil: Putting Green   **Clubhouse:** Food, Beer, Pavilion
Outings: Available   **Lessons:** Available   **Pro:** Mike Morrow, PGA

Directions: I-480 to SR 14 east (I-480 ends here); right (south) on SR 43 (Clev-Canton Rd.); left (east) on SR 59 past KSU campus.

Description With its small greens and thousands of trees, this course makes winners out of golfers good with their irons. It's a great place for outings, because skilled shooters win, and hackers are not overwhelmed. The trees here shape a number of holes and provide back settings at lots of greens. The place is old, built in 1929 by a local designer. Mike Morrow, PGA, brags about these small greens, claiming that they sometimes approach the quality found only in private clubs. It is No. 6 that will always challenge him, a 225-yard par 3 with a very small green. Missing the green leaves no good approach angle. "It's very hard to make a 3," the pro said.

Kent State University Golf Course

Links Golf Club ☎ (440) 235-0501

Area: **West**   City: **Olmsted Twp.**   Cost: $$$$$ Difficulty: ●●●

Address: 26111 John Rd., Olmsted Twp.

Tees	Ydg.	C/r	S/r	Pace
Back:	5000	63.6	107	3:19
Middle:	4500	60.6	96	
Forward:	3570	60.1	96	

Specials: Senior specials Mon–Fri until 2 p.m.

Season: Year-round **Hours:** Mon–Fri 7:30 a.m.–9:30 p.m.; Sat, Sun 6 a.m.–9:30 p.m.; shorter hours in winter **Tee times:** Required weekends, Recommended weekdays **Leagues:** Mon–Fri 4–6 p.m. **Ranger:** Daily **Practice facil:** Range, Putting Green, Chipping Green, Sand **Clubhouse:** Food, Beer, Liquor, Dining room, Pavilion, (men's showers only) **Outings:** Available **Lessons:** Available **Pro:** Vince Mastro

Directions: I-480 to Exit 6 for SR 252 (Great Northern Blvd.); south on SR 252 (becomes Columbia Rd.); right (west) on John Rd.; on right.

Description Going out, it plays into a trailer park; coming in, it wanders through the backyard of an old folks' home. This course has been a poorly maintained executive-length course (where they sometimes sprayed the greens . . . well, green) since it opened. Whether management is trying to repair a reputation for nonexistent customer service is unclear. The last time we played (and I do mean the last time) the starter was lounging in a cart behind the tee yelling for us to hit. Did he see the players in the middle of the fairway? Doubt it. It was asking too much for him to stand and look. That's a shame, because it could be a wonderful little course. The design is delightful, and its resistance to par could make it a fun course. But without management, it remains a goat farm.

PUBLIC 18+

Little Mountain Country Club   ☎ (440) 358-PUTT

Area: **Far East**   City: **Concord**   Cost: $$$$$$ Difficulty: ●●●

Address: 7667 Hermitage Rd., Concord

Tees	Ydg.	C/r	S/r	Pace
Back:	6615			4:15
Middle:	6200			
Forward:	5332			

Specials: Call for specials

Season: Year round **Hours:** Call for hours **Tee times:** Taken
Leagues: None **Ranger:** Some days **Clubhouse:** Food **Lessons:** Available
Pro: Jimmy Hanlin, PGA

Directions: I-90 to exit 200 for SR 44; left (south) on SR 44; right (west) on Auburn Rd.; right (northwest) on Girdled Rd. (becomes Hermitage Rd.); 1 mile on right.

Description   When the Hurdzan-Fry design team takes an assignment, the result is invariably great golf, and so it is here, where so many of the holes are exciting to see, challenging to play, and memorable. The course moves at a good pace over rolling woodlands, and features 82 bunkers that were super-sized. There are four sets of tees, bent grass is in the fairways, greens and tee boxes, and Kentucky blue grass in the rough. In addition to a three-acre lake, a stream meanders through five holes. The property drops 200 feet from south to north, and from the 17th and 18th tees, Lake Erie can be seen in the distance. Although plans are to take the course private, until the number of members reaches a certain point, the course is open to the public. It should not be missed.

Highlights   The opening hole is a wide and comfortable par 5 that starts at an elevated tee, bottoms out, and rises slowly to a tree-encircled green. It is the only hole without bunkers, and a great way to warm to the task.

No. 3, a 378-yard par 4, is one of the best holes on the front side, featuring a small landing area with lots of undulation and a rockwall in front of a small target green. No. 8 is also worthy of note: only 310 yards, it almost asks, as you're teeing it up, "feelin' lucky?" Big hitters can reach, but any miscalculation means the lake on the left of one of 10 big bunkers.

PUBLIC 18+

No. 10, some players think, is the premier hole on a course with lots of great holes. Played from the tips, it's a par 4 that stretches 470 yards and features a 70-foot deep ravine all the way down the left side. The green is big and accommodating, but it's surrounded by the biggest bunker on a course with lots of big bunkers.

The course record is held by Danny Ackerman, the pro from Longaberger, who shot a 65 last year. Head golf pro Jimmy Hanlin (who was married on the 18th green), also had a 5-under on the 18th tee, but his drive drifted right and his punishment was a bogey. Still, a 66 on this course . . .

Little Mountain Country Club

TIDYMAN'S TIDBITS #7

Best conditioned courses:
1) Painesville
2) Hawks Nest
3) Little Mountain
4) Fowlers Mill

Lost Nation Municipal Golf Course   ☎ (440) 953-4280

Area: **East**   City: **Willoughby**   Cost: **$$**$$$ Difficulty: ●●●

PUBLIC 18+

Address: 38890 Hodgson Rd., Willoughby

Tees	Ydg.	C/r	S/r	Pace
Back:	6440	69.4	113	
Middle:	6095	67.8	110	
Forward:	5700	70.9	112	

Specials: Senior & non-Senior specials Mon–Fri before noon

Season: Year-round **Hours:** Spring–fall: Mon–Fri 6:30 a.m.–sunset, Sat–Sun 6:15 a.m.–sunset; Winter hours: 8 a.m.–5 p.m. **Tee times:** Taken **Leagues:** Mon–Fri 4–6 p.m. **Ranger:** Daily **Practice facil:** Range, Putting Green **Clubhouse:** Food, Beer **Outings:** Available **Lessons:** Available **Pro:** Dave Moskalski

Directions: SR 2 to Lost Nation Rd.; north on Lost Nation Rd.; right at Hodgson Rd.; on right.

Description Lost Nation, built in 1928, has weathered wars, the Depression, good times and bad, and ... weather. Every once in a while, someone bounces a ball on the ice in front of No. 7 and aces the par 3. In fact, a great deal of winter golf is played here. That sounds unlikely, given the easterly location and nearness to the snowbelt, but the winds coming in off the lake push the snow farther south.

Highlights It's a relatively flat course, and, except for Nos. 1 and 9, the front nine is played on the other side of Hodgson Road. No. 1 is a 385-yard par 4. It begins just outside the clubhouse and heads for the Lost Nation Airport in the distance. It bends to the right toward a small green with a couple of traps on the right side. The hole is fairly open, with a driving range on the left and the entrance drive on the right.

At No. 4, the golf gets more challenging. It's a 400-yard par 4, a slight dogleg left. The left side is filled with thick woods, and, before the 150-yard markers, big grass bunkers sit on both sides of the fairway. A few more bunkers appear at the green—one grass and one sand.

No. 5, a 475-yard par 5, has a sneaky little water hazard that begins as a creek cutting across the fairway in front of the women's tees. When it finds the left rough, it turns up toward the green. On the right side of the fairway, big grass bunkers slow balls headed for the adjacent sixth fairway. Players with well-developed slices will share fairways on these two holes.

The back nine opens and closes with par 5s. It is the more difficult nine, because woods and water play a more important role, and the terrain rises and falls more on this side of the road.

Some people say the name of the course comes from an Indian tribe that found itself lost in these parts. That's hard to believe, given the nearness of both State Route 2 and Interstate 90.

Mallard Creek   ☎ (440) 236-8231

Area: **Southwest**   City: **Columbia Station**   Cost: **$$$**$$ Difficulty: ●●●

Address: 34500 Royalton Rd. (SR 82), Columbia Station

Tees	Ydg.	C/r	S/r	Pace
Back:	6622			4:30
Middle:	6199			
Forward:	5754			

Specials: Senior specials Mon–Fri before 3 p.m.; cart specials Mon–Fri before 7:30 a.m.

Season: Year-round **Hours:** Sunrise–sunset **Tee times:** Recommended
Leagues: Mon–Fri 3:30 p.m.–6:30 p.m. **Ranger:** Daily **Practice facil:**
Range, Putting Green, Chipping Green **Clubhouse:** Food, Beer, Pavilion
Outings: Available **Lessons:** Not available

Directions: I-480 to Exit 1B for Lorain Rd.; west on Lorain Rd. (becomes Butternut Ridge Rd. after crossing Root Rd.); left (south) on Island Rd.; left (east) on SR 82 (Royalton Rd.); on left.

OR I-71 to Exit 231 for SR 82 (Royalton Rd.); west on SR 82; on right.

Description Mallard Creek opened its first two nines on Memorial Day weekend, 1992. The third nine joined the family on Memorial Day weekend in 1995. Formerly farmland, the property consists of 350 acres. It is now one of the busiest courses in Northeast Ohio, which makes maintenance and conditioning problematic.

The course has gone through many changes over the past few years—not in the layout but in overall conditioning and improvements. For example, there are now cart paths throughout the entire 27 holes. This feature has taken some of the wear and tear off the fairways and allowed a more defined fairway/rough cut. Plate or disc yardage markers have been added in the fairways at 200, 150, and 100 yards. Course drainage problems have been addressed.

A fourth nine is scheduled to open this season. This nine will be similar to the third nine, with a lot of water from a newly-built 14-acre lake as the cornerstone of its design.

In the past, adequate water supply for course irrigation was a problem. That situation has been corrected with the addition of the new lake.

A beverage cart (with snacks) roams the course—a nice touch and good revenue producer. Three separate pavilions accommodate 150 people each and can be combined for larger groups. They have renovated the clubhouse, increasing the menu and providing more of a sports bar atmosphere.

PUBLIC 18+

Highlights More than half the 27 holes here are doglegs. No. 2 is a long par 4, at 424 yards, with a dogleg left. Trees on the right and left corner turn require length and accuracy off the tee. Trees continue on both sides to the green. No. 8, a par 4 of 318 yards, is not long but starts with a dogleg right. The key decision here is whether to lay up before the water or drive the corner towards the green.

No. 10 is a long dogleg right, a 438-yard par 4 with trees right and left, continuing from the turn all the way to the green. No. 12, a slight dogleg right, is a par 5 of 518 yards, and has trees on the right and left. A major obstacle is the large tree left of center in the fairway 300 yards from the tee. This signature-hole candidate has some water left of the tee but this shouldn't be a problem.

No. 20, a dogleg left, is a par 5 stretching 526 yards. It plays tough, with a lake on the right and trees located at the corner turn. These trees are about 250 yards from the tee. Failure to place the tee shot on the right side will bring the trees into play.

Mallard Creek is open every day except Christmas.

PUBLIC 18+

Manakiki Public Golf Course   ☎ (440) 942-2500

Area: **East**   City: **Willoughby Hills**   Cost: **$$**$$$ Difficulty: ●●●

Address: 35501 Eddy Rd., Willoughby Hills

Tees	Ydg.	C/r	S/r	Pace
Back:	6625	71.4	128	4:30
Middle:	6189	69.9	125	
Forward:	5390	72.8	121	

Specials: Senior (62+) & Junior specials; call about Golfer's Dollars.

Season: Mid-Mar–mid-Dec **Hours:** Sunrise–sunset **Tee times:** Taken, 5 days in advance, beginning at noon **Leagues:** Mon–Fri, various times **Ranger:** Daily **Practice facil:** Putting Green, Chipping Green, Sand **Clubhouse:** Food, Beer, Liquor, Dining room, Showers, Party rooms, Catering **Outings:** Available (Mon, Wed, Fri, Sat after 12 p.m.; call 440-942-2500) **Lessons:** Available **Pro:** Tom Kochensparger

Directions: I-90 to Exit 189 for SR 91 (SOM Center Rd.); south on SR 91; left (east) on Eddy Rd.

Description Donald J. Ross, the Scotsman from Dornoch, designed the course in 1928. (Ross apprenticed at St. Andrews under Old Tom Morris—the father to Young Tom Morris.)

Originally a private club, Manakiki has been turned into one of the premier public courses in the area. A great deal of work has been completed in recent years, and much more continues. Too bad a fungus attacked the greens last season, resulting in temporary greens at most of the holes. We'll see what sort of luck the course really has as it tries to recover.

A watering system is in place, as are cart paths, and several tees have been completely rebuilt. The challenging blue tee at No. 8, the number one handicap hole, was retrieved from the woods. Few players hit from that tee, however, because it calls for a drive few can produce on demand: a big, long, soft draw. No hook, please, or the ball is lost in the woods or water. No fade or slice, either, or the ball goes through the fairway and rattles around an equipment shed. No, this blue tee on No. 8 demands a great tee shot, and there's no negotiating.

In addition to a first-rate course, the club has a ballroom and recently gave the food concession to the restaurant company that operates Sammy's and the Metropolitan Club, among others. Prices for food at the turn doubled, but so did the quality and selection. Many foursomes finishing the last hole on Saturday afternoons climb the last few yards from the green and see newlyweds posing for wedding pictures while a reception awaits in the ballroom.

Manakiki Public Golf Course   (photo: Casey Batule/courtesy of Cleveland Metroparks)

Highlights No. 1 is the only homely hole on the course. A 375-yard par 4, it begins with a blind tee shot up a wide fairway. To the left front of the tee is the practice green; the practice range (available for a dollar) is to the right. A line of pines separates fairway from range, which is not o.b. About 170 yards from the tee is a large trap in the left rough, an easy hazard to find. The rising fairway crests near the 150-yard marker (4 x 4s with easy-to-read numerals—another improvement of recent vintage). There is sand on the right front of the green, which is flat.

No. 3 is one of four terrific par 5s on this layout. The driving area is very generous on the left side, but missing to the right can send the ball over the edge of a valley and into another fairway. Getting back can be difficult. From the tee of this 451-yard hole, the fairway dips and then rises until, about 225 yards from the tee, it drops away into a valley. Water cuts across the bottom of the valley 130 yards from the green. On the other side of the water, the ground rises just as suddenly as it fell, then levels toward the green. This green has a great deal of action in it; a huge dip in the front can make two-putting a monumental task.

No. 16 calls for extra thought before swinging. It is a 310-yard par 4 that starts left to the 150-yard mark, then drops into a valley. The hole bends back to the right and rises to the green. Missing the fairway to the left sends the ball into deep brush. Missing the fairway to the right puts tall trees between the ball and the green.

No. 18 resembles No. 10 because it plays in the same type of narrow, deep valley. At 392 yards its length is similar, too. But this valley is sun drenched, and players getting drives in the fairway have shots to the smallest green on the course (thought by many to be the smallest green in area golf!) Instead of being intimidating, it is an exciting hole. There is water crossing the fairway at 50 yards from the green. From there, the ground rises sharply.

Manakiki is a dramatic course marked by great golf history. It provides a wonderful ride over 18 very different holes.

PUBLIC 18+

TIDYMAN'S TIDBITS #8
Courses with cemeteries on the grounds:
1) Riverside
2) Medina
Courses with adjacent cemeteries:
1) Oberlin
2) Highland

Maplecrest Golf Club

☎ (330) 673-2722

Area: **Far South**   City: **Kent**   Cost: **$$**$$$ Difficulty: ●●●

PUBLIC 18+

Address: 219 Tallmadge Rd., Kent

Tees	Ydg.	C/r	S/r	Pace
Back:	6312	69.2	111	
Middle:	6016	67.9	108	
Forward:	5285	69.8	113	

Specials: None

Season: Mar 15–Dec 1 **Hours:** Sunrise–sunset **Tee times:** Recommended
Leagues: Mon–Fri 3:30 p.m. **Ranger:** Daily **Practice facil:** Range, Putting Green
Clubhouse: Food, Beer, Liquor, Lockers **Outings:** Available (outside banquet area only) **Lessons:** Not available

Directions: I-271 to Exit 18 for SR 8; south on SR 8 to I-76 east (in Akron); I-76 to Exit 31 for Tallmadge Rd.; left (west) on Tallmadge; on right.

Description Owner Jim Irving knows more about this course than anyone else, having caddied here as a kid and worked here since adolescence. Sensitive about the slope rating of 108, which would indicate a less-than-average golf challenge, he says, "Don't believe it. It's a helluva lot harder than that." He's right. It is. With five par 3s, par is 71. And what par 3s! On the front side, No. 3 is 210 yards, No. 6 is 184 yards, and No. 8 is 228 yards. On the back side, No. 13 is 182 yards, and No. 17 is 159. If you play the par 3s in par, you have a magnificent round going.

Highlights The course is lined with all sorts of trees, including flowering varieties, pines, maples (of course), the odd sycamore, and plenty of oaks. A stream meanders through and comes into play on five holes. In addition to the par 3s, two other holes are worthy of note: Nos. 7 and 10. The gorillas get out their clubs for the tee shot at No. 7. The creek is out there 213 yards, and driving it is a challenge difficult to ignore. No. 10 is a par 5 of 502 yards, and the creek is out about 260 yards from the tee; the dogleg left has o.b. down the right side. Three traps guard the green, which is noticeably narrow.

A hole in one on a par 4 is always noteworthy, and it occurred here a couple decades ago when a player on No. 1 let fly and his sliced ball finally bounced in the cup on No. 2.

TIDYMAN'S TIDBITS #9
Public courses with ballrooms on the grounds:
1) Springvale
2) Manakiki

Failures, Successes, and Gifts

Great Failures in Area Golf

1. The $20,000 membership fee at StoneWater GC, offered when the course was long on promise and short on cash. Members must have wondered when the clubhouse was going to rise (it has). When it did, the par 5 ninth hole had to be shortened. With new ownership, green fees were cut substantially. Twenty grand? It's a daily fee course.

2. Gene Lorenzo's putter, which featured a through-the-clubhead shaft and price tag of $185. Went nowhere.

3. *Ohio Golf Magazine*. Great idea. Bad magazine.

4. The Links at Renaissance. One of the great executive course designs, the Links suffers the failure to maintain or condition the course, along with nonexistent customer service.

5. Seneca Golf Course. The owner, Cleveland, runs this course like it runs its finance department.

Great Successes in Area Golf

1. The Tornado Tour, which put together cash purses and the most competitive players in the area.

2. Executive Women's Golf. The EWG has provided hundreds of women the opportunity to learn and enjoy the game.

3. Dorlon GC, where the owner as well as the head pro are dames.

4. Mike Kiely PGA, the caddymaster at Canterbury GC, who has made such a great and long-lasting impression on his charges while at the same time developing caddies who know how to caddy.

5. The premier courses at Cleveland MetroParks. Sleepy Hollow and Manakiki are two sparkling jewels in the Emerald Necklace.

Ten Great Gifts For Area Golfers

1. Custom-made persimmon woods from MacSmith Golf Company in South Euclid. The driver and the three- and five-wood, designed and built with only one player in mind, take a few weeks to create and last a lifetime. $450.

2. Two gift certificates for Windmill Lakes Golf Club in Ravenna. The first certificate for, say, $100, is best used at the annual end-of-season merchandise and clothing sale. Another for $75 lets the lucky recipient (and you?) enjoy lunch or dinner at the elegant Italian restaurant there, Cipriano's.

3. A playing lesson with Charlie Stone, Master Professional at Beechmont Country Club. $90 per hour and he always throws in a little lagniappe.

4. A round of golf and dinner at Springvale GC, where the new clubhouse, if you haven't yet seen it, will knock you out. First-class restaurant, so take a change of clothes.

5. Bud Boyer's Putt Bocci game—$22.95, guaranteed to polish your short game. As you know, short game equals money.

6. *The Golf Omnibus*, by P. G. Wodehouse. Thirty-one magnificent golf stories by the finest writer of golf stories in the history of writing and golf.

7. The 18th green at Little Mountain, the site of your wedding. And you won't be the first. Said pro Jimmy Hanlin pledged his troth there last year.

8. A one-year membership for the driving range at Bobick's in Willoughby. $450.

9. The first tee time on a summer morning at StoneWater. And to make it as wonderful as it can be, use a caddy. StoneWater is the only public course that offers the service. Green fees: $50, caddy fee $30 (plus tip, if the little street urchin performs acceptably).

10. Autographed copies of the *Cleveland Golfer's Bible* and *Golf Getaways from Cleveland*.

Oak Knolls Golf Club   ☎ (330) 673-6713

Area: **Far South**   City: **Kent**   Cost: $$$$$ Difficulty: ●●●

Address: 6700 SR 43, Kent

Tees	East Ydg.	C/r	S/r	Pace	West Ydg.	C/r	S/r	Pace
Back:	6882	71.8	118	4:15	6373	69.0	112	4:00
Middle:	6486	70.2	114		6172	68.0	110	
Forward:	5508	70.1	111		5588	71.3	112	

Specials: Special prices Mon–Thu before noon, all day Friday, Sat–Sun & holidays after 1 p.m.; 9-hole cart special all day Fri and Sat–Sun, holidays after 1 p.m.; Senior & student specials Mon–Fri before 4 p.m.

Season: Year-round **Hours:** Sunrise–sunset **Tee times:** Required
Leagues: Various times **Ranger:** Daily **Practice facil:** Range, Putting Green, Chipping Green **Clubhouse:** Food, Beer, Lockers, Showers, Pavilion
Outings: Available **Lessons:** Available **Pro:** Jon Wegenek

Directions: I-480 to SR 14 east (I-480 ends here); right (south) on SR 43 for 5 miles

PUBLIC 18+

Description Oak Knolls Golf Club, Inc., a privately held company, built the East Course in 1961. When land became available across the street in 1968, they built the West Course. State Route 43 bisects the tracks. The terrain is similar on both, though water shows up only on the West Course. More than 70,000 rounds are played here per season—a lot of golf. Older players in particular are courted here.

Highlights Howard Morrette designed the East Course, and he put in a couple exceptional par 5s: Nos. 1 and 9. The only way to play them is from the blues, from which the opening hole stretches 638 yards and No. 9 measures an even 600. The first hole sees more eagles because it plays slightly downhill and often has a bit of a tailwind. No. 9 plays uphill and into the wind. Trees planted in 1961 are big enough to add shape to the holes.

A couple of holes were improved in 1998: No. 6 was changed from a par 3 to a par 4 by cutting a fairway through the trees, and No. 7 was lengthened by 50 yards (to 400) by pushing the tee back—way, way back. There are two pavilions here for outings, and there's lots of league play on weeknights.

Jon Wegenek, PGA, designed the West Course; it is a finely balanced layout with generous landing areas and flat, medium to medium-fast greens. This is the side preferred by older players, a market segment important to management here.

PUBLIC 18+

Oak Knolls Golf Club

Orchard Hills Golf Course   ☎ (440) 729-1963
Area: **East**   City: **Chesterland**   Cost: $$$$$ Difficulty: ●●●

Address: 11414 Caves Rd., Chesterland

Tees	Ydg.	C/r	S/r	Pace
Back:	6409	71.1	126	4:00
Middle:	6206	70.2	124	
Forward:	5651	72.6	122	

Specials: Senior specials with Buckeye card

Season: Mar–Nov **Hours:** Sunrise–sunset **Tee times:** Required **Leagues:** Evenings **Ranger:** Most days **Practice facil:** Putting Green, Chipping Green, Sand **Clubhouse:** Food, Beer, Lockers, Showers **Outings:** Available **Lessons:** Available **Pro:** Dave Luithle

Directions: I-271 to Exit 34 for US 322 (Mayfield Rd.); east on Mayfield; left (north) on Caves Rd.; on left, one mile north of Wilson Mills Rd.

Description With a slope rating of 124 and the lovely, heavy scent of apples in the air, Orchard Hills in autumn must bear a strong resemblance to the fantasy some players have of heaven. It is as close to a private golf club as most golfers are likely to get without a sponsor and a substantial initiation fee. This semi-private layout, part of Patterson's Fruit Farm, has much to recommend it.

Orchard Hills attracts serious players, men and women who want to play the game well. It has a good little pro shop and a separate snack bar. When apples are in season, golfers play 18 holes, then grab a peck or two of apples and a gallon of cider before leaving the parking lot.

It is a very challenging layout, one that calls for course management, accuracy, and a deft touch on the greens. Ah, yes, the greens. Striking the ball well with woods and irons doesn't count for much here if the putting game is not decent. The greens roll fast and true.

It is a course notable for its physical beauty. The staff obviously works hard to keep it in excellent condition.

Highlights Players who walk this course regularly will be in good condition, too. The cardiopulmonary system gets a workout here, especially on No. 8, a 446-yard par 4, and its evil twin, No. 18—434 yards uphill.

Not all holes are as long or as demanding as these two, though. There are a few short, tempting par 4s: No. 1 (313 yards); No. 10 (290 yards); and No. 16 (306 yards). Nos. 1 and 10 are easy holes. No. 16 calls for two iron shots, the second over a small pond to a canted green. It was on the No. 16 tee many years ago that a player was shot to death. His assailant had lain waiting in the brush next to the tee box for hours. Police called it a gangland slaying, and no one argued.

Orchard Hills shares an important quality with a select number of courses: exciting design. Playing here is like a roller-coaster ride for grownups. And after playing the two last holes, players nod in agreement on hearing "It ain't over 'til it's over."

Even if the length and strength of the course discourage some players from walking, golfers are in for a treat each time they tee it up here.

PUBLIC 18+

Painesville Country Club   ☎ (440) 354-3469

Area: **Far East**   City: **Painesville**   Cost: $$$$$ Difficulty: ●●●

Address: 84 Golf Dr., Painesville

Tees	Ydg.	C/r	S/r	Pace
Middle:	5956	69.0	120	3:48
Forward:	5435	71.3	120	

Specials: Senior & Junior specials Mon–Fri before 2 p.m.

Season: Year-round **Hours:** Mon–Fri open 7 a.m.; Sat–Sun open 6 a.m.
Tee times: Taken **Leagues:** Mon–Fri afternoons; some traveling leagues on weekends **Ranger:** Weekends; weekday evenings **Practice facil:** Range, Putting Green, Sand **Clubhouse:** Food, Beer, Liquor, Dining room, Lockers, Pavilion, Club rental **Outings:** Available (steak roasts a specialty) **Lessons:** Available

Directions: I-90 to Exit 205 for Vrooman Rd.; north on Vrooman across Grand River; left (west) on Riverside Dr.; left on Golf Dr.

Description Family-owned businesses are supposed to self-destruct by the third generation. Not so here, where C. J. Alden's grandson, Rich, continues to improve on the original. Mr. Alden's touch with a mower is remarkable, and he turns ordinary fairways and rough into well-defined holes with eye appeal.

Much has changed since 1928, when the opening of the Painesville

PUBLIC 18+

Country Club was featured in *The Telegraph*. A clothing store ad on the same page offered men's suits for $22.50—an extra pair of trousers cost six bucks.

Much remains the same. It was a great little course then, and it's a great little course now. It looks and plays just as it did when it opened. It was designed by a Mr. Lamoran, according to old and yellowing news clips. He was the pro at Kirtland Country Club and supervised construction. This layout is a good example of the adage about designers discovering courses rather than building them—it is fitted to the land. The back is tighter than the front, and both enjoy dramatic changes in elevation.

The course and stone clubhouse were developed by C. J. Alden, then president of the Painesville Metallic Binding Co. His son, Dick, and grandson, Rich, run them today. The clubhouse has a snack bar and pro shop, as well as a large dining room with hand-carved woodwork saved from one of Cleveland's Millionaires' Row mansions. The mantel is easily 12 feet high. On one wall rests a huge moose head. Dick Alden likes to nod toward the beast and say in a confidential tone, "Shot him on the 14th fairway."

Notes for the 19th hole: the barroom here is the most comfortable in the area. It is not big. The bar itself could hold a dozen only if they were related. But the old wooden bar is handsome, and the windows on two sides make the room bright. Service is fast and friendly.

Highlights The opening hole is a 521-yard par 5. The tee is elevated, and the hole plays first across a shallow valley. The fairway rolls up and down until the 150-yard marker, where it swoops down to the green. Well behind the green is a ravine. There is plenty of sand on this hole—and on this course. Its small greens are of average speed.

It is a walk over the ravine to get to the tee at No. 2, a 394-yard par 4. This was designed as a straight hole, but over the last 50 years a couple of trees near the fairway have grown up and out; they make it look like it bends to the left. As at many of the greens here, mounds surround the putting surface. On this hole, losing the ball to the right or over the green sends it crashing down a ravine. Behind the green is the Grand River. It is at the bottom of a 100-foot cliff and encircles much of the course.

One of many virtues of this course is the dearth of development. There is but a single building visible to players on the round. And when the trees are in foliage, even that structure can't be seen. Play here is quiet, secluded, and beautiful.

There are two tees on No. 8, the famous "bell hole," to allow faster play. When the course is crowded (or when the original tee box just needs some time to recover from play), the second tee is used and it takes 50 yards off the 181-yard hole. There are two ponds, also, so there is water to clear regardless of the tee used. The green was originally cut in the shape of a bell with the bottom facing the tee. To serve as a clapper, a small evergreen was planted in front of the green. According to old news clips, some members disliked the hazard; others were charmed by it. The shape of the green has changed over the decades, but the doughty evergreen remains. It is substantial but not towering, and clearing it is not difficult.

No. 9 is a 340-yard par 4 that seems to wind to the green because of elevated terrain on the left side. But though mowed as a dogleg, it really isn't one. Playing a drive off the side of the hill is common. There is sand in the fairway, in the rough, and at the green. On this hole (and on several others) what is called an "extended approach" is cut before the green. It is cut shorter than fairway, longer than greens, and longer than the typical apron. It adds a handsome country-club touch and is a good example of what Rich Alden can do with a mower.

No. 11, a par 3, has a 100-foot drop from tee to green. But the green is still 239 yards away. Some golfers can't even *see* that far, let alone hit the green. Heavy trees line both sides and o.b. is on the right. The green was once half the size it is today. And it is not a large green. The right side was then protected by a tall pine. Back in the seventies, a disgruntled golfer slipped in under cover of darkness and chopped it down.

From the 18th tee, the stone clubhouse is visible in the distance. It is an especially pretty hole during the summer, when landing areas are trimmed and separated by rough.

Painesville Country Club is well worth the drive. Although it has provided challenge and delight for the better part of the 20th century, it is still largely undiscovered. And it is worth discovering.

PUBLIC 18+

Pine Brook Golf Club   ☎ (440) 236-8689

Area: **Far West**   City: **North Eaton**   Cost: **$$$**$$ Difficulty: ●●◐

Address: 11043 Durkee Rd., North Eaton

Tees	Ydg.	C/r	S/r	Pace
Back:	6162	68.3	113	3:38
Middle:	5741	66.8	110	
Forward:	5225	68.9	109	

Specials: Special prices Mon–Fri; Senior specials Mon–Fri before 11 a.m.

Season: Year-round **Hours:** 6 a.m.–10:30 p.m.; winter 7:30 a.m.–sunset
Tee times: Not taken **Leagues:** Mon–Fri 5–6:30 p.m.; one 9 always open for public
play **Ranger:** Most days **Practice facil:** Range, Putting Green, Chipping Green
Clubhouse: Food, Beer, Dining room, Pavilion **Outings:** Available **Lessons:** Available

Directions: I-480 to Exit 1B for SR 10 (Lorain Rd.); west on Lorain (becomes
Butternut Ridge Rd.); left (south) on Durkee Rd.; on left.

Description Interstate 480 makes Pine Brook Golf Club easily accessible. The clubhouse at this course was built in 1884. Of course, it wasn't built as a clubhouse, but as a barn. The course itself is young, having opened in 1964 with nine holes. The second nine was added a few years later. It is compact, beautifully maintained, and fun to play.

Highlights Let's begin with the important stuff: drainage. Five minutes after a downpour, you can tee it up here. The irrigation system has been improved so even during the dog days of August, the fairways are lush. The front side features three par 3s, three par 4s, and three par 5s. No. 2, a short, 485-yard par 5, tempts big hitters. The green can be had in two, but only by avoiding water, o.b., and trees that protect the green. Plenty of players dreaming of eagles when lining up for their second shots walk away with bogeys here. Prudence, perhaps an underrated virtue in public golf, is favored here.

No. 6, the second par 5 on the front side, measures 509 yards. It is a straightaway hole but unreachable in two for the overwhelming majority of golfers. By this hole, the dearth of sand becomes noticeable. Fink is mulling over the idea of additional grass bunkers, but not sand.

The back side measures a short 2,747 yards and has only one par 5, the 510-yard No. 11.

On No. 18 many players play from the blue tees. Then instead of a 300-yard par 4, it becomes 345 yards and much more challenging. The fairway slips down and away from the tee, then bends left around a lake, rising to an elevated green sitting in the shade of protective trees. A big drive to the right can go through the fairway; a big hook finds the lake and sleeps with the fish.

The specialty here is steak dinner outings.

Pine Hills Golf Club   ☎ (330) 225-4477

Area: **South**   City: **Hinckley**   Cost: $$$$$ Difficulty: ●●●

Address: 433 W. 130 St., Hinckley

Tees	Ydg.	C/r	S/r	Pace
Back:	6532	71.2	124	3:37
Middle:	6196	69.8	121	
Forward:	5685	74.3	126	

Specials: Senior specials Mon & Tue before 1:30 p.m.

Season: Apr 1–Dec 25 **Hours:** Sunrise–sunset **Tee times:** Recommended **Leagues:** Mon–Fri from 4 p.m. **Ranger:** Daily **Practice facil:** Putting Green, Chipping Green, Sand, Practice area (use your own balls) **Clubhouse:** Food, Beer, Liquor, Dining room, Lockers, Showers **Outings:** Available **Lessons:** Available **Pro:** Steve Brzytwa

Directions: I-71 to Exit 226 for SR 303 (Center Rd.); east on SR 303 to W. 130 St.; left (north) on W. 130; on right.

Description There is no shortage of area players who argue that Pine Hills is the best public course in Northeast Ohio. There is plenty of competition for that mythical title, of course, but little doubt Pine Hills would be a contender. It is not the toughest course, but it is a beautiful and demanding layout, a golf course for people who love to golf. Beginners and slowpokes are not welcomed. The pro here is one of the area's better teachers and provides all sorts of options for those who want to play better and enjoy golf more.

It is not an old course. Built in 1957, it was designed by Harold Paddock, Sr. (who also laid out Ironwood). The course record belongs to Joe Kruczek and Rick Nemecek, who each shot a 63 from the blue tees in 1989. It is tough to score well here without being adept with long irons and the putter. Kruczek's score is an eye-opener and his record will likely stand for a while.

Pine Hills is not a tight course, but it is compact and often hilly. The rough is not very rough, the fairways are cut short, and the greens are trimmed to be fast.

While it is always wise to get a tee time before setting out, getting one on weekend mornings is impossible. Permanent tee times belong to players who hold them more dearly than chili recipes or directions to a secret fishing hole.

Highlights No. 6 is one of the prettiest tee boxes here. It's a straight par 4, 411 yards long, and it rises and falls—mostly falls—getting to the green. A line of trees runs down the left sid,e and a deep forest is on the right. One of many dangerous greens on the course is found here. It is fairly large and pitched forward. Three-putting is made simple on greens like this.

No. 7 is the other par 5 on this side and, like No. 5, which plays to the left of it, has a blind tee shot. A stepladder at the tee provides a view of players ahead taking their second shots. The fairway on this 467-yard hole rises and slopes to the right. It parts company with No. 5 and goes its own way. Missing the fairway to the right sends the ball into a deep valley. About 175 yards from the green, the fairway suddenly drops, becoming part of the valley that lines the right side. The left side fills with trees and thick bushes. The valley bottoms out, then rises quickly and left to the green. It is not easy to hit in regulation or to hold. A player could shoot this hole six days in a row and play it well differently each day.

No. 11 offers a difficult tee shot. That's just one reason why it's the number three handicap hole. A valley sits in front of the tee on this 355-yard par 4. Deep, but not wide, it climbs quickly to a narrow fairway edged by trees, water, and deep rough. Missing the fairway means one thing: trouble. Even hitting the fairway is no guarantee—there are some sand traps and tall hardwoods on the right side of the fairway, both within range of decent drivers.

No. 18, a 420-yard par 4, can create heroes and break hearts. It begins with a pretty tee box, flowers on the right, and a split-rail fence in the rear. On the left side is the backyard of a residential neighbor. Straight out a few hundred yards is a stand of tall pines, a good aiming point. Staying in the fairway is vital on this hole because the approach shot must clear a couple of lakes where the hole turns 10 or 15 degrees to the left. With a decent tee shot, getting over the water can be done with a mid-iron. But that is only to get over. To hit and hold the green calls for a long iron, and the lakes, often home to a few dozen Canada geese, provide a physical as well as psychological barrier. There is only one chance to make this shot. There is sand at the green, a large target that leans down towards the water. While a heroic hole, it misses one virtue: beauty. Oh, it's handsome enough, but it's not a beautiful hole.

Conditions are excellent here, and play is brisk.

Pine Hills Golf Club   (photo: Jonathan Wayne)

TIDYMAN'S TIDBITS #9

Easiest courses for walking:

1) Bob-O-Links
2) Sweetbriar
3) Briardale
4) Hilliard Lakes
5) Royal Crest

IMG and Tiger

The year was 1958. The U.S. Open was being played at Southern Hills, in Tulsa, Oklahoma. The qualifiers from Northern Ohio included Bob Toski, George Bigham, Mark McCormack, and Bob Hamrich.

On the practice green there, Arnold Palmer said to McCormack, "You're a lawyer. You ought to do something for golfers."

Damn you, Arnold!

McCormack went on to found IMG, which, if memory, anecdote, and current events serve, stands for I Mean Greedy!

IMG's greed is a lesser variation of the same vice that made Standard Oil, Ford Motor, and U.S. Steel. In their incredible and fascinating stories, each of these industrial behemoths made and destroyed lives, neighborhoods, and careers. Each had a remarkable and lasting effect on American society. Each of them made history as well as money. Their contributions were both good and evil.

Too bad IMG's version of greed, international though it is, is so lacking in grace, power, vision, or influence. IMG's greed won't build libraries, fuel an economy, or make the middle class more secure. It will only make money for IMG. So what?

IMG's current prima donna, Tiger Woods, collects in excess of $50 million a year. According to him and his handlers at IMG, that's not enough. When the PGA Tour negotiated a new television contract, Tiger thought he should be cut in for a slice of the pie. Tiger also suggested that the PGA commissioner, Tim Finchem, was not as respectful to golf's prima donna as he might be. The commissioner, Tiger noted, never inquired as to his health, but called only when Tiger's presence was desired in a golf tournament.

Then there was the matter of PricewaterhouseCoopers using Tiger's picture when he won a tournament the company sponsored. Despite the contract calling for just such use, Tiger's agent, Mark Steinberg, said, "Those are the types of things that drive us absolutely crazy. Something like that is an implied endorsement. That's an infringement on Tiger's rights. It's stuff we won't stand for."

Mark? Shut up. There is only one thing that drives IMG crazy and that is failing to pick up any loose change on the table.

Anyway, $50 mil+ is enough for Tiger and the hell with his management company. It is too much. Way too much.

There are only two types of people who need all that and more. The first is the person who is going to live forever. Tiger is mortal. The second is the person who is going to take it with him. That's not Tiger.

Tiger, in his current incarnation, is little more than a tool for IMG, which makes millions of dollars every year off the kid. Dressed in the emperor's new clothes, Tiger can only hear the voices of IMG. IMG is not there to manage a person, but to maximize revenue.

It would have been asking far too much for IMG to be responsible for nurturing in this remarkable golf prodigy values such as gratitude, understanding, compassion, or sportsmanship. That would have been akin to asking a lawyer to understand the idea and ideals of justice.

Without contributing anything at all to American society, IMG has managed to alter one more game in which the essence of sport is blithely thanked and sent out the servant's entrance, never to be welcome again. In this latest chapter, Tiger is just one more tool.

Ironic, isn't it, that IMG would treat in such a despicable way the only game that bases its history, its attraction, and its future on a single virtue: honor. IMG is the latter-day money changer in the temple.

Is golf better for having IMG? Of course not. Golf was played long before IMG arrived and will likely be played long after the firm is a dull asterisk in sports history.

And Tiger. Is golf better for having him play? For all the excitement he brings to the game, it's too soon to tell. Golf was surely made better because Old Tom Morris played, and Donald Ross built courses, and Bobby Jones created one of golf's great tournaments. The common thread in these uncommon men was something neither IMG nor Tiger could understand: each was far more interested in giving to the game than taking.

If Tiger seeks to be a role model for kids—and clearly, he does—the lessons he teaches have about as much value as bacon fat at a health food store.

Feeding us this myth about bringing poor kids to golf courses is an admirable diversion, but let's face it: green fees are going up, not down. The prices charged for clubs (I'm not saying value, I'm saying price) continues to soar, and nobody is building golf courses adjacent to housing projects, so let's knock off the charade, okay?

The only lessons Tiger has been teaching are how to stamp one's feet, how to pout, how to threaten and demand that the rules be changed for him. If Tiger manages to alienate the ham-and-eggers who make up his audience, he'll have IMG to blame. For IMG to take advantage of a kid Tiger's age is deplorable.

Remember those wonderful television ads, the ones featuring kid after kid after kid, each one saying, "I'm Tiger Woods." Next time I see it, I'll say to each child, "No, you ain't, kid, and you don't want to be."

Pine Ridge Country Club

☎ (440) 943-0293

Area: **East**   City: **Wickliffe**   Cost: $$$$$ Difficulty: ●●●

Address: 30601 Ridge Rd., Wickliffe

Tees	Ydg.	C/r	S/r	Pace
Middle:	6132	68.9	114	4:15
Forward:	5330	70.5	119	

Specials: Senior specials available

Season: Year-round **Hours:** Sunrise–sunset **Tee times:** Taken
Leagues: Tue–Thu 3:45–6 p.m. start times; Tue Ladies League (mornings)
Ranger: Daily **Practice facil:** Putting Green, Chipping Green, Sand
Clubhouse: Food, Beer, Liquor, Dining room, Patio, Club storage, Club rental
Outings: Available **Lessons:** Available **Pro:** Tom Weiss, PGA

Directions: I-90 to Exit 189 for SR 91 (SOM Center Rd.); north on SR 91 to
SR 84 (Ridge Rd.); left (west) on Ridge; on right.

Description Lake MetroParks bought this former private club a few years ago. While playable, it's like Cinderella's ugly sister: no amount of makeup will make it beautiful.

Pine Ridge Country Club   *(photo courtesy Lake Metroparks)*

PUBLIC 18+

Pine Valley Golf Club   ☎ (330) 335-3375
Area: **Far South**   City: **Wadsworth**   Cost: **$$$**$$ Difficulty: ●●●

PUBLIC 18+

Address: 469 Reimer Rd., Wadsworth

Tees	Ydg.	C/r	S/r	Pace
Middle:	6097	68.5	109	
Forward:	5268	67.9	107	

Specials: Special prices & Senior specials Mon–Fri before noon

Season: Mar–Nov **Hours:** 7 a.m.–sunset **Tee times:** Required **Leagues:** Mon–Fri, various times **Ranger:** None **Practice facil:** Putting Green **Clubhouse:** Food, Beer **Outings:** Available (for small groups) **Lessons:** Not available **Pro:** Garland Parsons

Directions: I-77 to Exit 136 for SR 21; south on SR 21 to Minor Rd.; right on Minor to Medina Line Rd.; left on Medina Line; right on Reimer Rd., on right.

Description Pine Valley is an attractive little course tucked away in the farm country of Medina County and accessible from a two-lane blacktop. The Parsons family, who runs it, draws on a great deal of experience in golf course maintenance. For many years, Garland Parsons ran the Good Park course near Akron. When he left, he purchased land and created the Bath Golf Club on Medina Line Road, which is now being developed for housing.

The Parsons sold Bath in 1978 to Jim McCartney, who was later shot to death by his former wife. The women who take Table 1 in Pine Valley's small clubhouse still enjoy talking about the murder.

When the bulldozers arrived a few years ago to turn McCartney's course into a housing development, the Bath Men's Golf League switched to Pine Valley, resuming the 30-year-old league's relationship with Garland Parsons.

Of her husband and son, Mrs. Parsons says, "They could grow grass on concrete." The father-son team looks after the course that was built in 1962 and designed by Cliff Deming. It is not a long course, 6,097 yards and par 72. Water and sand are minimal. The forward tees are well groomed and provide substantial advantage. The greens are manicured but not particularly fast. It is a nice, relaxed course.

There are plenty of pines at Pine Valley (and more going in every year), but they share space with sweet birch, pin oak, ash, dogwood, hickory, and witch hazel. The witch hazel, which blooms in the fall, has forked branches said to divine water in the right hands. If the right hands happen to be in the area between the No. 5, No. 6, and No. 7 greens, water will surely be found—there is a large pond there. The additional pines being planted are going in to provide both guidance on holes and protection from errant shots.

Highlights No. 1 is Gary Parsons's favorite hole because, he said, it's the prettiest. It is one of many pretty holes here. Not only the trees that line almost every fairway, but the gently rolling farmland of this deep green course make it a beautiful layout to walk and play. The opening hole is a straight par 4 of 416 yards.

Two rules help quicken play here: the continuous putting rule (unless the ball or your feet interfere with another player's line, you're obligated to putt out), and the stand-aside rule (which calls for waving the next group up on par 3s).

A trip to Pine Valley is not made by those hungry for heroic shots. The course is peaceful and encouraging—plenty of opportunities for pars and even a few birdies. It is easily accessible and offers good value.

PUBLIC 18+

Pine Valley Golf Club

Pleasant Hill Golf Course   ☎ (440) 285-2428

Area: **Far East**   City: **Chardon**   Cost: $$$$$ Difficulty: ●●●

Address: 13461 Aquilla Rd., Chardon

Tees	Front & Middle 9s				Front & Back 9s				Middle & Back 9s			
	Ydg.	C/r	S/r	Pace	Ydg.	C/r	S/r	Pace	Ydg.	C/r	S/r	Pace
Middle:	6329				6295				6352			
Forward:	5447				5836				5599			

Specials: 27-hole special Mon–Fri; Senior specials Mon–Fri

Season: Mar 15–Nov 15 **Hours:** Sunrise–sunset **Tee times:** Taken
Leagues: Daily 5–6 p.m. **Ranger:** Most days **Practice facil:** Putting Green
Clubhouse: Food, Beer, Lockers, Showers, Pavilion
Outings: Available (banquet facilities for up to 300) **Lessons:** Available

Directions: I-271 to Exit 29 for Chagrin Blvd. (SR 87); east on SR 87; north on Ravenna Rd. (SR 44); right (east) on Butternut Rd.; left (north) on Aquilla Rd.; on right.

Description This layout has a few doglegs, a few hills, and some water. Many of the fairways here are wide and tempting. Sand is used judiciously, and the greens are kept in very good condition. It is a lovely course, and a good one to walk. Very playable, too, and many golfers finishing on the 18th green succumb to the temptation of another fresh nine holes.

Highlights No. 6, a long par 5 of 560 yards, is lined on the right side with woods. Just in front of the tee is a small lake with cattails filling the far shore. There are trees on the left side as well, but not so thick as to hide balls. The trees separate this fairway from the ninth fairway. This is a good birdie hole. Days probably go by without anyone getting on in two, but it's not difficult to get on in regulation, and there are no hazards in the way of the approach shot.

No. 9 is another long one, a par 5 of 603 yards. Reaching it in four is no shame. There is some water on the left side, the little lake that sits on the front of the sixth tee, but it is not a concern for straight hitters.

The finish is puzzling. Nos. 17 and 18 are par 3s, the former 165 yards and the latter 204 yards. Both tee shots go over water that should not come into play. No. 18 is the more difficult, not only for the length but because the hole plays uphill.

The third nine starts with a 402-yard par 4 that has a small lake on the right. The lake adds to the beauty of the course but should not add to the score. The left side is filled with hardwoods, but the right side is open.

Pleasant Hill is a very nice stroll through the woods, a course that doesn't demand golf prowess—only that players stay up with the foursome before them. But 27 holes in a day is a dream (or a daydream) for a lot of players. Give them tee times, they will come.

Pleasant Valley Country Club   ☎ (330) 225-2510

Area: **Southwest**   City: **Medina**   Cost: $$$$$ Difficulty: ●●●

Address: 3830 Hamilton Rd., Medina

Tees	Ydg.	C/r	S/r	Pace
Back:	6912	73.4	123	3:57
Middle:	6429	71.1	119	
Forward:	4984	68.9	113	

Specials: Senior specials weekdays

Season: Apr–until it snows **Hours:** 7 a.m.–7 p.m. **Tee times:** Taken weekends
Leagues: Mon–Fri evenings, Tue mornings **Ranger:** Some days
Practice facil: Putting Green **Clubhouse:** Food, Beer, Liquor **Outings:** Not available
Lessons: Not available

Directions: I-71 to Exit 222 for SR 3 (Hinckley/Medina); south off highway; right on Hamilton Rd. a little over a mile on left.

PUBLIC 18+

Description It is all golf here. There is no driving range and no lessons are offered. There are few price specials, and outings are discouraged. The pro shop has little more than a few sleeves of balls. But for golfers seeking to test their skills, Pleasant Valley offers a great deal.

The layout, designed by Jack Kidwell (who also designed Punderson), rolls through Medina County farmland, presenting holes that reward thinking golfers and penalize the careless.

It's a long course, and it's a mix: tough and challenging holes along with straight and generous ones. The rolling terrain, the water, and the wealth of old and sturdy hardwoods provide the setting. The layout takes advantage of each virtue and presents a course for the thinking player.

The fairways are trim and the rough is kept relatively short. Women are welcomed and provided a 1,500-yard advantage.

Highlights On No. 4, the course begins to show its personality. A 153-yard par 3 sounds easy, but this is not an easy hole to play. It is uphill, for starters, which makes club selection more important. Dense woods fill both sides, and a trap sits before the green.

At No. 5, a small lake and a weeping willow sit next to the tee. It's not unusual to find ducks paddling back and forth in the lake, especially early in the season. The fairway rolls a bit to another small lake, this one in front of the green. A bridge leads the way.

Nos. 16, 17, and 18 circle a large lake. No. 17 is a 180-yard par 3 across a steep valley. The big lake being circled here is on the right but does not come into play. Instead, at the bottom of the valley is another, smaller lake. This hole calls for nerve and a good swing.

The finishing hole, a 350-yard par 4, has the lake on the right side much of the way. The fairway bends sharply right; approach shots often have to carry the water's edge. That approach often adds drama and decides winners.

Pleasant Valley is a handsome and well-maintained course. Of course it's handsome—this is Medina County horse country. Good golf course management and rural beauty can co-exist very peacefully.

TIDYMAN'S TIDBITS #10

Courses where taking a cart is not always wimpy:

1) Ironwood
2) Hinckley
3) Brandywine
4) Thunder Hill

PUBLIC 18+

Powderhorn   ☎ (440) 428-5951 or (800) T-OFF-PGC

Area: **Far East**   City: **Madison**   Cost: $$$$$ Difficulty: ●●●

Address: 3991 Bates Rd., Madison

Tees	Ydg.	C/r	S/r	Pace
Back:	6004	68.5	117	
Middle:	5679	67.1	114	
Forward:	4881	67.6	113	

Specials: Several season pass options available; daily specials; Senior specials

Season: Year-round **Hours:** Sunrise–sunset **Tee times:** Taken
Leagues: Mon–Fri 4:30–6 p.m. **Ranger:** Most days **Practice facil:** Putting Green
Clubhouse: Food, Beer, Pavilion **Outings:** Available **Lessons:** Not available

Directions: I-90 to Exit 212 for SR 528 (River St.); north on SR 528;
right (east) on SR 84; right (south) on Bates Rd.; on left.

Description The course starts a little herky-jerky with a very difficult 411-yard par 4 followed by a dinky little 254-yard par 4. But after this brush with schizophrenia, Powderhorn takes a wonderful tour through the Lake County countryside.

The boss here is Larry Knowles, and he admits the opening hole, the number one handicap hole, is too difficult to be an opening hole. But he notes that switching nines would not help; No. 10 is the number two handicap hole.

If this is criticism, it's about all there is here to be critical about. It is a well-maintained course that offers plenty of good golf.

A sign in the parking lot reads "No Hunting on Golf Course Property," which gives an idea of the rural setting of this course. It wasn't always Powderhorn. First a nine-hole course named Whispering Pines was here (none of the original holes exists today). In the late 1980s, Powderhorn was designed by the Detroit architectural firm of Anderson, Lesniak & Associates.

Highlights After playing the course a few times, players might look forward to the first hole. It begins with water and ends that way, too. It is a narrow fairway and a handsome hole, though it will pale by comparison a few holes later. The water in front of the tee won't come into play, but the sizable water in front of the green allows no mistakes on the long-iron approach. The greens here are big and can be treacherous—all the more reason to play here a few times before rendering judgment. The opening hole here has opportunities for players who know that course management is the 15th club in the bag.

Looking out from the No. 4 tee over the 492-yard par 5, first-time players are taken with the view. It is one of the most beautiful holes around—and there is no shortage of competition. Woods, sand, and a little bit of water make this the number seven handicap.

Walking the front side is a snap; walking the back nine is a workout. No. 10 brings memories of the first hole. It is longer, at 433 yards, and this par 4 has fairway sand and plenty of water near the green. Again, course management can carry the day (if not the water).

The lone par 5 on the back side is No. 16—at 523 yards, a beautiful and long straightaway with a manicured fairway and woods down both sides.

The course finishes with one of its short par 4s, only 257 yards. Par here is 35–35, and total yardage is only 5,679 from the whites. There are only two par 5s. On paper, that might sound like a pushover. It isn't. This layout calls for thoughtful play.

Punderson State Park Golf Course   ☎ (440) 564-5465

Area: **Far East**   City: **Newbury**   Cost: $$$$$$ Difficulty: ●●●

Address: 11755 Kinsman Rd., Newbury

Tees	Ydg.	C/r	S/r	Pace
Back:	6815	72.9	119	3:55
Middle:	6600	72.0	114	
Forward:	6342	76.9	113	

Specials: Spring rates Apr–early May; winter rates late Sep–Nov; Senior rates w/ Buckeye card, discount after 3 p.m.

Season: Mar 1–Nov 1 **Hours:** Sunrise–sunset **Tee times:** Taken weekends, starting previous Thu **Leagues:** Minimal **Ranger:** Daily **Practice facil:** Range, Putting Green, Use own balls on range **Clubhouse:** Food, Beer, Pavilion, Punderson Manor available for overnight lodging; conference center also available. **Outings:** Available **Lessons:** Available **Pro:** Kip Freeman

Directions: I-271 to Exit 29 for SR 87 (Chagrin Blvd.); east on SR 87 (becomes Kinsman Rd. in Geauga County); enter Punderson State Park (on right, in Newbury Twp.); right on second main road in park to golf course.

Description Ohio cities and Ohio counties own and operate golf courses, so why not the state? The Department of Natural Resources, in addition to scraping roadkill off park roads, runs a beautiful golf course designed by Jack Kidwell and built in the spring of 1969. Course and park are named after Lemuel Punderson, the first permanent settler of Newbury. He worked for the Connecticut Land Company during the latter part of the 18th century. A direct descendant with the same name still lives in Newbury.

Punderson is a lot of golf course: 6,600 yards, par 72. But that doesn't mean a slew of lengthy par 4s. Much of the yardage comes from the par 5s; four of them total 2,158 yards. And both par 3s on the back side measure close to 200 yards.

The clubhouse looks more like a ski lodge and has a large porch from

PUBLIC 18+

which to sip a post-round beer, admire Mother Nature's woods, and watch players on the first tee. Special packages that include lodging in the Manor House or the cabins are delightful mini-vacations.

Punderson State Park Golf Course

Highlights No. 3 is one of the big par 5s—this one 550 yards. The fairway is beautiful from the tee. The hole plays straight, but the greenskeeper, with light mower, puts a wavy edge on the right side of the fairway and a straight edge on the left. Out on the left is a huge and ancient willow. There is water farther to the left (but it belongs to another hole, and unless a powerful snap hook is in a player's bag, it should not come into play). There are hills and dales in this green, and four traps around its borders. Behind it is the next tee. That's a lot of golf on a single hole.

No. 6, another 550-yard par 5, has a small lake in front of the tee. It's an open fairway for the first 200 yards before trees appear on the edges. The first two shots are blind because the slowly rising fairway doesn't crest until the 150-yard marker. This green is heavily bunkered.

On the back side, No. 11, a 390-yard par 4, is a magnificent hole. It is open but calls for an approach shot to clear a lake before the green. The lake is substantial and anchored on both sides by willows. This is another hole that gives pause to players when they stop to appreciate the fairways sculpted with light mowers.

The tee shot on No. 14, a 196-yard par 3, has to clear water covering much of the fairway and hold the green. There is fairway in front of the green for players unable to hit that shot. Among Punderson's many virtues are the challenging par 3s. None is easy; all are gorgeous.

No. 15, a 571-yard par 5, has a green virtually unreachable without three good shots. Deep woods line the right side, though that should not present problems because of a generous fairway here. A deep narrow valley opens up about 200 yards from the green. The valley is rough and cuts across the fairway. The second section of fairway picks up and heads straight to the green.

This is a first-class course and easy to get to.

PUBLIC 18+

Raccoon Hill Golf Club   ☎ (330) 673-2111
Area: **Far South**   City: **Kent**   Cost: **$$$$**$ Difficulty: ●●●

Address: 485 Judson Rd., Kent

Tees	Ydg.	C/r	S/r	Pace
Middle:	6068	68.3	112	4:00
Forward:	4650	65.4	101	

Specials: Senior specials Mon–Fri before 2 p.m.; Ladies get Senior rates Tues and Fri.

Season: Year round **Hours:** Sunrise–sunset **Tee times:** Recommended
Leagues: Mon–Fri evenings **Ranger:** Daily **Practice facil:** Putting Green, Chipping Green **Clubhouse:** Food, Beer, Liquor, Lockers, Pavilion
Outings: Available **Lessons:** Available **Pro:** Jim Beers

Directions: I-271 to Exit 18 for SR 8; south on SR 8 to SR 303; east on SR 303 (W. Streetsboro Rd.); right (south) on SR 91 (S. Main St.); left (east) on Norton Rd. (becomes Judson Rd.); on left, after Seasons Rd.

Description Purchased by Bill Snetsinger in 1989, this course has undergone a metamorphosis, including new cart paths, irrigation, and 2,500 new trees. It used to be Shawnee, and it used to be, as pro Jim Beers says, "a cow pasture."

Now, "It's a fun course," according to Solon resident Terry Uhl, whose regular foursome takes the first tee time every Saturday morning.

The course is meticulously maintained and features collars around the greens, which are themselves manicured and often, though not always, fast. There is lots of water here, but most of it won't come into play. There is sand here, too, though not so much as to slow you down. Women's tees are well maintained and give a substantial advantage—a difference of 1,418 yards.

Highlights No. 13 is the Z-hole, a par 5 of only 433 yards. It calls for three *very* accurate irons. It is followed by the L-hole, which demands a 200-yard drive and a sharp right turn. No. 18 is a heartbreaker, a par 3 of 187 yards with water in front.

PUBLIC 18+

Raccoon Hill Golf Club

Raintree Country Club   ☎ (330) 699-3232
Area: **Far South**   City: **Uniontown**   Cost: $$$$$ Difficulty: ●●●

Address: 4330 Mayfair Rd., Uniontown

Tees	Ydg.	C/r	S/r	Pace
Back:	6936	73.0	127	
Middle:	6391	70.6	121	
Forward:	5030	68.5	114	

Specials: Specials Mon–Thu before 9 a.m.

Season: Year-round **Hours:** Sunrise–sunset **Tee times:** Required
Leagues: Mon–Fri 3:30 p.m. **Ranger:** Daily **Practice facil:** Range, Putting Green,
Chipping Green **Clubhouse:** Food, Beer, Liquor, Dining room, Lockers, Showers,
Pavilion **Outings:** Available **Lessons:** Available **Pro:** David Cavalier

Directions: I-77 to Exit 118 for SR 241 (Massillon Rd.); south on SR 241;
left (east) on Wise Rd.; right (south) on Mayfair Rd.; on right.

Description Owner-developer John Rainieri thinks Raintree will serve
an emerging niche in the public player's market: golfers who want more
than what the average public course offers, but less than the pricey
amenities of a private club. There are some courses that serve that clien-
tele now, such as Tam O'Shanter in Canton and Sleepy Hollow in Broadview Heights.

"It's a trend [upscale public courses] that started about four years ago
in most parts of the country," Rainieri said. No debutante balls, of
course, but amenities such as showers, locker rooms, bag-drop areas,
and electric carts, as well as a first-rate course.

The clubhouse is worthy of mention because few clubhouses measure 20,000 square feet and have room for 500 guests. Maybe no debutante balls, but wedding receptions will fill the calendar on Saturdays.

"I could have saved a quarter million dollars building this if we just built a public golf course, but we were looking for more than that," Rainieri said. "More" included 140 traps and seven lakes and meant moving 125,000 cubic yards of earth.

And it included the services of young course designer/architect Brian Huntley. Huntley was delighted with the property and the opportunity to create a course with both links-style and northern golf course-style holes. "That's what we have," Rainieri said, "about half and half. And I liked his layout, I liked the way he put his traffic patterns around the clubhouse, along with the driving range and the parking lot and so on."

This thoughtful design insists many golf shots be available for a round. Mid-iron play will make a difference and so will the short game. Greenside bunkers, both grass and sand, along with steep mounds, will present most players with the opportunity to show off the downhill-sidehill pitch shot.

Once on the green, it's no picnic, either. These greens are fast, and about as predictable as a teenager. Most are big, too. After a round or two on these greens, one cannot help but admire the golf skills of Mike Rosseti, who fired the current course record: 65 from the blue tees.

Highlights The challenge begins with a 371-yard par 4 that shoots out of a hallway of trees almost 100 yards deep, then opens up rising and bending a bit to the left. There is fairway sand on the right that can be reached from the tee and rough that is troublesome. The fairway narrows near the green; mounds and grass bunkers appear over the final 40 yards.

No. 2, a 465-yard par 5, is mildly shocking and thoroughly delightful. The fun, however, comes not on the first go-round, but on subsequent rounds when players know what to expect and where to place the ball. The fairway slopes left and descends slightly. At about 200 yards, it turns to the right and narrows. While trees on both sides help players concentrate, the water on the left side near the green gives them something to worry about. The creek runs across the fairway, and a tree sits almost centered in front of the green. There are also mounds and a huge grass bunker. One last challenge: the green has a hogback ridge running horizontally across its surface.

The tee at No. 4, the first of the par 3s, provides the first view of traffic on I-77, though the player had better concentrate on proper club selection for this 160-yard hole where the wind can make a difference. There is sand at the green that can't be seen from the tee.

No. 6, the number one handicap, doesn't look difficult. It's a par 4 of 403 yards from the blues and 378 yards from the whites. Straight and wide open, it doesn't always play like a low-handicap hole, either. But the prevailing wind out of the southwest can make a difference; it makes this hole (and many others on the course) play much longer.

One of the more fun holes, No. 7, is a 500-yard par 5. There is o.b. on the right side as the fairway rises straight out from the tee. The fairway crests, then drops left toward the green, which is reached over a lake. Flying the green can send the ball onto private property and o.b. This hole looks as simple as arithmetic but has hazards, especially near the green, that will quickly sober the overconfident player.

The real signature hole here is No. 18, where most players will thank the Gods of Golf for a par and hustle to the clubhouse. Others, carding double and triple bogeys on this short, 459-yard par 5, will question their future in the game. Water bisects the fairway. Pick one side or the other at the tee and go for it. The next shots must cover all sorts of water and fairway traps. The water gets more troublesome as the fairway narrows. The green slopes sharply forward. With the pin in front, putting off the green suddenly becomes a realistic fear. It is a great finishing hole because two (or more) stroke swings make for memorable matches.

For all that Raintree offers, the price is surprising. When it was suggested to Rainieri that his greens fees provide an excellent value, he said, "The people in this community don't believe that. They think we're holding them up."

We should have more stick-up artists like Rainieri.

Red Tail Golf Club   ☎ 440-937-6286
Area: **West**   City: **Avon**   Cost: **$$$$$**   Difficulty: ●●●

Address: 4400 Lear Nagle Rd., Avon

Tees	Ydg.	C/r	S/r	Pace
Back:	7007	74.8	133	
Middle:	6590	72.3	129	
Forward:	6029	69.5	124	

Specials: Twilights possible; off-season rates Oct 1–May 14; Call for details

Season: Mar–Dec. weather permitting   **Hours:** Dawn to dusk   **Tee times:** Taken
Leagues: None   **Ranger:**   **Practice facil:** Range, Putting Green, Sand
Clubhouse: Food, Beer, Liquor   **Outings:** Available (Full service, small & large groups (some restrictions))   **Lessons:** Available   **Pro:** Bryan Huff, PGA

Directions: I-90 to Exit 156 for Cocker Rd.; left (south) on Cocker Rd.; right (west) on Detroit Rd.; left (south) on Lear Nagle Rd. to entrance of clubhouse on right.

Description This Robert Von Hagge–designed track, part of a huge luxury housing development, opened in 1999. The big and handsome clubhouse opened a little later and until the target membership for a private club is reached, this course is available on a daily fee basis.

Inside the 20,000-square-foot clubhouse are locker rooms, full service dining, and a pro shop. It's a very nice place for banquets, parties, and small weddings.

Lessons are offered here at a gorgeous range, and there are two practice putting greens. The two nines are separated by Lear Nagle Road, and the nines are different from one another.

The front side plays more open, more languorously, as it cruises over big landing areas. The first three holes are not only a delight to play, but a great way to warm to the course.

The back side tightens up considerably, often being hemmed in by luxury housing. While often fun to look at and envy, housing is more of a distraction to golf than anything else.

Management can't decide whether or not to keep the course "cart paths only," but has always leaned that way. What a shame. Cart paths only, not only slows play, leads to clubs being left behind in fairways, and adds difficulty to figuring yardage, but prevents the great senior players like Ed Preisler, Bill Close, and Bob Hamrich from playing. These guys (two of the three played in U.S. Opens) don't have the patience or the energy to leave the cart, haul three or four sticks across a fairway, and hope they have the right club.

To make it even more difficult, walking is (at least last season) not allowed until after 4 p.m. Can anybody tell me why walking, which is an essential part of golf, is banned at a daily fee golf course?

So, no walking and carts must remain on the paths. Hmmm. Someone's working here, but not at golf.

Highlights There is water on 13 holes, and 72 bunkers lie in wait. Head golf professional Bryan Huff loves No. 3 on the front side, and surely, they are worthy of affection. A par 5, played from the "way-backs," stretches 630 yards. For members, this dogleg left with thick woods down the left side, is 600 yards, so for the majority of us, it's more than a three-shotter; it's a three-good-shotter.

Huff points out that the par 3s here are four of the best par 3s in the area, and he's right. Each presents a different and handsome challenge.

On the back side, the signature holes might be No. 17 and the home hole. Seventeen is the last of the magnificent par 3s, and it's all carry over water. And No. 18? This par 4 begins with a slow ascent, then turns suddenly to tumble downhill, over a ravine, to a small green surrounded by sand. What a finish!

PUBLIC 18+

PUBLIC 18+

The Reserve at Thunder Hill

☎ (440) 298-3474

Area: **Far East**   City: **Madison**   Cost: **$$$$**$ Difficulty: ●●●

Address: 7050 Griswold Rd., Madison

Tees	Ydg.	C/r	S/r	Pace
Back:	7504	78.5	152	
Middle:	6437	72.5	137	
Forward:	4769	68.5	121	

Specials: Senior & Junior specials Mon–Fri before 2 p.m.; call for additional specials.

Season: Year round **Hours:** Sunrise–sunset **Tee times:** Required **Leagues:** Offered **Ranger:** Daily **Practice facil:** Range, Putting Green, Chipping Green **Clubhouse:** Food, Beer, Liquor, Dining room, Showers, Patio, Facilities for parties **Outings:** Available **Lessons:** Available **Pro:** Sam Kless, PGA

Directions: I-90 to Exit 212 for SR 528; south on SR 528; left (east) on Griswold Rd.; on right.

Description It started in 1976 when developer Fred Slagle fired up the bulldozer and took the first giant bite out of this rich Ashtabula County soil. He created a course that wended its way between an apple orchard and trout ponds, over hill and dale, and around stands of pine. Thunder Hill. A course of mythical proportions. Slope rating of 150, four-wheel-drive carts, a canine corps to find players lost in the rough, and with nearly 75 lakes and ponds, a bonanza for a golf ball salesman.

The name was truly delivered from the heavens. Slagle said he was on the bulldozer one day when a thunderstorm rolled across the property. A couple lightning bolts were followed by thunder close enough to bounce him around a bit.

After a few incarnations, the course is managed today by the Meadowbrook Golf Inc., which just dumped $3.3 million into improvements.

The renovation includes installation of cement cart paths throughout; irrigation improvements in the bunker areas; clubhouse/parking/grounds renovation; fairway conversion to bent grass (formerly bluegrass). That's on the course. In the clubhouse nearly $600,000 is being spent on new washrooms, showers, new carpeting, a full-service pro shop, a new banquet room, and a sports/snack bar combination.

A nice touch is the complimentary bucket of balls. The driving range, while small, is new and a good idea. There are five sets of tees here. The Thunder tees play more than 7,500 yards; the Champion plays 6,866; Reserve plays 6,437 yards; Challenge tees go 5,754; and the Sanctuary tees are 4,769.

Greens are large, undulating, and well maintained. A hole-by-hole booklet is attached to each cart, with drawings and yardage figures from various points.

The Reserve at Thunder Hill

PUBLIC 18+

Highlights For all its reputation, the front side here is not worthy of myth. It is a very challenging nine holes, but divine intervention is not necessary to score well.

The first hole looks out over a couple of ponds and runs straight until it meets a pine grove. The fairway then veers right. There are plenty of trees on the course, but very little underbrush. The rough is minimal, and chipping out from the woods is usually a simple matter. The last 150 yards of No. 1 are lined with hardwoods on the right and pines on the left. The green is surrounded by four sand traps.

No. 12, a 497-yard par 5, lets players stumble directly into harm's way. The fairway on this hole is filled with ambushes: one big tree, four ponds, four sand traps. Woods close in around the edges. It calls for remarkable accuracy and sound shot planning. Lady Luck can be a valuable partner here, as well.

At No. 14, a 377-yard par 4, vestiges of the orchard remain, and the rich smell of apples fills the summer air. This is no tee for a lapse in concentration. There is a valley in front of the tee, and beyond it the fairway is closely guarded on both sides by trees. The opening for the drive is only about 35 yards wide. Just a slight draw will send the ball into a pine grove.

The green on No. 16 is most unusual. Long and narrow, it has a huge hump near the rear. It's not likely the flag would be placed behind it (one would hope not, anyway). But putting from back there will be unimaginably difficult. Next to the green is a beautiful beech tree. Its bark is filled with what appear to be scars in the shape of putter heads.

And No. 17, an even 400 yards long, suggests strongly that there is brutal golf ahead. As it nears the 150-yard marker, a narrow fairway suddenly drops down and sharply to the right, then zooms up again to the green. About seven ponds can come into play on this hole. Thick groves of trees here are omnivorous, swallowing hooks and slices alike.

Ridge Top Golf Course   ☎ (330) 725-5500; (800) 679-9839

Area: **Far South**   City: **Medina**   Cost: $$$$$$ Difficulty: ●●●

Address: 7441 Tower Rd., Medina

Tees	Ydg.	C/r	S/r	Pace
Back:	6211	69.5	114	3:34
Middle:	5893	67.4	109	
Forward:	4968	67.9	107	

Specials: Weekday specials; Senior specials Mon–Fri

Season: Mar–Dec **Hours:** Sunrise–sunset **Tee times:** Taken **Leagues:** Mon–Thu 4–6 p.m. **Ranger:** Daily **Practice facil:** Putting Green **Clubhouse:** Food, Beer, Liquor, Dining room **Outings:** Available **Lessons:** Not available **Pro:** Larry Miksch

Directions: I-71 to Exit 218 for SR 18; west on SR 18; left (south) on River Styx Rd.; right (west) on Poe Rd.; left (south) on SR 57 (Wadsworth Rd.); bear right (south) on Tower Rd.; on left.

Description There are only two types of golfers, according to owner Bob Emery: considerate and inconsiderate. "Fifty percent of your golfers will repair the greens where the others will not." Like many other owner/operators, he takes great pride in those layered sand-and-soil gardens so fragile, yet so important to the game.

Ridge Top was Medina County farmland until the 1970s. Across Tower Road is a farm; its silo provides an aiming point on one of the tees. The course was designed by Bob Pennington and plays a surprisingly short 5,893 yards, par 71.

Highlights The front side is much more interesting than the back. It starts with a 360-yard par 4 that is not, despite its length, an easy warm-up hole. White o.b. stakes line the right side, and on the left the terrain drops to a valley where the next hole is played. The fairway is not narrow, though, and a decent drive (one that misses the big oak on the right edge of the fairway at the 150-yard marker) will suffice. Overshooting the green will send the ball into deep rough and nearly off the course. These greens are fast.

No. 3 is the first of several tough doglegs. It is a 384-yard par 4 with a sharp right turn about 200 yards out. The elbow is filled with trees and uneven ground; only very big hitters will succeed in cutting this corner. After the turn, the hole falls slightly to a narrow creek bed.

The back side begins with one of the more difficult and challenging holes on the course. No. 10 is a 425-yard par 4 that calls for two very good shots. From the tee, players look across a deep valley to the fairway, which bends left and slopes down to the green. All along the right side it is wide open. But all along the left are deep woods. Behind the green are tall hardwoods. It is the number four handicap hole and a real challenge to par.

There is a nasty little gorge just in front of the No. 11 tee, but unless players top the ball, it is only decorative. This hole was recently rebuilt into a 320-yard dogleg par 4. The left side is filled with deep woods; the right side is open, though playing to the right lengthens the approach. The green is nestled in thick woods, which were cleared to fit it—an expensive but valuable change.

Ridge Top is off the beaten path but worth the effort it takes to find. It has a great variety of holes, good prices, and enlightened management.

Ridge Top Golf Course

PUBLIC 18+

PUBLIC 18+

Ridgewood Golf Course   ☎ (440) 888-1057

Area: **South**   City: **Parma**   Cost: **$$$**$$ Difficulty: ●●●

Address: 6505 Ridge Rd., Parma

Tees	Ydg.	C/r	S/r	Pace
Back:	6299	70.3	115	3:54
Middle:	5825	67.9	110	
Forward:	5090	69.1	113	

Specials: Senior specials available

Season: Mar 1–Nov 30 **Hours:** Sunrise–sunset **Tee times:** Not taken
Leagues: Various times **Ranger:** Daily **Practice facil:** Putting Green
Clubhouse: Food, Beer, Liquor **Outings:** Available **Lessons:** Available

Directions: I-480 to Exit 15 for Ridge Rd. (SR 3); south on Ridge; on left.

Description There is an ancient oak next to the practice green here, and at the base of it is a plaque. It is inscribed "In memory of Howard A. Stahl, 1875-1930. A pioneer in the development of the City of Parma and builder of Ridgewood Golf Course."

Clearly this course has been around a while. It has not always been owned and operated by City Hall, however—Parma did not assume ownership until the mid-fifties. By that time, the original layout of the course had been sacrificed for some new homes. Instead of its original 6,306 yards, it now plays 5,825. What was a great course is now just a fair course.

LPGA player (and four-time Tour winner) Barb Mucha prepped here; so did Walker Team player Chris Wollman, who won the National Public Links Championship in 1996. Other players of note who have teed it up here include Arnold Palmer, Walter Hagen, Romeo Palumbo, Byron Nelson, Patty Berg, and Babe Didrikson Zaharias. In May 1950, Zaharias won the Weathervane Women's Open here.

Highlights Ridgewood's tees are well cared for and adorned with flower boxes. The flowers, like the greens, are watered by hand. During dry weather the greens are watered three times a day. This hand grooming produces healthy greens of average speed.

No. 5 is a very short par 5, only 435 yards. It's a beautiful hole from the tee, though the green is not visible. The fairway drops off from the tee and rumbles along for a few hundred yards. About 200 yards from the green, it begins rising and bending to the right. It's especially easy to measure length on this course, because the yardage markers appear to be hewn from telephone poles. They are placed on the edges of the fairway.

No. 12 is a 260-yard par 4 that appears to have been designed as an afterthought. The fairway is lined with trees and rises slightly to a green that appears jacked up four or five feet. Approaching from the left side puts the ball at odds with a tall tree near the green. There is plenty of sand at the hole.

Then it's through the W. 54th Street tunnel to No. 13, a brutal and exciting par 5 that covers hill and dale, woods and plain, and 575 yards. The first few hundred yards go straight out from the tee and up. At its crest, the fairway suddenly turns 90 degrees to the right and falls to a green marked by two sand traps on the left and one on the right. The length, the dogleg, and the hills on this hole give bragging rights to any birdie.

Most of the fairways here are generous; playing and staying on the short grass is not as difficult as it is on other public courses. Many Ridgewood veterans tell visitors, "You should have seen it before they chopped it up." Such is the price of progress.

PUBLIC 18+

Riverside Golf Club   ☎ (440) 235-8006

Area: **Southwest**   City: **Columbia Station**   Cost: $$$$$ Difficulty: ●●●

Address: 10005 Columbia Rd., Columbia Station

Tees	Ydg.	C/r	S/r	Pace
Middle:	5498	65.9	106	
Forward:	5162	68.9	111	

Specials: None

Season: Year-round **Hours:** Sunrise–sunset **Tee times:** Required
Leagues: Mon–Fri 4–6 p.m. **Ranger:** Most days **Practice facil:** Putting Green, Chipping Green **Clubhouse:** Food, Beer, Liquor, Lockers, Showers, Pavilion
Outings: Available **Lessons:** Available **Pro:** Jay Reid

Directions: I-480 to Exit 6 for SR 252 (Great Northern Blvd.); south on SR 252 (becomes Columbia Rd.); left (east) on Sprague; on right.

Description Riverside has a lot of golf history. Managing pro Ray Reid has shares of stock issued in 1928 for the Berea Golf & Country Club, the original name of the club. "We nestle in Nature," reads the prospectus (a quote from Ralph Waldo Emerson). The club got its current name from the west branch of the Rocky River. Baker and Robinson creeks also cut around and through the course.

More unusual than water is the small graveyard that rests next to the fairway on No. 9. Reid calls it the Baker Graveyard for the frequent appearance of that name on tombstones there. He guesses an influenza epidemic swept through the area because there are so many headstones for children. The graveyard is o.b.

Riverside is not a long course, but the top three handicap holes are anything but short. It is very walkable. League play has been regular here since the Riverside Golf Association scheduled tee times in 1937. The RGA continues today.

PUBLIC 18+

Highlights The first hole is a 363-yard par 4, with a straight and wide fairway. It is only slightly more challenging than a driving range. Markers at 150 yards are 4 x 4s and easy to find.

No. 2 is in the corner of the course. A 309-yard par 4, it begins from an elevated tee and falls into a shallow valley. Trees are a factor on this hole, especially close to the creek that cuts across close to the green. Down the right side is o.b., and a few trees stand in the left rough. But near the water, woods grow thick and close in suddenly, making the approach shot more demanding.

No. 3 is an unusual hole, a par 3 of only 101 yards (and depending where the tee is located, often less than 100.) The tee is shaded by an old triple-trunked sycamore. It is virtually a blind tee shot, because 10 or 15 yards in front of the green the terrain suddenly shoots straight up. None of the green can be seen. There is a large sand trap on the right front, and the green leans from back to front. Missing the green short means a steep uphill lie in deep rough, not the average player's favorite shot.

No. 9 is a 471-yard par 5 that begins with a wide and level fairway. All the way down the right side are deep woods, but to get a ball in there calls for a super slice. After 200 yards, the fairway bends left and the wooded area on the right falls away into a valley. At 120 yards from the green, a large grass bunker sits on the right side of the fairway. There are a couple of fairway traps and, at the green, three more traps. Off to the right of the green is the graveyard (whence lies the body of Uraniam Hickox, who threw off his mortal coil in 1860). This resting place is o.b. The green itself encourages careful play; one of the penalties easily meted out here is putting right off the green. The green is high in back, low in the front. It drops three feet very quickly. And it all falls to the right front corner, where a pine tree sits.

The back side here begins and ends with gorgeous par 3s. One in, and one over, a valley. No. 10 is 141 yards from an elevated tee to a generous green. The green is on the other side of a creek and is stuck in the corner of the valley. The terrain rises behind it. It's a climb out of the valley to the next tee. No. 12 is the number one handicap, a long but relatively undistinguished par 4. One hundred yards out on this 430-yard hole sits an Eisenhower tree on the right side of the fairway. Otherwise, it's wide open.

Riverside is a particularly good course for beginners and groups; it's also a good layout for women who don't hit the ball far. It would be a good choice, too, for mixed foursomes seeking an alternative to the usual Friday night routine.

Jimmy Hanlin, PGA

True story. Jimmy Hanlin is the head pro at Little Mountain Country Club, the new golf club in Concord. There's a threesome warming up, and it sends word to him it wants him to join and play. The threesome: Jim Brown, Austin Carr, and Reggie Rucker, three of the most recognizable names in Cleveland sports history. Hanlin passes on the offer and sends someone in his place.

He didn't pass because he didn't want to play with them. Messrs. Carr and Rucker are 6-handicaps as well as members of Little Mountain, and Jim Brown plays to an 8. It broke Hanlin's heart to decline, but in golf, as in all things, first things first. Hanlin is busier than a one-legged man at a butt-kicking contest, and his schedule was too jammed to allow for a round of golf, even with the luminaries who invited him.

In addition to teaching 18 hours a week, he supervises the work of five dozen employees, reviews finances with the accountant every week, sells club memberships, and shows housing lots for luxury homes around the course. He is deeply involved in construction of the clubhouse, which begins this fall. A couple times a week he'll have a working lunch with Terry and Hope Grant, the owners and developers, and Tom Scheetz, the course superintendent.

Hanlin manages the pro shop and arranges corporate golf outings.

He also solves the problems presented to him by members and guests, whether advising on the stiffness of a shaft, the fit of a pair of Armani slacks, or the recalcitrance golf balls exhibit as they get closer to the cup.

For all the glamour associated with golf—and the game has glamour—Jimmy Hanlin works harder and longer every week of the season than most indentured servants.

When the oaks and yews are bare and the flags rolled up and put away, and cold, rude winds start slapping us around, Hanlin gears down to a mere 40-hour week of selling club memberships, listening to the fervent pitches of golf apparel and equipment salesmen, putting together real estate deals at the course, and doing promotion and planning for the next season.

It's an unusual job, golf professional. The training and education are arduous and expensive. The hours are egregious. The money, at least until a head pro job or substantial teaching opportunities arrive, is nothing to write home about, and in any private club there are more bosses (read: members) than in any Mafia family.

Most club professionals started out with a different dream: the PGA Tour.

So it was with Hanlin, a Steubenville native who played the mini tours for two and a half years before deciding that his future, while it would be in golf, would not be on the PGA Tour.

"I had the sponsors and my game was improving," he said, "but I was 27 and if I didn't make the Tour, I would be going back as an assistant pro at age 30 or 31."

Sponsorship for Hanlin on the mini tours was about $60,000 per year, he said, "And I stayed in the southeast, I wasn't flying or traveling all over the country."

Sponsors know that their money will not likely return to them. They are there, Hanlin said, to "help and hope for" young players with potential. A successful player on the mini tours will win about $20,000 annually.

"There are plenty of pros here that can go out and shoot 65, spectacular players like Mitch Camp [Walden Golf & Tennis Club], Tom Atchison [Silver Lake CC], or Gary Trivisonno [Aurora CC]." On the Tour, though, "It's not just hitting the ball well, it's consistently hitting the ball well . . . a 72 is a bad round." Add to the playing demands the fact that there is more pressure on the Tour than can be created with a vise grip.

When he decided to seek work with a country club, one of his teachers, Danny Ackerman, now at Longaberger GC, was the head pro at Quail Hollow CC and hired his former student.

The idea of touring stayed with Hanlin, however. "I thought I'd work a summer, then go back to playing. Some members approached me and asked how much I needed. I was playing well at the time, but I turned it down."

One door closes. Another opens.

Terry Grant, owner and developer of Little Mountain, already had the Hurdzan Fry design team creating a spectacular course on the hills overlooking Lake Erie. The Grants wanted to bring in the course superintendent and the head golf pro a year before the gates opened late last year.

It was good thinking. Hanlin and superintendent Tom Scheetz were the only guys with golf experience. More important, golf pros and the superintendents rarely see eye to eye. The golf pro wants players on his course; the superintendent wants to protect the course. "Terry wanted us to grow together, and it's worked out very well."

Last year, just as he was getting comfortable with the vision the Grants created for Little Mountain, Hanlin was upended at a basketball game and came down on his elbow. "I thought I sprained it," he said. He had shattered the bone.

Dr. Tom Hunt, at the Cleveland Clinic, installed a fake elbow, and after lots of therapy, Hanlin was swinging again. But he was not playing well. He found out how difficult it can be for players who shoot in the 80s. Little by little, though, it came back, and today, with his artificial elbow, he swings as well as ever.

Royal Crest Golf Club   ☎ (440) 236-5644

Area: **Southwest**   City: **Columbia Station**   Cost: $$$$$$ Difficulty: ●●●

PUBLIC 18+

Address: 23310 SR 82, Columbia Station

Tees	Ydg.	C/r	S/r	Pace
Back:	6746	70.5	108	
Middle:	6205	68.0	108	
Forward:	5903	72.0	112	

Specials: Senior & Junior specials weekdays

Season: Apr 1–Oct 31 **Hours:** Sunrise–sunset **Tee times:** Not taken
Leagues: Every morning and evening **Ranger:** Most days **Practice facil:**
Putting Green **Clubhouse:** Food, Beer, Showers, Pavilion **Outings:** Available
(small groups; 16–72 players) **Lessons:** Available **Pro:** Trummie J. Hudson

Directions: I-71 to Exit 231 for SR 82 (Royalton Rd.); west on SR 82; on right.

Description This property has been in the Madak family since the turn of the century. The family farm was developed into a golf course in the late 1960s, and the barn into the clubhouse, which seats about three dozen players. More than 40 leagues play every week at Royal Crest.

It's a little longer than the average area course at 6,205, par 71, and the forward tees don't provide much relief. The number one and two handicap holes on the women's course are par 3s measuring 195 and 192 yards; many members of the LPGA would find those holes difficult. The terrain is generally level, and the course is well cared for. Clearly, the Madak family plans to keep this course for generations.

Highlights The first three holes do not call for heroics (though anyone holding the green on No. 2, a 207-yard par 3, deserves a round of applause). But they give a good indication of what the course is like. It is not fancy, but it is often challenging.

No. 4 is the only par 5 on the front side, a 544-yard dogleg left. The hole is played in the corner of the course; much of the right side is o.b. But it's a wide fairway until the last hundred yards. Cutting the corner of the dogleg is impossible. Another tee is near the elbow, and the area is marked with white stakes. It also has a stand of tall pines that would challenge even the biggest hitters. This is not a hole for risk taking. Three good shots will get the ball on the green.

The last hole on the front side is pure Royal Crest: long, straight, and lined with trees. No. 9 is a par 4 of 396 yards. The green is slightly elevated and behind it is a sand trap.

No. 16 is a fun par 5. A wide fairway and generous landing area tempt players to swing for the long ball. Big hitters not yet in control of their fades, however, might find either drive or second shot o.b. on the right.

Like many area courses, this is a family operation and likely to stay that way. Here, that's reassuring.

Seneca Golf Course   ☎ (216) 348-7274
Area: **South**   City: **Broadview Hts.**   Cost: $$$$$ Difficulty: ●●●

Address: 975 Metro Valley Pkwy., Broadview Hts.

Tees	A Course Ydg.	C/r	S/r	Pace	B Course Ydg.	C/r	S/r	Pace
Middle:	6559	71.2	118		6639	71.6	121	
Forward:	6387	74.6			6476	75.1		

Specials: Senior specials Mon–Fri until 3 p.m., Sat–Sun after 3 p.m.

Season: Mid-Mar–mid-Dec **Hours:** 6 a.m.–8 p.m. Mon–Fri, 5:30 a.m.–dusk Sat, Sun **Tee times:** Taken weekends **Leagues:** Mon–Fri 4–6 p.m. **Ranger:** Daily **Practice facil:** Range, Putting Green, Use own balls on range **Clubhouse:** Food, Beer, Dining room, Lockers, Showers **Outings:** Available (tent rental avail.) **Lessons:** Not available

Directions: I-77 to Exit 149 for SR 82; west on SR 82 (E. Royalton Rd.); left (south) on SR 176 (Broadview Rd.); left (east) on Metro Valley Pkwy.; on right.

Description In recent years, the mayor of Cleveland had threatened to privatize some city functions, including the operation of its two golf courses, Highland Park and Seneca. We'll see what Jane Campbell does with this and its East Side Siamese twin, Highland Park GC. Of course it should be privatized, and the sooner the better. Lots of cities and county and state agencies own and operate golf courses, and most of them do it very well. But Cleveland, which hands over hundreds of millions of dollars to owners of sports-as-business teams, couldn't care less about its two golf properties, which, if managed properly, could return a great deal of revenue to city coffers. As it is, city ownership of these two courses is shameful. Seneca doesn't have any of the essentials: manpower, equipment, or incentive. And that's a shame, because it could be a premier course. And it's a course with some history. Seneca was built under the Works Progress Administration during the mid-1930s and opened for play in 1940.

Highlights The number one handicap on B Course is No. 3. The 582-yard par 5 plays along a wide fairway with little trouble on either side. The tee shot is blind, as the terrain rises from the tee. A lake in front of the green is about 40 yards deep and easily 100 yards wide. Getting on in three is reserved for good players. B Course has only one par 5 and one par 3 per nine.

A few holes into the first nine, one gets used to the groundskeeping. The rough here is not long but is often filled with weeds. It has an unkempt look to it. The greens are sometimes in good shape, often in poor shape. The sand traps look as if they were never raked or filled with any new sand.

No. 6 is a 380-yard par 4 that rolls softly downhill toward a lake at the 150-yard marker. Often filled with more mud and cattails than water, the lake is as wide as the fairway. From the other side of the water the fairway rises slightly to a generous green.

Some of the trees on this old course are more than 100 years old and measure 15 to 20 feet around. Many of the holes are defined by trees, but woods don't become a problem except around the perimeter of the course.

The front side is unusually long for having no par 4s over 400 yards. The back is longer and has two monster par 4s.

No. 13, a 452-yard par 4, is another blind tee shot to a rising fairway. There is a fairway trap on the right and sand on the left side of the green as well. It's a long, long way for the average player to reach in regulation. No. 16 has a generous fairway, and it should. This par 4 is a long 449 yards to a green with sand on both sides.

All of B Course and the back side of A Course are played in an area east of the clubhouse. The front side of A Course is to the west. Unlike the other three nines, it does not have a wealth of century oaks; it plays a bit more open and is the side used for winter golf.

Sitting between the east and west sides of the clubhouse is a practice range and huge practice green. The clubhouse porch overlooks the practice areas and provides a good view of the 18th hole of A Course.

The back side of A Course is the only side here with two par 5s and two par 3s.

No. 17 is awfully long: straightaway 608 yards from tee to green. The fairway is wide and the green only slightly elevated. Except for the length, it's almost hazard free. But the length of this hole pushes many players to swing much harder than they normally might. The results rarely match one's hopes. A par on this hole is worth talking about.

The underlying features that once made Seneca a fine course are not lost. But the course's present owner has neither the resources nor the drive to make it playable again. It's time to let somebody else try.

PUBLIC 18+

TIDYMAN'S TIDBITS #11
Great short par 4s
1) No. 2 Pine Hills
2) No. 7 Forest Hills
3) No. 10 Berkshire Hills
4) No. 17 Sleepy Hollow
5) No. 18 Springvale

PUBLIC 18+

Shawnee Hills Golf Course   ☎ (440) 232-7184

Area: **South**   City: **Bedford**   Cost: $$$$$ Difficulty: ●●●

Address: 18753 Egbert Rd., Bedford

Tees	Regulation Course				Par 3 Course			
	Ydg.	C/r	S/r	Pace	Ydg.	C/r	S/r	Pace
Back:	6366	69.9	114	3:50		1:48		
Middle:	6175	68.7	112		1293			
Forward:	5884	72.5	116					

Specials: Golfer's Dozen: 12 rounds for the price of 10; Senior (62+) & Junior specials weekdays; special par 3 prices

Season: Mid-Mar–Dec 31 **Hours:** Sunrise–sunset **Tee times:** Taken, 1 out of 4 tee times kept open for walk-on players. **Leagues:** Mon–Fri, various times **Ranger:** Daily **Practice facil:** Range, Putting Green, Chipping Green, Lighted driving range **Clubhouse:** Food, Beer, Porch **Outings:** Available (weekdays and Saturday afternoons; call Golf Services at 440-232-2722.) **Lessons:** Available **Pro:** Jeff Staker

Directions: I-77 to Exit 153 for Pleasant Valley Pkwy.; east on Pleasant Valley (becomes Alexander Rd.); left (north) on Dunham Rd; right (east) on Egbert Rd.; on left.

Description The amenities offered at this 45-year-old Cleveland Metroparks course include a lighted driving range, a 40-seat clubhouse, and a four-minute response time from the Bedford Fire Department—especially valuable if players are prone to (or prone from) heart attacks. In addition to the 6,160-yard, par 71 course, Shawnee Hills also offers a 9-hole par 3 layout.

The grounds are very well tended here. Even driving to the course, if one drives from downtown, is a delight, because the road through the Metroparks Bedford Reservation is filled with beautiful woods, horse trails, picnic spots, and the picturesque Bridal Veil Falls, where wise newlyweds might pose for their wedding photos before changing clothes and heading to the first tee.

The deep woods are along the perimeter of the course, but the designers of Shawnee Hills kept as many of the old, tall, stately hardwoods on the course as they could. The trees provide guidance, protection, and hazards. Their stature gives the course a mature look.

Highlights No. 3 is a 347-yard par 4, a beautiful hole with a fairway that rises and falls a few times before it arrives at the green. Near the 150-yard marker it falls precipitously, and water cuts across at the bottom of the little valley. (Unusual note: this hole is one of three 347-yard holes on the course. A lucky number? The others are No. 5 and No. 15.)

The back nine starts next to the driving range. The 364-yard No. 10 is a straight par 4 and its fairway is littered with practice balls. Fortunately, the club uses yellow balls at the range. There is a lake behind this green, but it will have much more influence later.

No. 16 is the only par 5 on this side, 540 yards. It dips at the tee then rises to the right. The entire left side is filled with pines, and on the right a few trees separate this fairway from the adjacent 17th. The fairway slowly rises to the green.

It's a quiet course. A lovely, simple, and beautifully groomed course that doesn't present challenges so much as it offers players the pleasures of the game.

PUBLIC 18+

Shawnee Hills Golf Course   (photo: Casey Batule/courtesy of Cleveland Metroparks)

PUBLIC 18+

Skyland Golf Course
☎ (330) 225-5698

Area: **South**   City: **Hinckley**   Cost: **$$$**$$ Difficulty: ●●●

Address: 2085 Center Rd. (SR 303), Hinckley

Tees	Ydg.	C/r	S/r	Pace
Back:	6337			
Middle:	6115	68.9	113	
Forward:	5497	70.7	112	

Specials: Special prices Mon–Thu until 1 p.m.; Senior specials available

Season: Apr–Nov 15 **Hours:** Sunrise–sunset **Tee times:** Recommended
Leagues: Heavy play Tue–Fri 8–9:30 a.m., Mon–Fri 4–6:15 p.m.
Ranger: Most days **Practice facil:** Putting Green **Clubhouse:** Food, Beer, Liquor, Dining room, 2 pavilions **Outings:** Available **Lessons:** Available **Pro:** Tim Monroe

Directions: I-71 to Exit 226 for SR 303 (Center Rd.); east on SR 303; on left.

Description Across the street from the clubhouse is a dairy farm, a pastoral reminder of how close rural Ohio still is to Cleveland. Just down the street is an apple and cider market. At the course entrance is a big, blooming flower box built of railroad ties. This is a beautiful old layout, thought by some to be the oldest course in Medina County.

It brings with it some history. It was the first course in the area, owner Tim Rhodes said, to discard the "Women After Eleven a.m. Only" rule. "We thought that rule was one of the most arrogant things around. We were the first to break it. We didn't see any sense to it, and I have women with permanent tee times on Sunday mornings, as well as women's leagues."

Skyland was built by the father of owners Tim and Tom Rhodes. Every April, Tom leaves Hinckley to visit his favorite course: Augusta. He returns home inspired.

The first nine was built in the early thirties and the course was known as Hinckley Golf Course. When the second nine was added, in 1940, the name was changed to Skyland for the views available from some tees. "During the Depression, my mom and dad would charge 25 cents a round. Plenty of people would come out, five and six to a car, and play all day," Tim Rhodes said. The prices have changed, but the value remains.

Plenty of people still come out: 30 leagues play at Skyland. The oldest is the Hinckley Skyland Men's League, which first scheduled tee times in 1957. St. Bridget's Holy Name Society started playing in 1960. Both continue today.

The clubhouse, a large and airy brick one-story building, was erected in 1968. A brisk trade is done in outings. Tee times are available, but permanent weekend tee times are in the clutches of longtime regulars. "Some of these go back to 1956, when we first gave out tee times. Even if they move from the area, they find a way to move their friends into those tee times so they don't lose the slot."

Highlights The front side is much longer than the back.

No. 3 is a par 5 with a hilly fairway that is straight and tree lined. The tee box on this 480-yard hole is the site of one of the stranger golf stories picked up during the research for this book.

A regular foursome was making ready to tee off when one member began complaining about chest pains. He thought he was suffering a heart attack. His playing partners accused him of malingering and refused to do anything about his complaints. When he grew more frantic, his partners offered him a deal: they would walk him over to the rough on the adjacent No. 7 and lay him gently down. They would then play holes 4, 5, and 6. When they again reached him on the adjacent No. 7, they would inquire as to his health and, if he still feared he was dying, would take him in. So they resumed play as a threesome. A player from another group came across the heart-attack victim, and, after inquiring how he came to be prone in the rough on No. 7, rushed the man back to the clubhouse and medical assistance.

McReynold's Hex is No. 8, a 334-yard par 4, that calls for a blind tee shot to a wide and rising fairway that crests about 100 yards from the tee. The fairway slopes left; near the green is a lake on the left. From the lake a tiny creek—nemesis of a certain Mr. McReynold—cuts directly across the fairway. There is a stand of hardwoods in front of the water.

No. 11 is a very straight par 4, 404 yards. Two hundred yards from the tee, the fairway drops and rolls to a narrow creek cutting across. Then it rises and heads for the green. It is the toughest driving hole on the course, calling for accuracy not necessary on other tees. To miss right means deep underbrush where poison ivy and deer flies wait. To miss left means banging around a stand of trees with no chance of getting on in regulation. If ever a straight hit was needed, this is it. Smart players often tag 2-irons on this, the number three handicap hole.

Skyland is well into its second half century. It has long offered the golfing public a most wonderful walk in the woods. Management takes care of the big things, such as greens and fairways, and the little things, such as flower gardens and a warm welcome to the course. Just as it should be.

TIDYMAN'S TIDBITS #12

Best driving ranges that are part of a course:

1) Stone Water
2) Hawk's Nest
3) Sand Ridge

PUBLIC 18+

Sleepy Hollow Golf Course   ☎ (440) 526-4285

Area: **South**   City: **Brecksville**   Cost: **$$$**$$ Difficulty: ●●●

Address: 9445 Brecksville Rd., Brecksville

Tees	Ydg.	C/r	S/r	Pace
Back:	6702	72.7	132	3:43
Middle:	6301	71.3	127	
Forward:	5321	71.6	120	

Specials: Golfer's Dozen: 12 rounds for the price of 10; Senior (62+) & Junior specials

Season: Mid-Mar–Dec 31 **Hours:** Sunrise–sunset **Tee times:** Taken
Leagues: Mon–Fri 4:30–6:30 p.m. **Ranger:** Daily **Practice facil:** Range, Putting
Green, Chipping Green **Clubhouse:** Food, Beer, Liquor, Dining room, Lockers, Showers
Outings: Available (Mon, Wed, Fri) **Lessons:** Available **Pro:** John Fiander

Directions: I-77 to Exit 149 for SR 82 (E. Royalton Rd.); east on SR 82;
right (south) on SR 21 (Brecksville Rd.); on left.

Description With its polished clubhouse, bag drop, showers, phones, and hair dryers, Sleepy Hollow feels much more like a private club than a Metroparks layout.

It is also one of the toughest tracks in town. Not for beginners or players who are easily frustrated, this is a difficult and challenging lay-out with greens that are among the fastest and trickiest in Northeast Ohio public golf. Now if management could only speed play.

Highlights No. 2, the Par Three From Hell, is 220 yards to a two-tiered green. Along the right side is a shallow valley filled with dense under-brush and golf balls. The tee is elevated. Once over a small valley in front, the fairway rises slightly. There is sand to the right and near the green, which is long and rather narrow.

No. 3 is rated the number one handicap hole on the course, and with good reason. It is a 454-yard par 4, slightly downhill at first before the fairway drops more severely. A big drive has to stay left in order to see the green for the approach. Coming in from the right leaves a couple of tall trees in the way. In front of the green is a small but severe valley. On the left side, deep woods angle in, making the hole more narrow as it progresses. The generous green has sand to the left and right. A tourna-ment hole.

On the front side, it's generally clear where the ball should go. Not so on the back, which has a number of blind tees and very sharp doglegs. Taken as a whole, the two sides combine to present a sort of golfing trip through the Fun House—around every corner is a surprise.

No. 10 was shortened a bit when the tee box was rebuilt and moved as part of the driving range construction. The range now runs down its right side. The number two handicap, it's a 423-yard par 4. An unre-stricted fairway bends a bit to the right at the 150-yard marker. More troublesome than the bend is the grass valley that cuts across the fairway there. And sand surrounds the hole.

No. 14 begins by racing up the first 80 yards. It is a very blind tee shot—almost like shooting over a wall of grass—to a wide fairway that stretches out a couple of hundred yards before falling into a steep, small valley. On the right side of this 490-yard par 5 are deep woods. And when the fairway climbs up from the valley it takes a severe dogleg right; trees fill the elbow. The green can be reached in two great shots, the second a blind shot over tall trees to a smallish green. There is sand at the flat green. From any angle, this is a lot of golf hole.

Sleepy Hollow Golf Course   (photo: Casey Batule/courtesy of Cleveland Metroparks)

No. 17 is the rare tee here that does not require length, only accuracy. Well, that's not always true. For lack of length, Paul Rowland, a retired librarian at the *Plain Dealer*, once hit eight consecutive tee shots into the small lake in front of the tee. Rowland saved himself an ignominious 30 by dropping a long putt, penciling in a 29. He still answers when people ask for the Legend of Sleepy Hollow. Once over the pretty lake on this 272-yard par 4, the fairway takes a 90-degree left turn. In the elbow of the dogleg are tall trees, so cutting the corner is virtually impossible.

No. 18 is a 364-yard par 4, a straight hole with few difficulties. A couple of trees mark the rough on the sides, and the fairway dips a bit before the green. At the sloped green are sand traps. Like many of the holes at Sleepy Hollow, this one calls for big hitting and fearless putting.

On any ranking of area courses, Sleepy Hollow will rank very high. With the new clubhouse and related amenities, it has been transformed from just a very tough course to a glamorous one. It is easy to forget that this course and facility are owned and operated by the government. It sets a standard for all public courses.

Springvale Golf Course ☎ (440) 777-0678

Area: **West**   City: **North Olmsted**   Cost: **$$$**$$ Difficulty: ●●●

PUBLIC 18+

Address: 5873 Canterbury Rd., North Olmsted

Tees	Men's Tees				Women's Tees			
	Ydg.	C/r	S/r	Pace	Ydg.	C/r	S/r	Pace
Back:	6303	69.0	112	3:35	6303	73.4	123	
Middle:	6033	67.8	110		5586	71.4	118	
Forward:	5586	66.4	108		5077	67.7	110	

Specials: Call for specials.

Season: Year-round **Hours:** Sunrise–sunset **Tee times:** Taken **Leagues:** Mon–Fri 3–6 p.m. **Ranger:** Daily **Practice facil:** Range, Putting Green, Chipping Green, Sand, Six target greens **Clubhouse:** Food, Beer, Liquor, Dining room, Lockers, Patio, Ballroom dancing Wed, Fri, Sun nights **Outings:** Available **Lessons:** Available **Pro:** Jerry Ludvik

Directions: I-480 to Exit 6 for SR 252 South (Olmsted Falls); south on SR 252; right (west) on Butternut Ridge Rd.; left (south) on Canterbury Rd.; on left.

Description Built in the early part of the twentieth century, this club is still influenced by the 1930s: in addition to serving the passion for golf, it is also home of the Springvale Ballroom, where big bands play four nights a week.

The clubhouse is old-fashioned and very comfortable. The dark woodwork is handsome, and the card room downstairs is a wonderful throwback to another era. A long bar dominates the room, and stuffed fish and game trophies cover the walls. A screened-in porch almost the width of the clubhouse provides a view of the first tee.

Springvale Golf Course, Banquet, Dance and Meeting Facility. What an overblown name for a golf course! While the name is fancier than the amenities here, the course provides a few noteworthy holes and a good challenge to area players. It also provides big band music for people who appreciate the box step. A most elegant combination.

Highlights A local rule is often invoked on No. 1, a 323-yard par 4. Just in front of the tee is a lake. Players dribbling their balls into the water have to shoot from the forward tee on the other side of the water hazard. It speeds play. Once over the water, the hole is straight with some fairway sand on the left side and more sand at the green. The greens here are fast.

No. 5, a 334-yard par 4, bends to the right. An Eisenhower tree is in the fairway near the bend, favoring left-to-right players. On this end of the course it is not unusual to halt play, especially in the evening or early morning, to let deer trot across the fairway.

No. 11, a 476-yard par 5, is the signature hole on this course. The fairway is wide and flat to begin with, but drops near the 150-yard marker to a crossing valley and creek. Beyond the water, the green is jammed in the side of a hill, sloping forward. An interesting hole, a very different hole. Some players find it an unfair hole because the average player has to hit a drive, a wedge to the edge of the valley, then a 6- or 7-iron over the valley and the water to a green that is very difficult.

St. Denis Golf Club   ☎ (440) 285-2183

Area: **Far East**   City: **Chardon**   Cost: $$$$$ Difficulty: ●●●

PUBLIC 18+

Address: 10660 Chardon Rd. (US 6), Chardon

Tees	Ydg.	C/r	S/r	Pace
Back:	6640	71.7	117	
Middle:	6375	69.9	115	
Forward:	5800	72.5	117	

Specials: Specials for 2 golfers with cart for 18 holes; Senior specials Mon–Fri

Season: Mid-Apr–mid-Nov **Hours:** 7 a.m.–9 p.m. **Tee times:** Taken
Leagues: Mon-Thu 3:30-6:30 p.m. **Ranger:** Most days
Practice facil: Putting Green, Chipping Green **Clubhouse:** Food, Beer, banquet facility w/ full menu **Outings:** Available **Lessons:** Not available

Directions: I-90 to Exit 189 for SR 91 (SOM Center Rd.); south on SR 91 to Chardon Rd. (US 6); left (east) on Chardon Rd; on left.

Description There are many reasons to visit this quiet town in Geauga county: maple syrup in the spring, the town square with the opera house on one end … but coming to Chardon to play St. Denis is right up there.

Course superintendent Bill Griesmer and his father, Scotty Foecking, have built and manage a course that is an absolute delight. Father and son had the design done by Harry Burkhart, the veteran who designed Astorhurst, Shawnee, and Thunderbird.

Mr. Foecking purchased 135 acres for the course in 1966. His orders to the designer were simple: "We just wanted a regulation 18-hole golf course that the average golfer could really enjoy."

That is just what he has today. A big, comfortable one-story clubhouse contains pro shop and snack bar. Flowers are everywhere. Flower pots hang from the ceiling and fill tee boxes. The fairways are meticulously manicured. The holes roll with the terrain. It is gently hilly. It is not short, at 6,375 yards, but it often looks more challenging than it plays. Walking these 18 is a fine cardiovascular workout.

Highlights No. 5, one of two holes favored by Mr. Foecking as signature holes, is a 400-yard par 4 with a narrow landing area. It is largely downhill until 80 yards before the green when it zooms up and right.

Between the No. 7 green and the No. 8 tee is a small grove of apple trees. When the trees are producing, a garbage can is set out for cores.

No. 14, the number one handicap hole, is Mr. Foecking's other great hole. The challenge on this 410-yard par 4 is at the tee. An inability to land the drive accurately means fishing the ball from the stream that gurgles diagonally across the fairway. Missing here can tarnish an otherwise good round.

No outings here, and that's fitting. This course is far too nice for the boorish behavior that marks most outings.

StoneWater Golf Club   ☎ (440) 461-4653

Area: **East**   City: **Highland Hts.**   Cost: **$$$$$**   Difficulty: ●●●

Address: One Club Dr., Highland Hts.

Tees	Black/Gold/White				Green/Green/Silver			
	Ydg.	C/r	S/r	Pace	Ydg.	C/r	S/r	Pace
Back:	7000	74.8	138	4:30	5630	68.0	122	4:30
Middle:	6659	73.0	132		5630	72.6	132	
Forward:	6211	70.6	127		4915	69.2	123	

Specials: Call for specials

Season: Apr 1–Dec 1 **Hours:** Tues–Sun: 7 a.m.–7 p.m.; Mon: 11 a.m.–7 p.m.
Tee times: Recommended, Non-members may call 1 week in advance;
tee times more than 1 week in advance subject to privilege fee. **Leagues:** None
Ranger: Daily **Practice facil:** Range, Putting Green, Chipping Green, Sand,
(available for warming up prior to round) **Clubhouse:** Food, Beer, Liquor,
Lockers, Patio service; clubhouse to open for the 2000 season **Outings:** Available
(member-sponsored only) **Lessons:** Available **Pro:** Jon Boland, PGA

Directions: I-90 to Exit 187 for Bishop Rd.; south on Bishop; left (east) on Aberdeen
Blvd. for 1/2 mile; on left. OR I-271 to Exit 36 for Wilson Mills Rd.; west on Wilson Mills;
right (north) on Bishop Rd.; right (east) on Aberdeen Blvd. for 1/2 mile; on left.

Description At long last, the clubhouse is up and running at this magnificent course, where management has been a bit on the … loony side. Originally created as an upscale daily fee course, the dedication round wasn't played, but memberships for $20,000 were offered. The membership fee provided discounts on the greens fees, access to a trailer/locker room, and the privilege of making tee times far in advance. StoneWater dumped hundreds of thousands into a global positioning system on its carts and a goose-chasing dog, while players, paying close to a hundred bucks a round, were changing their shoes in the parking lot. When the site for the clubhouse was finally selected, it was deemed too close to the ninth fairway, so the long and powerful par 5 had its legs cut out from under it. Still, with this design and with caddies in white coveralls, the golf experience here can be memorable. If you don't mind playing through yet another housing development.

When you arrive, the bag boy takes your sticks for you. He straps them onto a cart that has your name on it. Freshly laundered towels are on board. The driving range is all grass, 300 yards deep, and stocked with Pro Staff balls. The starter arrives at the range to lead your foursome to the first tee. Starting times are every ten minutes.

That's the way a round begins at this singular upscale club, honored by *Golf Digest* as one of the top four new courses in 1997 and featured in *Golf Magazine*. Designed by Dana Fry of the Fry/Hurdzan Design Group, this course takes stonework to a level not seen before. Bridges, sand traps, tee boxes, and lakes are lined with sandstone, quarried on site as the course was being built.

StoneWater Golf Club   *(photo: Henebry Photography)*

PUBLIC 18+

Highlights The front side is open and suggests to players that the path to par is without difficulty. While the landing areas for tee shots are generous, the challenges to par are both subtle and devious. Gamblers welcome here; risk and reward taken to new heights.

The opening hole is 397 yards and water plays an important role. It begins next to the green and gurgles down the right side until it cuts across the fairway and continues down the left side.

No. 3 is the signature hole on this side, a gorgeous par 3 over water and marsh to a stonewalled green. Mallards often dine here and the big egret from No. 7 drops in on occasion.

The cottage at the turn provides food and drink, but players are encouraged to eat and run.

The back side is far different, marked by drama, high adventure and great challenge. These nine holes were carved from woods and it will be on the last four holes that matches are decided.

The home hole is the signature hole on this side, though No. 16 provides competition. Each has water and distinct landing areas. Each calls for excellent iron play, and par on either hole is satisfying.

At the end of a match, the bag boy utters a line never heard on public courses: "Clean your clubs, sir?"

Sunny Hill Golf & Recreation ☎ (330) 673-1785

Area: **Far South**   City: **Kent**   Cost: $$$$$ Difficulty: ●●●

Address: 3734 Sunny Brook Rd., Kent

	1st & 2nd nines				3rd nine			
Tees	Ydg.	C/r	S/r	Pace	Ydg.	C/r	S/r	Pace
Back:	6224	68.4	110					
Middle:	5919	66.8	107		2273	30.7		
Forward:	5083	68.4	107		2084	31.5		

Specials: Senior specials Mon–Fri; Guys & Dolls special Sat–Sun after 3 p.m.

Season: Apr 1–Dec 31 **Hours:** Sunrise–9 p.m. **Tee times:** Taken **Leagues:** Various times **Ranger:** Daily **Practice facil:** Range, Putting Green, Chipping Green **Clubhouse:** Food, Beer, Liquor, Pavilion **Outings:** Available **Lessons:** Not available

Directions: I-77 to I-76; east on I-76 to Exit 31 for Tallmadge Rd.; east on Tallmadge; right (south) on Sunny Brook Rd.; on left.

Description The front side here is the tough side. It's short and very, very, tight, and its greens are all elevated. Little room for error. Lots of short holes; if you're good with short irons you can chew it up. The back side is more open, and greens are more amenable to play: flatter and more forgiving.

TIDYMAN'S TIDBITS #13
Great short par 4s
1) No. 2 Pine Hills
2) No. 7 Forest Hills
3) No. 10 Berkshire Hills
4) No. 17 Sleepy Hollow
5) No. 18 Springvale

More ... Than ...

Golf is more ...

Mental than psychotherapy.

Delightful than a children's choir.

Peaceful than a cemetery.

Uncomfortable than a prostate exam.

Healthy than Jack La Lanne.

Eagerly anticipated than the Second Coming.

Frustrating than false labor.

Humiliating than getting caught.

Unforgiving than a Browns fan.

Stern than a highway patrol officer.

Dependable than a Boy Scout.

Demanding than the Teamsters.

Deceiving than Congress.

Hopeful than sunrise.

Colorful than autumn.

Exciting than NASCAR.

Faithful than a dog.

Sweetbriar Golf Club at Legacy Point   ☎ (440) 871-0822

Area: **West**   City: **Avon Lake**   Cost: **$$$**$$ Difficulty: ●●●

Address: 750 Jaycox Rd., Avon Lake

	Courses 1&2				Courses 1&3				Courses 2&3			
Tees	Ydg.	C/r	S/r	Pace	Ydg.	C/r	S/r	Pace	Ydg.	C/r	S/r	Pace
Back:	6491	68.7	106		6075	66.3	100		6292	67.5	104	
Middle:	6311	67.8	105		5895	65.5	99		6112	66.7	102	
Forward:	5612	68.9	105		5505	68.0	105		5411	68.3	104	

Specials: Weekday specials

Season: Year-round **Hours:** Sunrise–sunset **Tee times:** Taken weekends
Leagues: Daily **Ranger:** Daily **Practice facil:** Range, Putting Green **Clubhouse:** Food, Beer, Pavilion **Outings:** Available **Lessons:** Available **Pro:** David Mealey

Directions: I-90 to Exit 153 for SR 83; north on SR 83 (Center Rd.);
SR 83 briefly joins Chester Rd. then turns north; continue east on Chester;
left (north) on Jaycox Rd.; on left.

Description The west side of Cleveland is about to enjoy its first upscale daily fee course. It was worth waiting for.

Always a playable course, but never a memorable track, the 27 holes here are undergoing a transformation that will make this flat track a wonderful place to play, to dine, to shop, and to enjoy outings.

Unlike lots of other courses that tried to go too fast too soon (Gleneagles and StoneWater come to mind immediately), management here has a plan that calls for steady growth.

First, the new clubhouse. The old clubhouse wasn't bad—a small eating area and a large merchandise area. But it was leveled. The new place is as stylish as a country club. It offers a full-service dining room, a grill room, locker rooms, and a nice patio bar area. The pro shop is filled to overflowing with high-end merchandise, and the chef is up to the task, whether you want a grilled cheese sandwich or sea bass with the appropriate wine.

Would you like to set up an account? Suddenly this old course will be a place for business entertaining.

The first nine holes to be reworked used to be the third nine, holes 19 through 27, which played like a beginner's pleasant course. Not any more. Michigan designer Don Childs went to work, and the new nine bears no resemblance at all to the old. Suddenly it's almost 3,400 from the tips, features water on 6 of 9 holes, and has 33 traps and greens that will delight players.

The original 18 are next to be redone, and hopes must be high, based on the work Childs has already completed.

Luxury housing is being built there by Kopf Builders, and it will include single-family homes, villas, and chateaus.

Highlights The strengths of Sweetbriar begin on No. 3, a 449-yard par 4—not beautiful, but tough with out-of-bounds down the left side. The hole starts out to the right and then bends back to the left. It's a wide fairway, but a long way in to the elevated green. Not a gorgeous hole, but a real challenge to par.

No. 6 is a blind tee shot, a par 4 of 386 yards and a dogleg right. There is plenty of room on the left side to land a drive. Drivers with "lazy wrists" or slices will find themselves between trees and mounds, unable to go for the green. A wide creek passes in front of the green.

The second nine opens with a 349-yard dogleg left. This par 4 requires a drive to the right side of the fairway for a clear approach. Trees make the hole more narrow at the dogleg. On the left side of the fairway is the driving range. Many players will break a Rule of Golf here by hitting stray practice balls back to the range.

No. 17, a 522-yard par 5, has some water in front of the tee that is merely decorative. The fairway begins bending to the left after 120 yards or so. From 300 yards in to the green, stands of trees line the rough on both sides.

Management here understands that golf is not a seasonal malady but an addiction that must be sated year round. If the snow is not deep, there is play here. And then the clubhouse provides all the coffee needed to warm up—on the house.

PUBLIC 18+

Valleaire Golf Club   ☎ (440) 237-9191

Area: **South**   City: **Hinckley**   Cost: $$$$$ Difficulty: ●●●

Address: 6969 Boston Rd., Hinckley

Tees	Ydg.	C/r	S/r	Pace
Back:	6442	70.2	117	
Middle:	6067	68.4	113	
Forward:	5552	70.9	116	

Specials: Senior specials Mon–Fri

Season: Apr–Nov **Hours:** Sunrise–sunset **Tee times:** Required weekends
Leagues: Mon–Fri 4–4:30 p.m. **Ranger:** Daily **Practice facil:** Putting Green
Clubhouse: Food, Beer, Liquor, Lockers, Showers, Pavilion
Outings: Available **Lessons:** Not available **Pro:** Jason Martin

Directions: I-71 to Exit 226 for SR 303; east on SR 303; left (north) on SR 3 (Ridge Rd.); right (east) on Boston Rd.; on right.

Description Golf courses are built for all sorts of reasons: as a family business, for a land bank, to fill a market niche. Here the course was built because the Knights of Columbus were having difficulty securing tee times for their traveling league. Members purchased property in the north of Medina County and built a gorgeous little course.

Valleaire is very playable, a course where average golfers will find themselves looking at a few birdie putts. Only one hole is longer than 500 yards. It's a beautiful layout, cut from softly hilly forest and manicured with a professional touch. Recent improvements include a computerized watering system and paved cart paths.

Highlights Representative of the holes to follow is No. 2. At the tee of this 447-yard par 4, civilization is suddenly left behind. Getting on this green in regulation is very difficult for reasons of distance alone. The fairway narrows as it heads toward an elevated green, one of the trademarks of this course. The 150-yard markers are the best in the area: wooden planks hanging from pipes in the rough. In addition to being elevated, this long and narrow green also has a stand of pines behind it.

No. 9 is a par 3 of 148 yards, much of it over water. Shade is provided at the tee by an old and stately oak tree, and the lake separating the tee from the green has a fountain. Some Canada geese regularly lounge about, close to water's edge and unaffected by the spouting from the fountain or the occasional curses from the tee.

Water is much more important on the back side than on the front. The course takes advantage of the land, especially the beautiful old hardwoods, and offers players a slightly hilly round of golf. The greens, most of them elevated, are kept in good shape, and six holes have sand around them. The two-story clubhouse is comfortable, like an old K of C hall.

Valleaire Golf Club

Valley View Golf Club   ☎ (330) 928-9034

Area: **Far South**   City: **Akron**   Cost: **$$$**$$ Difficulty: ●●●

PUBLIC 18+

Address: 1212 Cuyahoga St., Akron

	Valley-River				Lakes-River			
Tees	**Ydg.**	**C/r**	**S/r**	**Pace**	**Ydg.**	**C/r**	**S/r**	**Pace**
Back:	6293	68.8	111		6183	68.2	110	
Middle:	6006	67.4	109		5871	66.2	102	
Forward:	5322	69.1	113		5277	68.6	112	

Specials: Senior specials Mon–Fri before 11 a.m.

Season: Mar–Dec **Hours:** 6 a.m.–10 p.m. **Tee times:** Required weekends, Recommended for weekdays. **Leagues:** Mon–Fri 4:30 p.m. **Ranger:** Weekends **Practice facil:** Putting Green, Chipping Green **Clubhouse:** Food, Beer, Pavilion **Outings:** Available **Lessons:** Not available

Directions: I-271 to Exit 18 for SR 8; south on SR 8 exit for Cuyahoga Falls Ave.; southwest on Cuyahoga Falls; right (west) on W. Tallmadge Rd.; right (north) on Cuyahoga St.; on left.

Description It was Carl Springer and his family who started building these 27 holes known as the Valley, River, and Lake nines 40 years ago, and the course will likely stay a family operation. Maintenance and course conditioning are hallmarks here. The course is playable; the hosts are gracious.

Highlights On the Valley nine, it's No. 2 that confounds players. It is only a 370-yard par 4, but the green sits on a hill. This nine has rolling terrain, and sand shows up on only a half dozen holes. Pines here are 30 years old and oaks are 35 to 40, but this nine is largely open.

The River nine is the flattest of the three, and it is hole No. 7 that provides a noteworthy challenge. It's a short par 5, only 459 yards from the whites, but the river floats through about 320 yards out. On the Lake nine, No. 2, another short par 5, gets the nod. It plays along the river to an elevated green and is a bit of a dogleg right.

TIDYMAN'S TIDBITS #14
Friendliest staffs:
1) Painesville
2) Skyland
3) Powderhorn
4) Erie Shores
5) Legends at Massillon

Western Reserve Golf & Country Club ☎ (330) 239-9902

Area: **Far South**   City: **Sharon Center**   Cost: **$$$**$$ Difficulty: ●●●

PUBLIC 18+

Address: 1543 Fixler Rd., Sharon Center

Tees	Ydg.	C/r	S/r	Pace
Back:	5923	68.1	108	
Middle:	5545	66.1	104	
Forward:	4516	64.7	101	

Specials: Senior specials Mon–Fri

Season: Year-round **Hours:** 6 a.m.–10 p.m. in summer **Tee times:** Taken
Leagues: Available (various schedules) **Ranger:** Weekends **Practice facil:**
Putting Green **Clubhouse:** Food, Beer, Lockers, Showers, Pavilion
Outings: Available (up to 150 people) **Lessons:** Available **Pro:** Bill Giles, USGTF

Directions: I-71 to Exit 218 for SR 18; east on SR 18; right (south) on Boneta Rd.;
left (east) on Fixler Rd.; on left.

Description The clubhouse sits above the practice green and looks down on the course. It's a wide building with an equally wide porch in front. The course and the clubhouse have an old-fashioned informality about them that is fun. Clearly, the mortgage doesn't rest on a game of golf here. Golf is played for the pleasure of it.

This course used to be a farm. It is a short and tight layout with a couple of holes that make little sense, but who's to criticize? Plenty of league play fills the tees from Monday through Friday. Between a growing (and laudable) juniors program, the league play, and the regulars, the first tee here can be a busy spot.

Highlights Play opens on the number one handicap hole, a 394-yard par 4 and big dogleg right. Neither short nor tight, this hole makes plenty of sense. In the elbow of the dogleg a stream meanders between the first and 10th fairways. Over on the left side of the bend there is deep rough and a small pond. About 180 yards from the green there are two fairway traps on the left side. A nicely trimmed apron leads up to a large green. A tough opening hole.

At 415 yards, No. 5 is one of the shortest par 5s around. It is a straight hole with water near the green. Just before the apron, a small pond cuts into the fairway. There are some mounds at the green but no sand here. A real birdie opportunity.

No. 8, a 352-yard par 4, is straight 100 yards before it bends sharply left. In the corner are trees, deep rough, and o.b. It's a hole of questionable design. The right side—the edge of the course—is o.b. as well. Pines and an occasional oak tree line the hole on the left side, and the green, with a large sand trap on the front left, is slightly elevated.

No. 9 is a difficult hole for club selection. This third par 3 on the front is only 162 yards, but all of them steeply uphill. It is virtually a blind tee shot. In front of the tee is a small pond, and over to the right is a trash dump. Missing the green short and left can send the ball into a valley filled with trees and thick underbrush.

Like many area courses, Western Reserve was transformed from farmland to fairway. It is reached via a couple of two-lane blacktops and rarely promotes itself. A good little hideaway for the salesperson who keeps sticks in the trunk. While not especially notable, neither is it pretentious. And it has a great front porch.

PUBLIC 18+

Wicked Woods Golf Club   ☎ (440) 564-7960
Area: **Far East**   City: **Newbury Township**   Cost: **$$**$$$ Difficulty: ●●●

Address: 14085 Ravenna Rd. (SR 44), Newbury Township

Tees	Ydg.	C/r	S/r	Pace
Back:	6439	71.8	125	
Middle:	6280	70.3	123	
Forward:	5140	69.8	118	

Specials: Senior specials Mon–Fri

Season: Year-round **Hours:** Sunrise–sunset **Tee times:** Taken
Leagues: Available **Ranger:** Weekends **Practice facil:** Putting Green, Chipping Green, 2-hole practice area **Clubhouse:** Food, Beer, Liquor, Dining room, Lockers, Showers **Outings:** Available (weekdays & weekends, small groups) **Lessons:** Available **Pro:** George Zimmer

Directions: I-271 to Exit 29 for SR 87 (Chagrin Blvd.); east on SR 87; left (north) on Ravenna Rd. (SR 44); on right, after Pekin Rd.

Description Formerly known as Pleasant View Golf Club, Wicked Woods was carved out of 180 acres of dense woods in 1991 by Tucker Pfouts and sold to golf pro Paul Tirpak in 1997. The layout assumes players can make a ball follow directions. The hills assume walking players are in good condition.

There are eleven doglegs to contend with, and the only flat lies are on the tees. The fairways are lined with woods, and trees often surround greens. Colored stakes and fairway plates are at 200, 150, and 100 yards. Tough greens here.

Recent work on the course includes one new green and a few upgraded tees.

Highlights No. 4, a stunning 510-yard par 5, twists, rises, and falls. Much of the way it is lined with old and beautiful trees. There is water on the left and a big, sand-free green surrounded by mounds.

No. 9, a par 5 of 490 yards, is a dogleg left with the fairway sloping right. Between tee and green there are ravines to carry, and the green on this hole drops six feet from back to front.

Windmill Lakes Golf Club ☎ (330) 297-0440

Area: **Far South**   City: **Ravenna**   Cost: **$$$$$**   Difficulty: ●●●

Address: 6544 SR 14, Ravenna

Tees	Ydg.	C/r	S/r	Pace	Tournament tees Ydg.	C/r	S/r	Pace
Back:	6503	71.8	124	3:48	6936	73.8	128	
Middle:	6132	69.7	118					
Forward:	5368	70.4	115					

Specials: Senior specials Apr–May Mon–Fri; Jun–Aug Mon & Tue; Sat–Sun before 1 p.m.

Season: Late Mar–late Oct (pro shop open all year) **Hours:** 7 a.m.–9 p.m.
Tee times: Taken, credit card guarantee for advance booking **Leagues:** Various times **Ranger:** Daily **Practice facil:** Range, Putting Green, Chipping Green
Clubhouse: Food, Beer, Liquor, Dining room, Lockers, Showers, Pavilion, Cipriano's restaurant, Banquet facilities **Outings:** Available **Lessons:** Available **Pro:** Jim Wise

Directions: I-271 to Exit 27 for US 422; east on US 422 to SR 44; right (south) on SR 44 (Painesville-Ravenna Rd.); left (east) on SR 14 (merges with SR 44); on left.

Description This home course of the Kent State University golf team, opened in 1970, was designed by Maryland golf architect Edward Ault, Sr. Herb Page, manager at Windmill Lakes, describes the style of the layout as "typical of that period, with big, rolling greens. Ours average 7,000–8,000 square feet. Three sets of men's tees, big tee boxes. Fifty-four greenside bunkers. And whether you like it or not, it's a big maintenance style."

From the tournament tees (Windmill Lakes hosts qualifying matches for the USGA Public Links Championship), it plays 6,936, par 70. That is a lot of golf course. The course record is held by Hogan Tour pro Karl Zoller, who helps Page coach at KSU. A few years ago, he fired a 63. The average score posted there is close to 90, Page said. "That's strictly a guess," he said, adding that the typical player at Windmill is an above-average golfer. That could be. Ravenna is off the beaten path, and many players consider the trip to be more than a round at the closest public course. It is one well worth planning.

Highlights The first hole is a 398-yard par 4 (from the tournament tees it measures 450 yards). The slight dogleg right slopes down from the tee and then bends right. Near the 150-yard marker on the left is a small lake. Oak trees fill the right side of the fairway and traps mark the green. The green on No. 1 is indicative of the rest: fast, true, and undulating. And the fairway on No. 1 has features that will become familiar as the round goes on. The turf is thick and healthy, grass cut to about half an inch. It is beautifully manicured, and the difference between fairway and rough is substantial. The rough is not of U.S. Open length, but it is rough. The value of staying in the fairway is at a premium. Such grooming also adds to the physical beauty of the game and can best be appreciated with a view from the tee.

No. 8 is a beautiful par 3. A big pond lies in front of the green, the largest on the front side. Behind the green is dense underbrush. Along the right side of the hole are tall trees that can be troublesome.

The experienced player, reflecting on the difficult greens of the front side, will likely opt for simply chipping the ball directly into each cup on the back side, dispensing with even trying to read them. That only slows play.

The only par 5 on the back side is No. 16, a 495-yard hole with a fairway that rises ever so slightly and bends as slightly to the right. From the tee, an average player hitting a good shot will clear the soft turn and save a few yards. A particularly troublesome sand trap yawns right in front of this green.

Many of the tees at Windmill Lakes have flower boxes; No. 17 is one. Beside gorgeous flowers is a sign: "Any person seen to be hitting golf balls at the tower will be lawfully prosecuted to the fullest extent of the law." The warning refers to a tower, off the course to the left, that is about three stories high and resembles a water tower. It is pockmarked by hundreds of dents from outlaw golf balls. Likely the sign and its stern warning incite this tempting crime.

There are amenities here not found at other clubs—the best known is Cipriano's, a restaurant and lounge frequented by area residents as well as players. Herb Page also runs one of the best pro shops in Northeast Ohio. The NOPGA once named him "Merchandiser of the Year." Tee times are not so important during the week but are very important on weekends and holidays, when the course offers a credit-card guarantee.

PUBLIC 18+

TIDYMAN'S TIDBITS #15

Courses where the finishing hole is a par 3:
1) Raccoon Hill
2) Berkshire Hills
3) Tam O' Shanter
4) Ridgetop

Public Courses
FARTHER AWAY BUT WORTH THE DRIVE

Avalon Lakes Golf
☎ (330) 856-8898

Area: **Farther East**   City: **Warren**   Cost: **$$$$$**   Difficulty: ●●●

Address: One American Way, Warren

Tees	Ydg.	C/r	S/r	Pace
Back:	7001	74.3	127	
Middle:	6453	71.7	122	
Forward:	5324	70.1	116	

Specials: Twilight rates after 4 p.m.

Season: Apr–Nov **Hours:** 8 a.m.–sunset **Tee times:** Required, taken up to 1 year in advance **Leagues:** None **Ranger:** Daily **Practice facil:** Range, Putting Green, Chipping Green **Clubhouse:** Food, Beer, Liquor, Dining room, Lockers, Showers, Pavilion **Outings:** Available (Avalon Travel, Inc. offers full-service travel agency; restaurant seats 200; Grand Pavilion available for outings or banquets, seats 300.) **Lessons:** Available **Pro:** John Diana

Directions: I-271 to Exit 27 for US 422; east on US 422; east on SR 82 for 9 miles; left (north) on Howland Wilson Rd.; right (east) on E. Market Rd.; 1/2 mile on left.

Description We are blessed to have bragging rights to a couple of Pete Dye courses, and this one, built in 1967, is a gem. Dye had not yet developed his penchant for railroad ties, but he built courses that demanded a great deal from players. He built one of those at Avalon Lakes, now owned by Avalon Holdings Company.

A couple years ago, Dye returned to upgrade his course, and the new version is one of the great 18 holes in Northern Ohio. His work with mounding and sand traps is gorgeous as well as intimidating.

Highlights Instead of tee markers in red, white, and blue, the new version has Position 1, which at 4,904 yards is the shortest, Position 2, which plays 5,458, Position 3, 6,491, Position 4, 6,932, and the Big Daddy of the all, Position 5, which stretches and stretches and stretches until it plays 7551 yards. The maintenance and conditioning of the tee boxes alone is noteworthy.

The opening hole is the number two handicap, a par 4 of 406 yards from Position 3, which might be equal to the white tees on other courses. Play has barely begun when players realize something special is going on.

When Dye was reworking his magic, he was often asked, "What's the signature hole going to be?" He answered, "It's not the hole, it's the whole course. There are no signature holes here."

Sez him. No. 6, a 504 yard par 5 from the Position 3, is an easy hole. But playing it from Position 5 means a carry of 275 to get to the fairway. No. 8, a wonderful par 3 over water to a stonewalled green that sticks out from the land, is another signature, because it's beautiful and calls for the proper club selection as well as a successful swing. No. 11 is another tee over water, this one a par 5 with a big lake in front. It asks, "How much would you like to bite off?"

Chippewa Golf Club   ☎ (330) 658-6126

Area: **Farther South**   City: **Doylestown**   Cost: $$$$$ Difficulty: ●●●

Address: 12147 Shank Rd., Doylestown

Tees	Ydg.	C/r	S/r	Pace
Back:	6273	69.1	109	
Middle:	5933	67.4	107	
Forward:	4877	67.0	103	

Specials: Mon–Thu seasonal breakfast special; special prices Sat–Sun after 2 p.m.

Season: Year-round **Hours:** Dawn–dusk **Tee times:** Required
Leagues: Weekday evenings **Ranger:** Most days **Practice facil:** Range, Putting Green, Chipping Green **Clubhouse:** Food, Beer, Liquor, Pavilion
Outings: Available **Lessons:** Available **Pro:** Don Olney, Jr.

Directions: I-77 to Exit 136 for SR 21; south on SR 21; left (east) on Clinton Rd.; left (north) on Shank Rd.; on right.

Description How could a relatively short course play so tough? Answer—the Bermuda Triangle is here: Nos. 14 (364 yards, par 4), 15 (381 yards, par 4), and 16 (383 yards, par 4). No. 14 is on the cover of the scorecard. This dogleg right has a clearly defined landing area, and missing the fairway means no shot to the green. Oh, there's a shot, but launching one from the rough to a green fronted by water is risky business.

Furthermore, as Bob Gainer says, "all the Triangle greens are two-tiered and slick as ice." Gainer, who runs a hair salon in nearby Barberton, didn't take up golf until his three kids were old enough to fend for themselves. Today he is among the game's most passionate proselytizers. He is, of course, a student of the Triangle. "If you're even through the Triangle, you have some skins coming," he says.

Lots of matches are determined at No. 18, a 408-yard par 4 that plays into a westerly breeze and finishes on a two-tiered green.

Owner Kevin Larizza keeps the rest of the greens here reasonably slick and keeps rangers on the course to maintain fast play. With the ups and downs, the fast greens, and the troublesome rough, this is not a course for hackers or beginners.

Hawks Nest   ☎ (330) 435-4611
Area: **Farther South**   City: **Creston**   Cost: $$$$$ Difficulty: ●●●

PUBLIC 18+ WORTH THE DRIVE

Address: 2800 E. Pleasant Home Rd., Creston

Tees	Ydg.	C/r	S/r	Pace
Back:	6680	71.5	124	4:10
Middle:	6200	69.2	121	
Forward:	4767	67.9	110	

Specials: Senior specials Mon 7–11 a.m.; Ladies specials Thu 7–11 a.m.

Season: Apr–Nov **Hours:** 7 a.m.–sunset **Tee times:** Recommended **Leagues:** Weekdays after 4:30 p.m. **Ranger:** Daily **Practice facil:** Range, Putting Green **Clubhouse:** Food, Dining room, Pavilion **Outings:** Available **Lessons:** Available **Pro:** Chris McCormack

Directions: I-71 to Exit 204 for SR 83; south on SR 83 to New Canaan; east on SR 604; right (south) on SR 3 for 3 miles; on left.

Description Chris McCormack, PGA, former assistant at Wooster CC, is the pro here.

Betty Hawkins built the course. It was designed by Steve Burns, who clearly had a ball transforming 200 acres of rolling farmland into 18 holes of rolling golf course. Burns also designed Fox Meadows, and there are some players who think the Hawk got the better of the Fox.

Ms. Hawkins, an avid golfer, always wanted a golf course. She had been looking for land and had been playing at Hillcrest, but that course was sold and the property developed. This land came up at auction one day, and she and her husband came out and bought it.

The first round was played in July 1993; the next year the back nine was opened. Four sets of tees here, and "ready golf" is the norm.

The prevailing wind comes out of the southwest and is always a factor. When it's blowing, it makes the long par 4s play longer.

Eighty percent of the trade comes from towns north of here. From Cleveland to the first tee it's one stop sign and one stoplight. The trip takes about 45 minutes and is well worth it.

Golf Digest magazine gave Hawks Nest a 4½-star rating and also ranked the course among Ohio's top five public courses.

Highlights The only homely hole is the first one, a straightaway par 4 of 365 yards; two-lane blacktop is the left-side border. But once that's out of the way, this course provides one of the great rides in public golf.

Holes 3, 4, and 5 are the Shotmaker's Trinity.

At 522 yards, No. 7 begins with an uphill drive, then a blind second shot that sets up an approach over a lake and creek to the green. It's one of those holes that should be played a half dozen times in order to play it best.

No. 13, par 5, 520 yards. One of the toughest holes in the county. A dogleg left, players have to be long and straight; woods follow the curve of the fairway to an elevated green.

No. 14 is another hole that is surprising and delightful. Only 323 yards, the drive on this par 4 heads toward the edge of a cliff. The flag and the green are at the bottom, and the flag stick is 12 feet long, the better to see it from a distance.

PUBLIC 18+
WORTH THE DRIVE

Hemlock Springs Golf Club ☎ (800) 436-5625

Area: **Farther East**   City: **Geneva**   Cost: $$$$$ Difficulty: ●●●

Address: 4654 Cold Springs Rd., Geneva

Tees	Ydg.	C/r	S/r	Pace
Back:	6812	72.8	129	3:46
Middle:	6520	72.0	127	
Forward:	5453	73.8	116	

Specials: Weekday specials; Senior & Junior specials

Season: Mar–Nov **Hours:** Mon–Fri 7 a.m–7 p.m.; Sat–Sun 5:30 a.m.–7 p.m.
Tee times: Recommended **Leagues:** Yes **Ranger:** Daily
Practice facil: Range, Putting Green **Clubhouse:** Food, Beer, Liquor, Lockers, Pavilion **Outings:** Available **Lessons:** Not available

Directions: I-90 to Exit 218 for SR 534; south on SR 534 for 3 miles; left (east) on Cold Springs Rd.; 1/2 mile on right.

Description Nestled in the heart of Ohio wine country is this course built in the early sixties. Without sounding like a shill for the Ashtabula County Chamber of Commerce, can we suggest a day of golf followed by dinner? In this part of the state, they go together.

In its December 1997 issue, *Golf Digest* magazine had high praise for the course: "The championship bent grass greens are a pure joy to putt."

Good marketing spoken here. Rangers will present discount coupons to players replacing divots or repairing ball marks. The coupon is good for 15 percent off in the pro shop. For every $100 spent in the shop, a round of golf is included in the change. And I never saw a golf course so clean, so free from litter, cigarette butts, ball sleeves, soda cups . . .

Highlights This is a lot of course, and has everything it needs: woods, water, changes in elevation, and good design. The Stimpmeter usually reads 8.5, so the greens can be quick. No. 11, a par 3, 186 yards, takes all those virtues into account. It's the signature hole. An elevated tee overlooks a lake and a narrow tree-lined fairway. The elevated green is guarded in front by two sand traps. In the past 20 years it has been aced only once. Great home hole: 530-yard par 5 is a dogleg right with a lake to the right of the fairway and in the landing area.

Hemlock Springs is one of golf's better values.

Hemlock Springs Golf Club

Legends of Massillon

☎ (330) 830-4653

Area: **Farther South**   City: **Massillon**   Cost: $$$$$ Difficulty: ●●●

Address: 2700 Augusta Dr., Massillon

Tees	Ydg.	C/r	S/r	Pace
Back:	7002	73.7	121	4:30
Middle:	6390	70.9	116	
Forward:	5627	72.3	108	

Specials: Special prices May–Sep Mon–Thu before 1 p.m.; Senior specials Mon & Tue & weekend afternoons

Season: Apr–Nov **Hours:** Dawn to dusk **Tee times:** Required
Leagues: Mon–Fri 3–6 p.m. **Ranger:** Daily **Practice facil:** Range, Putting Green, Chipping Green, Sand **Clubhouse:** Food, Beer, Liquor, Dining room **Outings:** Available **Lessons:** Available **Pro:** Ray Bush

Directions: I-77 to exit for SR 21; south on SR 21; east on US 30; left (north) on SR 627; left (west) on Nave St. (adjacent to US 30); right (north) on Veterans Blvd.; left (west) on Augusta Dr.; on left.

PUBLIC 18+
WORTH THE DRIVE

Description Now there are two Legends of Massillon. Paul Brown, of course, is the first; this course is the second. Recently, the starter took a player's arm on the way to the first tee and asked, "Ever play here before?" When the player said he had not, the starter's face brightened and he said, "You're going to love it!" All courses should have staff that committed to the club. The starter was right. The course is worthy of a golfer's love. At least it is now. But housing tracts are going up fast, and that development will take away from the beauty of the course. A new nine is due to open this year, and between the 27 holes will be 83 sand bunkers, and water will appear on 17 holes.

TIDYMAN'S TIDBITS #16
There's one thing missing at ...
1) Hilliard Lakes ... Tee Times
2) Pine Hills ... Slice of Humble Pie
3) Manakiki ... Course Conditioning
4) Big Met ... Customer Relations training for staff

Why I Love Playing Golf with Women

1. Women show up on time. Nothing is as upse[t]
    playing partners flying into the parking lot t[o]
    tee time, nearly rolling the car as they try to p[ark, then racing]
    out to the first tee, untied shoes on their feet, sticks clicking
    and clacking, and innocently huffing, "What's the bet?" Women
    have too much regard for the game, as well as for other
    players, to let that to happen.

2. I'm not saying it doesn't happen, but I have yet to see a woman
    playing golf pull out a cell phone and clear her messages. Men
    talking on cell phones while playing golf should be sterilized.
    The men, not the phones. The gene pool doesn't need them.
    The men, not the phones.

3. Women dress for it. Not only do they dress for the game, they
    often dress well. Their dress adds an element of grace to the
    game.

4. Women are easily satisfied. Women don't play to avenge loss,
    win drinking money, or garner bragging rights. They play
    because it's a pleasure to play. With a few nice tee shots, a few
    good chips, and the occasional long putt, women players are
    happy.

5. Women are sympathetic when the putter in a man's hand
    becomes recalcitrant. Women are good sports. They smile often
    and sincerely. They rarely leap into the air, after a particularly
    good shot, screaming, "Ye-e—e-e-s-s-s-s-s-s-s-s!!!" Best of all,
    they play fast. The women I've played with play faster than
    most men.

6. Women won't give unsolicited advice. A while back, my
    Babycakes and I went to play Little Met—a nice executive-
    length course often used by beginners. The starter put us with
    two guys. At the first tee, I looked in their bags. These guys are
    bums, I thought to myself. The tipoff? They had sets of great
    sticks and they were playing Little Met. As soon as my
    Babycakes took her first swing, each had advice for her. They
    shut up on the third tee when she outdrove both of them.
    Unsolicited advice is like a headache looking for a forehead to
    slam into.

7. Not only are women more peaceful on the course, they rarely swear and they never curse their equipment. Do I have to add they never toss the sand wedge thirty yards in any direction? I used to play with a radio newsman who, early in his golf affair, had a bit of a temper. At one outing, on the 18th green of a course he had never played before, he missed an important putt. He turned, launched his putter, and only then realized he had just launched it over the parking lot. He watched help-lessly as the misbehaving putter turned, grip over clubhead, on its descent. He cringed as he watched the clubhead plow through the windshield of a luxury car—a car owned by one of the players in his foursome. Women don't create situations where the probability of humiliation is high. That's a guy thing.

TIDYMAN'S TIDBITS #17
Government-owned courses:
1) Gleneagles (Twinsburg)
2) Springvale (North Olmsted)
3) Briardale Greens (Euclid)
4) Seneca & Highland (Cleveland)
5) The Six Cuyahoga County MetroParks Courses
6) Erie Shores and Pine Ridge CC (Lake County MetroParks)
7) Ridgewood (Parma)
8) Grantwood (Solon)
9) Good Park (Akron)

Mill Creek Park Golf Course   ☎ (330) 740-7112

Area: **Farther East**   City: **Boardman**   Cost: $$$$$ Difficulty: ●●●

Address: 1 West Golf Dr., Boardman

Tees	South Course				North Course			
	Ydg.	C/r	S/r	Pace	Ydg.	C/r	S/r	Pace
Back:	6511	71.8	129	3:44	6412	71.9	124	3:46
Middle:	6302	70.7	122		6173	70.7	122	
Forward:	6102	74.9	118		5889	74.4	117	

Specials: Coupon books available; Senior specials; autumn rates after Sept 30

Season: Apr–Dec **Hours:** Sunrise–sunset **Tee times:** Taken **Leagues:** Weekdays
Ranger: Daily **Practice facil:** Putting Green, Chipping Green, Sand **Clubhouse:** Food, Lockers, Showers, Pavilion **Outings:** Available **Lessons:** Available **Pro:** Dennis Miller

Directions: I-80 to exit for SR 11; south on SR 11 to exit for SR 224 (Boardman); east on SR 224; left (north) on West Golf Drive at park entrance.

PUBLIC 18+
WORTH THE DRIVE

Description Just a couple years before the Depression, Donald Ross finished work on a pair of courses at Mill Creek Park. The North and South courses are owned and maintained by the Mill Creek Metropolitan Park District.

Highlights Pro Andy Santor says most players think the South course is more challenging than the North, but the North, he points out, has two great finishing holes, 9 and 18 and the North better reflects the style of the Scotsman from Dornach: small greens, mounding, and a demand for accurate iron play. Number 9 is a 440-yard par 4 with a creek in the middle of a fairway, a narrow landing area and a green, the pro says, "about the size of your desk." Pure Ross. And it is on the home hole on the South course, a 450-yard dogleg par 4, that many matches are settled. Par is 70 on both courses.

Sawmill Creek

☎ (419) 433-3789

Area: **Farther West**   City: **Huron**   Cost: **$$$$$**   Difficulty: ●●●

Address: 600 Mariner Village, Huron

Tees	Ydg.	C/r	S/r	Pace
Back:	6702	72.3	128	
Middle:	6321	70.3	125	
Forward:	5124	69.4	115	

Specials: None

Season: Apr 1–Nov 1   **Hours:** 7 a.m.–10 p.m.   **Tee times:** Taken
Leagues: Mon–Thu evenings on one 9 only, varied times   **Ranger:** Daily
Practice facil: Putting Green, Intermediate pitching area   **Clubhouse:** Food, Beer, Liquor, Dining room   **Outings:** Available   **Lessons:** Available   **Pro:** Chris Bleile

Directions: SR 2 to exit for Rye Beach Rd.; right (north) on Rye Beach; left (west) on Cleveland Rd. W.; on right.

PUBLIC 18+
WORTH THE DRIVE

Description Few courses are as well cared for as this resort in Huron, hard by Lake Erie. Your lawn should look like the rough here. It is a great neighborhood for golf, as well. In the vacation villages that line the lake are a number of good fish houses. This means 18 holes at a Tom Fazio course followed by fresh walleye or a big plate of fresh perch. It's like the commercials featuring a bunch of guys standing around a campfire saying "It doesn't get any better than this." Except in this case it would be true.

This course is eminently playable but by no means a pushover. It's a resort course, so it is not supposed to overwhelm players. But good scores here only come from very good play. Most of the greens are elevated and have sand on both sides. The greens are the most demanding feature here; getting on in regulation hardly means an automatic par. The greens are very big, quite fast, and full of undulation. While the rough is manicured, make no mistake—it is rough. Leaving the comfort of the fairway rarely means losing a ball, but once the ball nestles down in the thick grass, the possibility of par drifts away.

Highlights Play begins with two straightaway par 4s: the opening hole of 340 yards and No. 2, which stretches out 425 yards. Both have fairway bunkers. Properly warmed up, players then face a series of doglegs and holes that flirt with the marshes and inlets. Fazio took every advantage of the local physical beauty, which is augmented by a nearby bird sanctuary. There is nothing unusual here about watching a hawk circle above, or a cardinal or barn swallow work for dinner. When the Canada geese are arguing and a train is murmuring in the distance, the game becomes a delight for all the senses.

Holes 12 and 13 are the signature holes here. Both have water, both call for exacting tee shots, and both are noteworthy for their views from the tee box. They are the Big Brother and Little Brother of the Back Side. No. 12 is a par 5 of 566 yards and features a narrow landing area and marsh on the left and water on the right. No. 13 is a short par 3, only 142 yards, but it carries water the entire ride.

Sawmill Creek has a reasonable pro shop, and a very good lounge called A. Mulligan's Pub.

Tam O'Shanter Public Golf Course   ☎ (800) 462-9964

Area: **Farther South**   City: **Canton**   Cost: $$$$$$ Difficulty: ●●●

PUBLIC 18+
WORTH THE DRIVE

Address: 5055 Hills and Dales Rd. NW, Canton

	Hills Course				Dales Course			
Tees	Ydg.	C/r	S/r	Pace	Ydg.	C/r	S/r	Pace
Back:	6362	69.4	115	4:10	6538	70.4	117	4:10
Middle:	6054	68.1	112		6143	68.6	114	
Forward:	5070	67.5	108		5012	67.5	108	

Specials: Season golf and cart passes available; hotel packages available; Senior specials Mon–Fri before noon

Season: Year-round **Hours:** Sunrise–sunset **Tee times:** Recommended, as far in advance as requested; credit card guarantee Sat, Sun **Leagues:** Mon–Fri 8:30–9 a.m., 4–6:30 p.m. **Ranger:** Daily **Practice facil:** Range, Putting Green, Chipping Green, Sand, 8 covered tees **Clubhouse:** Food, Beer, Liquor, Dining room, Lockers, Showers, Pavilion **Outings:** Available (up to 150 people) **Lessons:** Available **Pro:** Martin Roesink, PGA

Directions: I-77 to Exit 109 for Everhard Rd./Whipple Ave.; west on Everhard; left (south) on Dressler Rd.; right (west) on Hills and Dales Rd. NW; on right.

Description Management at Tam O'Shanter works hard to stand out from the crowd. Here, aspiring professionals play under tournament pressure, golf vacationers come from as far away as Boston, and the dining room and pro shop are first rate. It is the only course taking a billboard on Interstate 77 to brag about itself.

Tam O'Shanter boasts a pair of distinctly different 18-hole layouts, classic golf course architecture, and a country-club atmosphere. The clubhouse should be surrounded by magnolias; it is an old-fashioned, three-story house with a half-dozen tall columns supporting the broad porch roof.

The courses were built as part of a housing development, the Hills and Dales project, which is just across the street. Had the project been successful and a building boom continued, backyards and basements would today be where a driving range and practice green are. Development was slowed first by the Depression, then by World War II.

"The Dales course opened in 1928," former general manager Chuck Bennell said, "and the Hills course opened in 1931. When Hills opened,

Mr. T. K. Harris, the developer, added some hoopla because of the Depression. He brought Walter Hagen and Gene Sarazen in from the Western Open to play the dedication round. And a Massillon bootlegger made sure the refreshments were spirited."

Bennell pointed out the style of golf architecture that marks these 60-year-old layouts. "They say the old-time architects didn't design courses so much as they found them." The Dales Course was designed by Leonard Maycomber, the construction superintendent for Donald Ross when Ross created Canton Brookside in the early twenties. The Hills Course was designed by Merle Paul.

Highlights Holes 4 and 5 are good examples of what the Dales course is like. No. 4 is a straight 411-yard par 4. The last few hundred yards of fairway are lined on both sides with pine trees. The old hardwoods to the right of the green should not be a hazard—they protect the next tee. To the right of the green is a new staircase built of wood pieces the size of railroad ties. It leads to the No. 5 tee.

There, the drive is a blind shot. This 348-yard par 4 can delight as well as confound. The fairway does more than rise—it has a steep hill in the middle of it. Hitting over the hill is not difficult and provides an easy shot to the green, but missing a tee shot can be costly. This is one of many holes that plays better with practice.

The back side starts off with a very challenging par 4; No. 10 is 439 yards bending to the right almost off the tee. Players grateful for the opportunity to use their slices learn quickly that accuracy does not lose its value here. It is a narrow, hilly fairway and landing area. There is fairway sand to the right front of the green and more sand on the right side of the green. The green is elevated and calls for a most difficult approach: a high, long iron.

No. 15, a 405-yard par 4, tumbles down into a valley, turns right, and climbs the side of a hill. This is a blind tee shot (make sure the players in front of you have cleared the landing area!) with o.b. on the left. The green has sand on the right side. This is certainly one of the holes that the course architect "found."

After Dales, real golfers relax over lunch and maybe take a brief nap before heading out to the first tee on the Hills Course. It is more open than Dales, and shorter, too. No. 1 is a 381-yard par 4 that plays straight, though not level. Even in the heart of the fairway, unlevel lies are to be expected. Near the green is sand on the right front; getting out of it is a matter of lofting the ball eight feet.

No. 5 is only 434 yards, a very short par 5. But the fairway narrows on this dogleg right and there are o.b. stakes all the way down the right side. In the last 150 yards, the rough on both sides rises, giving the hole a riverbed look. Tall trees close in as golfers near the green, and hardwoods form a backdrop for the approach.

It's a bit of a drive to Canton, but the only regret of most players making the trip is not playing both layouts the same day. Counting club-

PUBLIC 18+
WORTH THE DRIVE

house, courses, and history, Tam O'Shanter would have to be considered one of the top public courses in Northern Ohio.

Tannenhauf Golf Club
☎ (800) 533-5140

Area: **Farther South**   City: **Alliance**   Cost: $$$$$ Difficulty: ●●●

Address: 11411 McCallum Ave. NE, Alliance

Tees	Ydg.	C/r	S/r	Pace
Back:	6694	71.3	121	4:30
Middle:	6290	69.4	119	
Forward:	5595	65.4	106	

Specials: Breakfast special Mon–Fri before 11 a.m. (non-holidays); special prices Sat–Sun after 1 p.m.; Senior & Junior specials Mon–Fri

Season: Apr–Oct **Hours:** Sunrise–sunset **Tee times:** Recommended
Leagues: Mon–Thu 4–6 p.m.; Women's League Thu a.m. **Ranger:** Weekends
Practice facil: Range, Putting Green, Chipping Green **Clubhouse:** Food, Showers, Pavilion **Outings:** Available **Lessons:** Available **Pro:** Lanny Snode, PGA

Directions: I-77 to Exit 188 for SR 241; north on SR 241; right (east) on SR 619 (becomes Edison St.); right (south) on McCallum Ave.; on right.

Description The name comes from the Swiss word for pine trees; it refers specifically to a pair of pines in front of the old farmhouse. Manager Rick Snode's father, uncle, and aunt created the course on what was once a family dairy farm. That was in 1957, and the layout designed by James Harrison and Fred Garbin is aging well. The course has grown a bit tighter, as trees planted a couple decades ago are now big enough to knock down errant shots.

Twilight golf on Friday nights, when there is no league play, is delightful. The course is a good one for walking, and course conditions are excellent. Soft spikes are encouraged. Every August, when the Alliance Carnation Festival is in full swing, the course hosts the Carnation Scramble event; during play, the Queen of the Court tours the course. That's the sort of stuff that makes small towns special (though Alliance is fast moving away from small-town status).

Highlights The first and tenth holes are parallel, separated by the home hole. No. 1 features a lake 240 yards out. Most players lay up (most players can *only* lay up) on this 501-yard straightaway par 5. It's during Carnation Week, when the Scramble is on, that many players try to fly the water, which means 280 yards of carry. No. 3, usually the number one handicap hole, is a long one from the blues at 605 yards and 545 from the whites. When the wind is out of the north, this dogleg plays much longer.

PUBLIC 18+
WORTH THE DRIVE

Tannenhauf Golf Club

Thunderbird Hills ☎ (419) 433-4552

Area: **Farther West**   City: **Huron**   Cost: **$$**$$$ Difficulty: ●●●

Address: 1316 Mud Brook Rd., Huron

Tees	North Course				South Course			
	Ydg.	C/r	S/r	Pace	Ydg.	C/r	S/r	Pace
Back:	6347	70.3	109		6534			
Middle:	5973	74.0	121		6368			
Forward:			5008					

Specials: Couples specials; Senior specials Mon–Fri; call for winter rates

Season: Year-round **Hours:** Seasonal **Tee times:** Required **Leagues:** Weekdays: various times mornings and afternoons **Ranger:** Most days **Practice facil:** Range, Putting Green, Chipping Green **Clubhouse:** Food, Beer, Pavilion **Outings:** Available (catering avail.) **Lessons:** Available **Pro:** Ryan Spicer

Directions: SR 2 to exit for Huron/Mud Brook Rd.; right on Mud Brook; on right.

Description Owner Bruce Palmer was so pleased with the operation of one course that he created a second. They are called North and South. South is the new layout, opened just a few seasons ago and still wrestling with growing pains. It is not as hilly as North and features bent grass on tee boxes, fairways, and greens. In its former life it was farmland.

North, the older sibling, is known for pine trees and irrigation. The trees help define the holes here. There is no sand and very little water— just some feeder streams from the Huron River. Fairways are generous.

Greens are medium to small and will play faster than in recent years thanks to a new superintendent. North is open year round.

Nice and playable as these layouts are, the claim to fame here comes from the pro shop, named every year for the last decade as one of the best 100 pro shops in the country by *Golf Digest*. Manager Will Spence makes it sound easy: "Customer service is the key. We can get anything for anybody. We have 4,000 square feet filled with 1,500 pairs of shoes and 400 bags. We have a full line of clothing and clubs and there's no hassle on returns. We take care of you."

Willow Creek Golf Club   ☎ (440) 967-4101

Area: **Farther West**   City: **Vermilion**   Cost: **$$**$$$ Difficulty: ●●●

Address: 15905 Darrow Rd., Vermilion

Tees	Ydg.	C/r	S/r	Pace
Back:	6356	68.1	108	4:15
Middle:	5957	66.2	105	
Forward:	5419	68.0	111	

Specials: Special prices Mon–Fri before 2 p.m.; Senior specials

Season: Mar–Dec **Hours:** Sunrise–sunset **Tee times:** Taken weekends
Leagues: Mon–Fri early mornings, evenings until 6 p.m. **Ranger:** Most days
Practice facil: Range, Putting Green, Chipping Green **Clubhouse:** Food, Beer, Pavilion
Outings: Available (catering avail.) **Lessons:** Available **Pro:** Frank Cisterino, PGA

Directions: I-90 to SR 2; SR 2 to SR 60; south on SR 60 (Vermilion Rd.); left (east) on Darrow Rd.; on left.

Description Century oaks provide dramatic and beautiful scenery here, whether budding in spring, providing deep shade in the summer, or lining the forest floor with golden leaves in autumn. Owner Frank Cisterino calls the trees his greatest asset here. In addition to the oaks and willows there are a half dozen apple trees. In the late summer and fall, they produce a sweet and crisp fruit, favored by a few golfers as well as families of deer that live around the course.

The course is nearly an antique; the first nine was carved out of the woods at the end of World War II. Twenty years later, a second nine was created.

Eighteen leagues call Willow Creek home, and outings regularly use the pavilion. There are both driving range and practice green. The pro shop is moderately well stocked, and the snack bar offers all that players need. Tee times are taken for league play, and Cisterino is available for players needing lessons.

Highlights From the first hole on, it is a beautiful course to walk. No. 1 is a long par 4, 396 yards with a leftward bend. It plays into a setting sun in the early evening. But most of the course is laid out north-and-south, adding a distinct measure of comfort to the round. The green is small at the first hole, but lush and of average speed. Getting down in two should be routine.

No. 9 is the signature hole here, but not for its length or difficulty, though a par 4 of 440 yards is no piece of cake. It's a dogleg left crossed diagonally in front of the tee by a creek, which continues up the left side near the green. An old willow squats next to it there. Players don't get to see the green until the second shot.

No. 12 is a very tough par 4 of 315 yards. About halfway, the hole turns right. That can't be seen from the tee. A maple sits almost in the middle of the fairway and forces tough choices on the tee. Most players leave the driver in the bag and opt for a more controlled shot.

No. 18 is a par 4 of 413 yards. It is a straight hole, with woods continuing down its left side. On the right are more apple trees—they produce quite a crop. A creek cuts across the fairway in front of the green, which is slightly elevated, and a willow rests on the left side.

Willow Creek is an attractive old course in good hands. It will likely provide great golf for another half century.

PUBLIC 18+ WORTH THE DRIVE

TIDYMAN'S TIDBITS #18
Private courses I'd most like to play:

1) *Elyria CC.* It is one of the classic courses in northeast Ohio and none is more beautiful.

2) *Hawthorne Valley CC.* This is my pick as the best of the Donald Ross courses.

3) *Lakewood CC.* This is the only A.W. Tillighast course in the area. Short on drama, but long on challenge.

4) *Canterbury GC.* While it will always be more course than I am golfer, it's here you walk where giants walked.

5) *Sand Ridge GC.* If ever there was a reason to grow rich, membership here is it. Like Canterbury, a course for players dedicated to the game.

Public Courses
9-HOLE, PAR-3 AND EXECUTIVE-LENGTH

Aqua Marine Resort & Country Club
9 holes, par 3

Area: **Far West**　City: **Avon Lake**　Cost: **$**$$$$　☎ **(440) 933-2000**

Address: 216 Miller Rd., Avon Lake

Tees	Ydg.	C/r	S/r	Pace
Back:	1398			
Middle:	1544			
Forward:	1283			

Specials: Senior & Junior specials Mon–Fri; other specials vary by season

Season: Year-round　**Hours:** Sunrise–sunset　**Tee times:** Taken　**Leagues:** Various times　**Ranger:** Weekends　**Practice facil:** Putting Green, Chipping Green　**Clubhouse:** Food, Beer, Liquor, Dining room, Lockers, Showers, Pavilion　**Lessons:** Available

Directions: I-90 to Exit 151 for SR 611 (Colorado Ave.); west on Colorado; right (north) on Miller Rd. for 2 miles; on left.

Casement Club
9 holes

Area: **Far East**　City: **Painesville**　Cost: **$$$**$$　☎ **(440) 354-4443**

Address: 349 Casement Ave., Painesville

Tees	Ydg.	C/r	S/r	Pace
Middle:	3047	69.8	119	
Forward:	3047	74.0	127	

Specials: Senior & Student specials Mon–Fri before 3 p.m.

Season: Year-round　**Hours:** 6 a.m.–sunset　**Tee times:** Recommended　**Leagues:** Weekdays 3:30–6 p.m.　**Ranger:** Some days　**Practice facil:** Range, Putting Green　**Clubhouse:** Food, Beer, Liquor, Dining room, Lockers, Showers　**Lessons:** Not available

Directions: SR 2 to Painesville exit for Richmond St.; south on Richmond; left (east) on E. Erie St. across Grand River; right (south) on Casement Ave.; on right.

Cherry Ridge Golf Course   9 holes

Area: **Far West**   City: **Elyria**   Cost: **$$**$$$ ☎ **(440) 324-3713**

Address: 1211 W. River Rd., Elyria

Tees	Ydg.	C/r	S/r	Pace
Middle:	2813			
Forward:	2558			

Specials: Senior specials Mon–Fri

Season: Mid-Mar–Oct **Hours:** Sunrise–sunset **Tee times:** Taken weekends
Leagues: Mornings and evenings **Ranger:** Weekends **Practice facil:** Putting Green
Clubhouse: Food, Beer, Enclosed patio **Lessons:** Not available

Directions: I-90 to Exit 145 for SR 57; south on SR 57; left (east) on SR 113/SR 57
(Northeast Bypass); left (north) on W. River Rd.; on right.

Emerald Valley Golf Course   9 holes

Area: **Far West**   City: **Lorain**   Cost: **$$$**$$ ☎ **(440) 282-5663**

Address: 4397 Leavitt Rd., Lorain

Tees	Ydg.	C/r	S/r	Pace
Middle:	3225			

Specials: Senior specials before 5 p.m.

Season: Year-round **Hours:** Sunrise–sunset **Tee times:** , Not required
Leagues: Mon–Fri 5:00 p.m. **Ranger:** Weekends **Practice facil:** Putting Green,
Chipping Green **Clubhouse:** Food, Beer, Liquor, Dining room, Nightclub open
noon–2:30 a.m. **Lessons:** Available

Directions: I-90 to SR 2 west (I-90 splits off to merge with the Ohio Turnpike);
north on Leavitt Rd. (SR 58); on right, after Jaeger Rd.

**PUBLIC 9,
EXEC, PAR 3**

TIDYMAN'S TIDBITS #19
Home Holes of note:
1) *Orchard Hills.* Designed by Sisyphus.
2) *Skyland.* Par 4s don't get much longer.
3) *Pine Hills.* Drama spoken here.
   To par here calls for two very good shots.
4) *Manakiki.* A drive into a narrow valley
   followed by an approach to an elevated
   green with sand front left and right.
   This green is the smallest green in the area.
5) *Fowlers Mill.* A big, beautiful, classic,
   sand-studded, dog-legged par 5.
6) *Red Tail CC.* A wonderful dog left that begins
   with the fairway rising and then, suddenly,
   turning a hard left and tumbling downhill and
   over a ravine to the green. Whew!

Firestone Golf Course   9 holes
Area: **Far South**   City: **Akron**   Cost: $$$$$ ☎ **(330) 724-4444**

Address: 600 Swartz Rd., Akron

Tees	Ydg.	C/r	S/r	Pace
Back:	3008	67.8	109	
Middle:	2880	66.6	107	
Forward:	2386	66.2	105	

Specials: Senior specials Mon–Sat

Season: Year-round **Hours:** Summer: 7 a.m.–9 p.m.; winter: 10 a.m.–7 p.m.
Tee times: Taken **Leagues:** Available **Ranger:** Daily **Practice facil:** Range,
Putting Green **Clubhouse:** Food, Beer, Liquor, Dining room, Pavilion,
Hackers Bar & Grill **Lessons:** Available

Directions: I-277 to Exit 3 for S. Main St.; south on S. Main; east on Swartz Rd.
(Swartz is directly opposite eastbound exit for S. Main); on right.

Geauga Hidden Valley Golf Course   9 holes
Area: **Far East**   City: **Thompson**   Cost: $$$$$ ☎ **(440) 298-3912**

Address: 17261 Thompson Rd., Thompson

Tees	Ydg.	C/r	S/r	Pace
Middle:	3206	35.1		
Forward:	2600	35.9		

Specials: Senior & Junior specials available

Season: Mar–Nov **Hours:** Sunrise–sunset **Tee times:** Not taken
Leagues: Wed 5 p.m. **Ranger:** Some days **Practice facil:** Putting Green
Clubhouse: Food **Lessons:** Not available

Directions: I-90 to Exit 212 on SR 528; south on SR 528 to Thompson Rd.;
east on Thompson Rd.; on right.

Green Hills Golf Course   9 holes
Area: **Far South**   City: **Kent**   Cost: $$$$$ ☎ **(330) 678-2601**

Address: 1105 Tallmadge Rd., Kent

Tees	Ydg.	C/r	S/r	Pace
Back:	3461			
Middle:	3192			
Forward:	2573			

Specials: Weekday specials available; Senior & Junior specials weekdays only

Season: Apr–Nov **Hours:** Sunrise–sunset **Tee times:** Taken weekends **Leagues:**
Mon–Fri 4 p.m. **Ranger:** Weekends **Practice facil:** Putting Green, Chipping Green
Clubhouse: Food, Beer, Dining room, Pavilion **Lessons:** Not available

Directions: I-271 to Exit 18 for SR 8; south on SR 8 to exit for Hudson/SR 303; left
(east) on SR 303 (W. Streetsboro Rd) to Hudson; right (south) on SR 91; left (east) on SR
59 to Kent; right (south) on Middlebury Rd.; right (west) on Tallmadge Rd.; on right.

PUBLIC 9,
EXEC, PAR 3

Green Ridge Public Golf Course

9 holes, exec

Area: **East**   City: **Wickliffe**   Cost: **$$$$**$ ☎ **(440) 943-0007**

Address: 29150 Ridge Rd., Wickliffe

Tees	Ydg.	C/r	S/r	Pace
Middle:	2250			
Forward:	2060			

Specials: Senior specials Mon–Fri

Season: Year-round **Hours:** Sunrise–sunset **Tee times:** Not taken
Leagues: Various times **Ranger:** Most days **Practice facil:** Putting Green
Clubhouse: Food, Pavilion **Lessons:** Not available

Directions: I-90 to Exit 187 (Bishop Rd.); north on Bishop; right (east) on Ridge Rd.; on right.

Johnny Cake Ridge Golf Course

9 holes, exec

Area: **East**   City: **Willoughby**   Cost: **$$**$$$ ☎ **(440) 946-3154**

Address: 7134 Mentor Ave., Willoughby

Tees	Ydg.	C/r	S/r	Pace
Back:	1888			2:00
Middle:	1724	28.5	90	
Forward:	1586	29.2	89	

Specials: Senior & Junior specials available

Season: Year-round **Hours:** Sunrise–sunset **Tee times:** Taken
Leagues: Various times **Ranger:** Some days **Practice facil:** Putting Green,
Chipping Green **Clubhouse:** Food, Covered deck **Lessons:** Available

Directions: I-90 to Exit 190 for SR 306; north on SR 306 to US 20 (Mentor Ave.); left (west) on Mentor Ave. for 1 mile; on left.

Leisure Time Recreation

9 holes, exec

Area: **Far South**   City: **Stow**   Cost: **$**$$$$ ☎ **(330) 688-4162**

Address: 4561 Darrow Rd., Stow

Tees	Ydg.	C/r	S/r	Pace
Middle:	2144			

Specials: Senior & student specials Mon–Fri before 5 p.m.

Season: Mar–Nov **Hours:** 8 a.m.–10 p.m. **Tee times:** Not taken **Leagues:** Mon–Fri
6–6:30 p.m. **Ranger:** None **Practice facil:** Putting Green, Chipping Green
Clubhouse: Food, Beer, Dining room, Showers, Restaurant, Motel **Lessons:** Available

Directions: I-271 to Exit 18 for SR 8; south on SR 8 to exit for SR 303/Hudson;
left (east) on SR 303 (W. Streetsboro Rd) to Hudson; right (south) on SR 91 (becomes
Darrow Rd. in Stow); on left.

PUBLIC 9,
EXEC, PAR 3

Little Met Golf Course

9 holes, exec

Area: **West**   City: **Cleveland**   Cost: **$$**$$$ ☎ **(216) 941-9672**

Address: 18599 Old Lorain Rd., Cleveland

Tees	Ydg.	C/r	S/r	Pace
Middle:	2535			

Specials: Golfer's Dozen: 12 rounds for the price of 10; Senior (62+)
& Junior specials available

Season: Mid-Mar–mid-Dec **Hours:** Sunrise–sunset **Tee times:** Taken weekends
Leagues: Mon–Fri, various times **Ranger:** Daily **Practice facil:** Putting Green,
Club rental **Clubhouse:** Food, Beer **Lessons:** Not available

Directions: I-480 to Exit 9 for Grayton Rd.; north on Grayton; left (west) on Puritas Rd.
into Rocky River Reservation; right (north) on Valley Pkwy. past Big Met Golf Course;
right (east) on Old Lorain Rd.; on right.

Little Met Golf Course   *(photo: Casey Batule/courtesy of Cleveland Metroparks)*

**PUBLIC 9,
EXEC, PAR 3**

Mastick Woods Golf Course

9 holes, exec

Area: **West**   City: **Cleveland**   Cost: $$$$$ ☎ **(216) 267-5626**

Address: 19900 Puritas Ave., Cleveland

Tees	Ydg.	C/r	S/r	Pace
Back:	1900			
Middle:	1827	31.0		
Forward:	1755	31.0		

Specials: Golfer's Dozen: 12 rounds for the price of 10; Senior (62+) & Junior specials Mon–Fri

Season: Mid-Mar–mid-Dec **Hours:** Sunrise–sunset **Tee times:** Taken weekends, until noon **Leagues:** Mon–Fri, early & late **Ranger:** Most days **Practice facil:** Putting Green **Clubhouse:** Food, Beer **Lessons:** Not available

Directions: I-480 to Exit 9 for Grayton Rd.; north on Grayton; left (west) on Puritas Rd. into Rocky River Reservation; on left.

PUBLIC 9, EXEC, PAR 3

Mastick Woods Golf Course

photo: Casey Batule/courtesy of Cleveland Metroparks

Meadowood Golf Course

18 holes, par 3; 9 holes, exec

Area: **West**   City: **Westlake**   Cost: $$$$$ ☎ **(440) 835-6442**

Address: 29800 Center Ridge Rd., Westlake

Tees	Ydg.	C/r	S/r	Pace	Ydg.	C/r	S/r	Pace
Middle:	2635	66.8	118		2845	56.2	80	
Forward:								

Specials: Senior & Junior specials Mon–Fri

Season: Year-round **Hours:** Sunrise–sundown **Tee times:** Not taken
Leagues: Mon–Thu afternoons **Ranger:** Some days **Practice facil:** Putting Green
Clubhouse: Food, Beer, Pavilion **Lessons:** Not available

Directions: I-90 to Exit 156 for Crocker Rd./Bassett Rd.; south on Crocker;
right (west) on Center Ridge; on right.

North Olmsted Golf Club

9 holes, exec

Area: **West**   City: **North Olmsted**   Cost: $$$$$ ☎ **(440) 777-0220**

Address: 5840 Canterbury Rd., North Olmsted

Tees	Ydg.	C/r	S/r	Pace
Middle:	1681	57.1	80	
Forward:	1427	54.6	74	

Specials: Senior specials Mon–Fri 10 a.m.–4 p.m.; Junior specials available

Season: Apr 1–Dec 1 **Hours:** Sunrise–sunset **Tee times:** Required weekends
Leagues: Mon–Fri 7:30–10 a.m.; 4–5:30 p.m.; other times vary **Ranger:** Weekends
Practice facil: Putting Green **Clubhouse:** Food, Beer **Lessons:** Available

Directions: I-480 to Exit 6 for SR 252 (Great Northern Blvd.); south on SR 252;
right (west) on Butternut Ridge Rd.; left (south) on Canterbury Rd.; on right.

PUBLIC 9, EXEC, PAR 3

Old Pine Golf Course

18 holes

Area: **South**   City: **Richfield**   Cost: $$$$$ ☎ **(330) 659-4900**

Address: 3770 Broadview Rd., Richfield

Tees	Ydg.	C/r	S/r	Pace
Middle:	1900			

Specials: Senior & Junior specials on weekdays noon–4 p.m. and Sat until noon

Season: Mar 15–Nov 31 **Hours:** Sunrise–sunset **Tee times:** Taken
Leagues: Traveling **Ranger:** Daily **Practice facil:** Putting Green
Clubhouse: Food **Lessons:** Not available

Directions: I-77 to Exit 143 for Wheatley Rd.; west on Wheatley (becomes
Broadview Rd./SR 176 after Brecksville Rd.); on left.

Pepperidge Tree Golf Course   9 holes

Area: **Far East**   City: **N. Madison**   Cost: **$$$**$$ ☎ **(440) 428-1398**

Address: 6825 N. Ridge Rd., N. Madison

Tees	Ydg.	C/r	S/r	Pace
Middle:	3048			

Specials: Senior specials available

Season: Year-round **Hours:** Sunrise–sunset **Tee times:** Taken
Leagues: Mon–Fri 5 p.m. **Ranger:** Some days **Practice facil:** Putting Green
Clubhouse: Food, Beer, Pavilion **Lessons:** Not available

Directions: I-90 to Exit 212 for SR 528 (River St.); north on SR 528;
right (east) on N. Ridge Rd. (SR 20); on left.

Riverwoods Golf Course   9 holes, exec

Area: **Far South**   City: **Akron**   Cost: **$$**$$$ ☎ **(330) 928-2669**

Address: 1870 Akron-Peninsula Rd., Akron

Tees	Ydg.	C/r	S/r	Pace	Ydg.	C/r	S/r	Pace
Back:	2145				2370			
Middle:	1876				2201			
Forward:	1589				1852			

Specials: Senior (62+) specials Mon–Fri before 2 p.m.

Season: Mar–Dec **Hours:** Sunrise–sunset **Tee times:** Not taken
Leagues: Mon–Thu, various times **Ranger:** Daily
Practice facil: Range, Putting Green, Chipping Green, Sand, Lighted range,
Grass tees, Covered tees **Clubhouse:** Food, Beer **Lessons:** Available

Directions: I-77 to Exit 138 for Ghent Rd.; west on Ghent; right (east)
on Yellow Creek Rd. under I-77; right (east) on W. Bath Rd.; right (south) on
Akron-Peninsula Rd.; on right.

Sycamore Valley Golf Course   9 holes, exec

Area: **Far South**   City: **Akron**   Cost: **$$$$**$ ☎ **(330) 928-3329**

Address: 1651 Akron-Peninsula Rd., Akron

Tees	Ydg.	C/r	S/r	Pace
Middle:	1839			

Specials: Senior (65+) specials Mon–Fri before noon

Season: Year-round **Hours:** Sunrise–sunset **Tee times:** Not taken
Leagues: Ladies league only **Ranger:** Some days **Practice facil:** Putting Green
Clubhouse: Food, Beer **Lessons:** Not available

Directions: I-77 to Exit 138 for Ghent Rd.; west on Ghent; right (east) on Yellow Creek
Rd. under I-77; right (east) on W. Bath Rd.; right (south) on Akron-Peninsula Rd.; on left.

**PUBLIC 9,
EXEC, PAR 3**

Private Courses

Acacia Country Club

☎ (440) 442-2686

Area: **East**   City: **Lyndhurst**   Difficulty: ●●●

Address: 26899 Cedar Rd., Lyndhurst   **Pro:** Chris Wagner, PGA

Tees	Ydg.	C/r	S/r	Pace
Back:	6701	72.5	129	3:40
Middle:	6395	71.1	126	
Forward:	5736	73.3	129	

Directions: I-271 to Exit 32 for Cedar Rd.; west on Cedar; on right.

Description "The Anniversary Waltz" was played at Acacia in 1996, when 75 candles were lit. And as soon as the plates were cleared, plans were finalized for some renovation. There had been some speculation that this storied course would be sacrificed to retail development. That's not the case; Acacia will be here for a long, long time.

A good thing, too. This Donald Ross design challenges and rewards finesse players as it rolls up and down 6,400 yards from the blues.

Of course, not everyone who played here was known for finesse. Brawny baseball slugger Babe Ruth played his one and only pro match here on August 17, 1937, in the True Temper Open.

And talk about a foursome! Tris Speaker, Billy Burke, and Tommy Armour rounded out the group.

Ashtabula Country Club

☎ (440) 964-7952

Area: **Far East**   City: **Ashtabula**   Difficulty: ●●●

Address: 4338 Lake Rd. W., Ashtabula   **Pro:** John Lucansky

Tees	Ydg.	C/r	S/r	Pace
Back:	5971	68.6	120	3:43
Middle:	5805	67.9	119	
Forward:	5378	71.1	118	

Directions: I-90 to Exit 223 for SR 45; north on SR 45 (becomes Center Rd.); right (east) on Lake Rd.; on right.

Description This is a short track at 5,805 from the whites, but par is only 70. The club was founded in 1923 and has 220 members.

Aurora Golf & Country Club ☎ (330) 562-5300

Area: **Southeast**   City: **Aurora**   Difficulty: ●●●

Address: 50 Trails End Rd., Aurora   **Pro:** Gary Trivisonno, PGA

Tees	Ydg.	C/r	S/r	Pace
Back:	6642	72.9	134	4:15
Middle:	6249	71.4	131	
Forward:	5486	72.8	129	

Directions: I-271 to Exit 27 for US 422; east on US 422; right (south) on SR 306 (Chillicothe Rd.); left (east) on SR 82 (Garfield East Rd.); right (south) on Hudson Rd.; left (west) on Trails End Rd. to entrance.

Description The course record here, 64, is shared by a trio of out-of-towners: Arnold Palmer, Bruce Devlin, and Charles Coody. When the Cleveland Open was a tour stop, Aurora CC was the site three times. Glancing at the scorecard, you may think this course looks easy, at only 6,200 yards. That's until you realize there are only three par 5s and three par 3s on this course; there are plenty of long par 4s.

On No. 1, players meet for the first time a creek that will meander through a half dozen or so holes as the match proceeds. Lots of bunkers near the greens, too. Head pro Gary Trivisonno describes his course as "sporty, tight, and somewhat hilly. It has small greens and it plays longer than 6,200 yards." Trivisonno is one of the longest-hitting pros in the area. His reputation for being genuinely nice is well deserved, as well.

PRIVATE

Avon Oaks Country Club ☎ (440) 871-4638

Area: **West**   City: **Avon**   Difficulty: ●●●

Address: 32300 Detroit Rd. (SR 254), Avon   **Pro:** Judd Stephenson, PGA

Tees	Ydg.	C/r	S/r	Pace
Back:	6735	72.7	129	3:53
Middle:	6436	71.3	127	
Forward:	5623	74.1	128	

Directions: I-90 westbound to Exit 156 for Crocker Rd./Bassett Rd.; left (south) on Crocker to SR 254 (Detroit Rd.); right (west) on Detroit; on right.

OR I-90 eastbound to Exit 153 for SR 83 (Center Rd.); south on SR 83; left (east) on Detroit Rd. (SR 254); on left.

Description Avon Oaks plays 6,436 from the member tees, so this is no short layout. In addition, the demands on tee shots are substantial. Fairways and landing areas are narrow. Making the course play longer is the prevalence of elevated greens. A few years ago, the course added gold tees. From these new championship tees, Parma resident Rob Moss fired a 66 for the course record. From the blue tees, the record of 63 is shared by a small group of players.

Head pro Judd Stephenson, PGA, picks No. 12 as his favorite hole. From the back of the box, it stretches 170 yards and has water and bunkers. Reaching it is not easy, and once there you're putting on the layout's most undulating green.

Barrington Golf Club   ☎ (330) 995-0667
Area: **Southeast**   City: **Aurora**   Difficulty: ●●●

Address: 350 N. Aurora Rd., Aurora   **Pro:** Rich DeLaat

Tees	Ydg.	C/r	S/r	Pace
Back:	7138	74.6	135	3:54
Middle:	6595	71.3	125	
Forward:	5272	69.8	117	

Directions: I-271 to Exit 27 for US 422; east on US 422; right (south) on SR 306 (Chillicothe Rd.); right (west) on Treat Rd.; left (south) on N. Aurora Rd. (SR 43); on left.

Description Barrington was built in 1994 and named by *Golf Digest* as one of the top 10 new courses. Having Jack Nicklaus serve as designer, whether he does any of the real design work or not, doesn't hurt in such matters.

PRIVATE

Beechmont Country Club   ☎ (216) 831-9100
Area: **East**   City: **Beachwood**   Difficulty: ●●●

Address: 29600 Chagrin Blvd., Beachwood   **Pro:** Charlie Stone, Master PGA

Tees	Ydg.	C/r	S/r	Pace
Back:	6648	72.3	131	3:40
Middle:	6359	70.8	128	
Forward:	5845	73.4	130	

Directions: I-271 to Exit 27 for SR 87 (Chagrin Blvd.); east on Chagrin; on right.

Description First things first. Try hard to get Ed Preisler, the skinny nonagenarian, in your foursome. He is older than many of the hardwoods that line the fairways here and just as resilient. Every club should have a member like him. Every club should have a pro like Charlie Stone, Master PGA Professional. He is a hands-on pro whose teaching program is absolutely first rate. His philosophy behind teaching bears repeating: "The basic reason for lessons is to increase the pleasure of playing," he says. Outings at this classic track are first rate, as well, because, as the pro says, "I don't do outings. I do tournaments. If you treat an outing like you would treat a tournament, you can't miss."

Two tips should always be kept in mind here. First, this is not a course for aggressive putting. In most cases, the smart play is to lag putt. Getting down in two is nothing to be ashamed of here. Mr. Preisler counsels, "A guest here would be wise to ask where the ball should be putted." Second, at one point or another, you will find yourself behind one of the gorgeous oaks. Ignore what your ego says and chip back to the short grass.

"There are more shots wasted because you think you're going to make that shot over the tree," Mr. Preisler cautions. Wasted shots count, too.

Charlie Stone has good advice as well. "The first few holes are very difficult," he says. "No. 1 is long (412 yards), No. 2 is tight, No. 3 is a long par 3 (184 yards), and No. 4 (at 440 yards) is the longest par 4 on the course. It would be easier if you could play the back nine first."

Last year the club had the bunkers redesigned to better fit the course, and a new and more playable sand was put in. A little water was taken out and some fairway bunkers installed. A few tees were moved back. Always a beautiful course, the improvements maintain and improve the beauty.

Beechmont Country Club

Canterbury Golf Club   ☎ (216) 561-1000

Area: **East**   City: **Shaker Hts.**   Difficulty: ● ● ●

Address: 22000 S. Woodland Rd., Shaker Hts.   **Pro:** Craig Murray

Tees	Ydg.	C/r	S/r	Pace
Back:	6942	73.9	138	3:54
Middle:	6471	71.7	130	
Forward:	5830	68.8	125	

Directions: I-271 to Exit 27 for SR 87 (Chagrin Blvd.); west on Chagrin; right (north) on Green Rd.; left (west) on S. Woodland Rd.; on left.

Description This is the course where Jack Nicklaus won his 14th major, one of many records in his trophy case. It is here that the PGA and the USGA have come for championship play. This is not a country club; it is a golf club. An example of that could be seen in the 1996 U.S. Senior Open. The best senior professionals played the course just as it is played every day by its members. It is a big and powerful course, with three finishing holes that try the souls of the best players in the game. To be a guest here is quite an honor. It is also home to one of golf's greatest friends, Mike Kiely PGA, the caddymaster whose charges learn the game in the classic manner and who often return, years later, as members. Kiely is self-effacing, intensely proud of his club and a joy to talk golf with.

Chagrin Valley Country Club   ☎ (440) 248-4314

Area: **Southeast**   City: **Chagrin Falls**   Difficulty: ● ● ●

Address: 4700 SOM Center Rd. (SR 91), Chagrin Falls   **Pro:** Michael Heisterkamp

Tees	Ydg.	C/r	S/r	Pace
Back:	6614	72.9	131	3:53
Middle:	6410	72.1	130	
Forward:	5211	69.3	120	

Directions: I-271 to Exit 27 for US 422 (east) to SR 91 (SOM Center Rd.); north on SR 91; on left.

Description When veteran member Phil Kish thinks about the joys of golf, his mind's eye focuses on No. 4, the 170-yard par 3. The green is elevated and surrounded by shelf rock. Flowers brighten the stone and trees provide the background. "It's a well-defined hole, easy to see the challenge. It's a beautiful hole, too, and playing No. 4 is memorable. Finally, it's a satisfying hole. Most players who walk away with par are smiling." He birdies it a few times every season.

PRIVATE

This club, nestled in heavy woods, began in 1921 when the Chagrin Valley Country Club Company built its first nine holes on the former Mapes family farm. That course later became the Moreland Hills Golf Course, a public track on the east side of SOM Center Road. The club built a course and clubhouse on the west side of SOM Center in 1928.

Columbia Hills Country Club   ☎ (440) 236-5051

Area: **Southwest**   City: **Columbia Station**   Difficulty: ●●●

Address: 16200 E. River Rd., Columbia Station   **Pro:** Jim Wise

Tees	Ydg.	C/r	S/r	Pace
Back:	6432	70.9	134	3:59
Middle:	6045	69.0	130	
Forward:	5471	72.6	130	

Directions: I-71 to Exit 231 for SR 82 (Royalton Rd.); west on SR 82 for 5 miles; left (south) on E. River Rd. (SR 252); 1 mile, on right.

Description One of many virtues here is the landscaping. Few other clubs can match the incredible size, variety, color, or quality of the flower and plant displays throughout this course. This is a hilly layout and a fairly short one, only 6,068 yards from the members' tees. The steep inclines make it play lots longer than it measures, though. Much work has been done on the severe flooding problem, including the installation of an irrigation system. The clubhouse has been renovated and carts are now electric.

The Country Club   ☎ (216) 831-9252

Area: **East**   City: **Pepper Pike**   Difficulty: ●●●

Address: 2825 Lander Rd., Pepper Pike   **Pro:** Jack McKelvey

Tees	Ydg.	C/r	S/r	Pace
Back:	6908	73.5	130	3:51
Middle:	6558	71.9	125	
Forward:	5684	72.2	123	

Directions: I-271 to Exit 29 for Chagrin Blvd.; east on Chagrin to Lander Circle; north on Lander Rd.; on right.

Description This ancient (for these parts) club and course (1889) is joined at the hip with Pepper Pike Club, and each serves a distinct purpose: Pepper is the course for Cleveland corporate executives; Country is truly a country club, with a wonderful course and all the amenities, including facilities for debutante balls. A walk through the locker room

PRIVATE

and cursory examination of the names on the lockers reveals an impressive representation of WASP royalty. Some people believe the management and staff here were the inspiration for *Upstairs, Downstairs.*

Country Club of Hudson   ☎ (330) 650-1192
Area: **Southeast**   City: **Hudson**   Difficulty: ●●●

Address: 2155 Middleton Rd., Hudson   **Pro:** Jim and Jeff Camp

Tees	Ydg.	C/r	S/r	Pace
Back:	6732	71.7	122	3:48
Middle:	6442	70.4	120	
Forward:	5519	70.9	120	

Directions: I-480 to Exit 37 for SR 91 (Darrow Rd.); south on SR 91; left (east) on Middleton Rd. for 1/2 mile; on left.

Description As this Geoffrey Cornish design nears the 40-year mark, it only gets better. The layout has always been a good one, but the course was built on Summit County farmland—and on high ground, as well. With no trees, it had a "Scottish links" look and all the challenges wind can bring. But the thousands and thousands of trees subsequently planted here are now slowing the wind, defining holes, and adding more character every season.

Eight ponds dot the course, and the greens, usually kept to a 9 on the Stimpmeter, can reach 10 and faster. No. 11 is the signature hole here, a classic par 4 of more than 400 yards. It narrows near the green, which has bunkers on both sides and white stakes on the left. Bud Nauffts, a good player in these parts for many, many years, birdied No. 14 last year but said it took him a driver and a 3-wood to get on.

Better-known players who have golfed here include John Daley and Phil Mickelson, who were winners in the annual Junior Invitational played here.

PRIVATE

TIDYMAN'S TIDBITS #20
Best bang for a buck in a private club:
1) Oberlin GC
2) Little Mountain CC
3) Rosemont CC
4) Spring Valley CC

Country Clubs of Fox Meadow (Meadow Course)
☎ (330) 723-4653
Area: **Southwest**   City: **Medina**   Difficulty: ●●●

Address: 6416 Wadsworth Rd. (SR 57), Medina   **Pro:** Scott Campbell, PGA

Tees	Ydg.	C/r	S/r	Pace
Back:	6918	73.1	125	3:58
Middle:	6325	71.5	120	
Forward:	4788	68.9	117	

Directions: I-71 to Exit 218 for SR 18; west on SR 18; left (south) on River Styx Rd.; right (west) on Sharon-Copley Rd.; left (south) on Wadsworth Rd. (SR 57); on right.

Description This track, designed by Steve Burns and built on softly rolling farmland, is not as challenging as its sister course, Weymouth. Still, to have two distinct courses for a single membership is intriguing. Fox Meadow has almost two dozen homes as part of the development, and plans call for more than 500 once the last roof tile is hammered down. Members at Fox Meadow are also members at Weymouth (see separate listing). The courses share Scott Campbell, PGA, as golf pro and superintendent Tim Cunningham.

PRIVATE

Country Clubs of Fox Meadow (Weymouth Course)
☎ (330) 725-6297
Area: **Southwest**   City: **Medina**   Difficulty: ●●●

Address: 3946 Weymouth Rd., Medina   **Pro:** Scott Campbell, PGA

Tees	Ydg.	C/r	S/r	Pace
Back:	7007	74.5	134	3:58
Middle:	6639	71.7	127	
Forward:	5243	71.0	121	

Directions: I-71 to Exit 222 for SR 3; south on SR 3 (Weymouth Rd.); on right.

Description From 1969 until 1986 this was a pretty good public track. Once it went private, traps were added until the count reached 80, fairways were contoured, trees were moved around, and designer Geoffrey Cornish added his two cents. It is now a very good private track. Length is not yet determined, but it will likely play around 6,400 yards from the member tees and par is 72.

Members at Weymouth are also members at Fox Meadow (see separate listing). The courses share Scott Campbell, PGA, as golf pro and superintendent Ken Aukerman, who has tended the greens and fairways at Weymouth for a quarter century.

Elyria Country Club   ☎ (440) 323-8225

Area: **Far West**   City: **Elyria**   Difficulty: ●●●

Address: 41625 Oberlin-Elyria Rd., Elyria   **Pro:** Rich Casabella, PGA

Tees	Ydg.	C/r	S/r	Pace
Back:	6731	72.1	130	3:47
Middle:	6326	70.4	125	
Forward:	5625	72.0	123	

Directions: I-480 take Exit 1A for SR 10 (I-480 ends here); west on SR 10 for 14 miles; right (north) on Lagrange Rd.; left (south) on Oberlin-Elyria Rd.; on left.

Description This is among the most beautiful courses in an area blessed with beautiful courses.

The designer was William F. Flynn, whose work includes Shinnecock Hills in New York and Burning Tree in Maryland. In the Greater Cleveland area, Mr. Flynn also created courses at The Country Club in Pepper Pike and Pepper Pike Country Club.

Play here calls for every stick in the bag, as the course rolls and pitches over ravine and hillock. Two memorable tees are No. 11, an elevated par 3 of 168 yards that shoots down over water, and No. 15, which calls for a big draw over the east branch of the Black River to a tree-lined fairway.

Fairlawn Country Club   ☎ (330) 836-5541

Area: **Far South**   City: **Akron**   Difficulty:

Address: 200 N. Wheaton Rd., Akron   **Pro:** Frank Wharton, PGA

Tees	Ydg.	C/r	S/r	Pace
Back:	6277	70.4	126	3:42
Middle:	5917	68.6	123	
Forward:	5242	69.7	115	

Directions: I-77 southbound to Exit 138 for Ghent Rd.; right off circular exit (east) on Ghent Rd.; left (east) on W. Market St.; left (north) on N. Wheaton Rd.; on left. I-77 northbound to Exit 132 (White Pond Dr.); right (north) on White Pond; right (east) on Frank Blvd.; left (north) on W. Market St.; right (east) on N. Wheaton Rd.; on left.

Description This is a classic old course that reeks of character. Greens are small and well bunkered; the Stimpmeter usually measures around 10. Few courses are better conditioned. At just a little under 6,000 yards from the white tees, this course bobs and weaves enough that good scores are posted only by players who make few mistakes.

PRIVATE

Firestone Country Club

☎ (330) 644-8441

Area: **Far South**   City: **Akron**   Difficulty: ●●●

Address: 425 E. Warner Rd., Akron   **Pro:** Mark Gore, PGA

Tees	South Ydg.	C/r	S/r	Pace	North Ydg.	C/r	S/r	Pace	West Ydg.	C/r	S/r	Pace
Back:	7139	75.1	128	3:44	7060	74.7	131	3:55	6663	72.4	130	3:46
Middle:	6379	71.2	122		6422	71.8	126		6156	70.1	124	
Forward:		5609	72.1		124		5049			69.9	121	

Directions: I-77 to Exit 120 for S. Arlington St.; north on S. Arlington; left (west) on E. Warner Rd.; on left.

Description If you play the South Course of parallel holes from the tips, you'll play 7,139 yards, par 70. Big deal. Only one type of game plays well here: long.

Harvey Penick used to say, "The woods are filled with long hitters." Here, long hitters can wind up in an adjacent fairway, which, while not the preferred method, is not always a bad place to be.

The signature hole is No. 16, a 625-yard par 5. Sand is found on both sides of the fairway, which finally buttonhooks around water to get to the green. Many players find themselves in the water in four.

The greens here have caused more headaches and expense than any other part of the club. They appear to finally be free of disease and other problems.

The North course, thought by many to be more difficult than South for its dramatic changes in elevation, leaning fairways, and "water, water, everywhere," is lots more fun. Middle and low handicaps will find themselves creating shots that they didn't know were in their bags.

Management at this storied course has generously seen fit to add a nine-hole course and allow the hoi polloi to play there. How thoughtful.

PRIVATE

TIDYMAN'S TIDBITS #21
Best courses for beginning players:
1) Pine Brook
2) Riverside
3) Brentwood
4) Little Met
5) Mastick Woods

Hawthorne Valley Country Club   ☎ (440) 232-1400

Area: **Southeast**   City: **Solon**   Difficulty: ●●●

Address: 27840 Aurora Rd. (SR 43), Solon   **Pro:** Dave Pezacov, PGA

Tees	Ydg.	C/r	S/r	Pace
Back:	6340	71.1	133	3:51
Middle:	6102	69.9	131	
Forward:	5753	73.4	126	

Directions: I-271 to Exit 26 for Rockside Rd.; east on Rockside; right (south) on Aurora Rd. (SR 43); on right.

Description Almost sold to Bertram Wolstein, the developer whose lack of regard for wetlands and environmental law is legend, this wonderful Donald Ross course was saved by developer Fred Rzepka, who bought it and immediately set about improving it. While it was member-owned, outings were rare—a shame, because in a town with a fistful of Ross courses, this is likely the most beautiful and challenging. The prohibition on outings is one of many changes Mr. Rzepka has instituted. FYI, outings are available on Mondays and Friday mornings. But Friday mornings only if it's a shotgun start beginning before 8 a.m.

The kitchen, always a good one, is suddenly en route to greatness: three new chefs, an executive, sous, and banquet, are on board, and their degrees from culinary schools are on the wall.

Among the physical changes is the new veranda, a big, wide and sweeping affair than hangs over the ninth fairway. Heated in the cold weather, lighted when it's dark. More improvements and changes are in the ballroom, the club room, the card room the casual dining porch.

This is a hilly course, and two of the outstanding holes use elevation. No. 14 is a 207-yard par 3 that begins at an elevated tee—be ready for 23 wooden steps up to the tee box—and ends at an elevated green. No. 16 inspires awe. A drive of a couple hundred yards on this par 4 leaves an approach of a couple hundred more, as the fairway suddenly leans left and careens steeply to a green.

PRIVATE

Kirtland Country Club   ☎ (440) 951-8422

Area: **East**   City: **Willoughby**   Difficulty: ●●●

Address: 39438 Kirtland Rd., Willoughby   **Pro:** Tim Bennett

Tees	Ydg.	C/r	S/r	Pace
Back:	6842	73.6	135	3:58
Middle:	6437	71.7	130	
Forward:	6006	69.5	123	

Directions: I-90 to Exit 193 for SR 306; south on SR 306 for 1/2 mile; right (west) on Kirtland Rd.; on left.

Description The two most difficult consecutive holes in the area are to be found in the Chagrin River Valley, on the back nine of this magnificent course. No. 11 is a par 3 of 225 yards and No. 12 is a par 4 of 440 yards. Uphill. To a double-tiered green. If a great golf hole has to be difficult as well as beautiful, the back nine here easily has more examples—seven, at my count—than any club around. It is the site of the U.S. Open sectional qualifier. From the back tees, the slope is 135 and the course rating a stern 73.6, so don't look for red numbers.

Lake Forest Country Club   ☎ (330) 656-3804

Area: **Far South**   City: **Hudson**   Difficulty: ●●●

Address: 100 Lake Forest Dr., Hudson   **Pro:** John Goodson, PGA

Tees	Ydg.	C/r	S/r	Pace
Back:	6736	72.9	129	4:02
Middle:	6337	71.1	125	
Forward:	5709	72.8	126	

Directions: I-271 to Exit 18 for SR 8; south on SR 8; left (east) on Boston Mills Rd.; left (north) on Lake Forest Dr. to dead end.

Description The magnificent clubhouse here was designed by H. O. Fullerton, who cut his design teeth on the Van Sweringen mansion in Shaker Heights. The course was designed by Herbert Strong, the maestro behind Canterbury Golf Club in Shaker Heights.

The club's first pro, Densmore Shute, teamed up with Walter Hagen to challenge Tommy Armour and Horton Smith three days before the course's opening in 1930. At the time, Lake Forest, at 6,890 yards, was the longest course in Ohio.

The foursome arrived by Goodyear blimp on the spectator-lined first hole (now the driving range). Shute and Hagan made short work of

PRIVATE

their opponents, winning by five strokes. Shute went on to win two PGAs and the 1933 British Open.

Guests should speak in reverential tones here; the course is purely wonderful. No. 10 is the most striking tee in the area. And No. 14 is a great par 5: 500 yards over two creeks while descending a narrow fairway, with an approach to a two-tiered green.

Lakewood Country Club   ☎ (440) 871-5338
Area: **West**   City: **Westlake**   Difficulty: ●●●

Address: 2613 Bradley Rd., Westlake   **Pro:** Tom Waitrovich, PGA

Tees	Ydg.	C/r	S/r	Pace
Back:	6800	72.9	136	4:00
Middle:	6357	70.9	131	
Forward:	5966	74.4	133	

Directions: I-90 to Exit 156 for Crocker Rd./Bassett Rd.; left (south) on Crocker; right (west) on SR 254 (Detroit Rd.); left (south) on Bradley Rd.; on left.

Description After all these years, this course remains a challenge.

The 1921 design was done by A. W. Tillinghast, whose other golf treasures include Winged Foot Country Club and Baltusrol Country Club in New York and Baltusrol Golf Club in New Jersey.

Nothing's unfair about the layout, but its route through woods and over water definitely makes it a course for better players.

PRIVATE

Legend Lake Golf Club   .   ☎ (440) 285-3110
Area: **Far East**   City: **Chardon**   Difficulty: ●●◐

Address: 11135 Auburn Rd., Chardon   **Pro:** Reece Alexander

Tees	Ydg.	C/r	S/r	Pace
Back:	6568	71.2	128	3:47
Middle:	6322	70.1	125	
Forward:	5570	72.1	124	

Directions: I-271 to Exit 34 for US 322 (Mayfield Rd.); east on US 322, past SR 306; left (north) on Auburn Rd. for 2 miles; on left.

Description Six days out of seven, this Chardon club fulfills its mission: "We help golfers golf." The club is short on pretense and expense, high on course maintenance and promotion of the game.

Legend Lake Golf Club

PRIVATE

Madison Country Club
☎ (440) 953-1964

Area: **Far East**   City: **Madison**   Difficulty: ●●●

Address: 6131 Chapel Rd., Madison   **Pro:** Tom Fussaro

Tees	Ydg.	C/r	S/r	Pace
Back:	6458	71.1	127	3:47
Middle:	6145	69.7	124	
Forward:	5288	70.0	116	

Directions: I-90 to Exit 212 for SR 528; north on SR 528 past US 20; left (west) on Chapel Rd.; on left.

Description This was not always Madison Country Club. It began in 1923 as Madison Golf Lakelands, a summer retreat for Pennsylvania families from Pittsburgh and Sharon. When a home was purchased, club membership went along with the deal. Designer Grange Alves laid this course out on rolling terrain. Nearby Lake Erie provides scenery— and warmth. Thanks to the warm lake, the playing season often goes until Thanksgiving. Woods are minimal; sand is substantial. While golf is the club's mainstay, the family is the force behind the activities here, which include swimming, tennis, and excellent dining.

Mike Kiely

Getting Mike Kiely to talk about himself is like wrestling with a greased pig: Just when you think you have him, he slips away.

That's because Kiely, for all his exuberance, energy, and affection for the game, would much rather talk about his golf club, Canterbury, or his charges, the caddies there.

He joined the storied golf club thirty-five years ago as an assistant pro and golf teacher. Over the next few years, he found time to fall in love and marry. At that point, he needed a steadier check, so he took over the caddy program.

It would be difficult to count the thousands of boys and girls who have slung bags on shoulders and looped the championship course. And anyway, Kiely doesn't want to talk about numbers; he wants to talk about his caddies.

"Some of my caddies today are the second generation," he says, obviously delighted. "I have members here, successful professional men, who caddied as they were growing up. My personal physician, Dan Breitenbach, M.D., used to caddy for me and now he's the doctor for the caddy program as well."

Every spring, about 150 boys and girls will knock on the caddymaster's door, visions of double sawbucks dancing in their heads. By the middle of June, the ranks are thinned to 75 or 80 who will stick with the program.

"We don't turn anyone away," Kiely says. "And we only have two caddy categories, A and B. The A caddy makes $30 per bag per round, the B caddy makes $20. I like to keep the rates on the low side, because the caddies know members here will reward them for great caddying." It generally takes two years for a caddy to develop.

Kiely's daughter Colleen—one of his three children—not only caddied but developed into one of the area's premier junior players. She went to Northwestern University on a golf scholarship.

Kids who caddy here not only get to watch the area's best players at play, they get to be an important part of classic golf. There are no cart paths, no gimme's, and no Mulligans. A demanding yet fair course, Canterbury has been the site for 14 major championships.

Kiely's favorite story, chosen from among hundreds of great golf stories at Canterbury, goes back to 1979, when the U.S.G.A. National Amateur Championship was played at his course. Northeast Ohio sent two players: Bobby Lewis (now playing at Country) and Wink McLaughlin, Kiely's brother-in-law as well as current head golf professional at the Oakwood Club.

"Can you believe that?" Kiely asks. "Wink was a caddy. A caddy playing in the national amateur!"

Mayfield Country Club

☎ (216) 382-3958

Area: **East**   City: **South Euclid**   Difficulty: ●●●

Address: 1545 Sheridan Rd., South Euclid   **Pro:** Charlie Wood, PGA

Tees	Ydg.	C/r	S/r	Pace
Back:	6631	73.0	133	3:57
Middle:	6308	71.4	131	
Forward:	5745	73.8	134	

Directions: I-271 to Exit 32 for Cedar Rd.; west on Cedar; right (north) on Richmond Rd.; left (west) on Mayfield Rd.; left (south) on Sheridan Rd.; on left.

Description Want to create a mood for your game? At Mayfield, the historic club tucked away in South Euclid, you can begin by having a cup of coffee with Charlie Wood, the club's longtime pro.

This shotmaker's course was designed by Bertie Way, an Englishman by way of Scotland. There have been a few changes since the dedication round in 1911, but nothing major. Mr. Way, incidentally, also did the original layout at Firestone South as well as the Detroit Country Club.

Medina Country Club

☎ (330) 725-6621

Area: **Southwest**   City: **Medina**   Difficulty: ●●●

Address: 5588 Wedgewood Rd., Medina   **Pro:** Scott Schreck, PGA

Tees	Blue-Green Ydg.	C/r	S/r	Pace	Blue-Red Ydg.	C/r	S/r	Pace	Green-Red Ydg.	C/r	S/r	Pace
Back:	6906	73.4	134	4:04	6365	70.2	122	3:45	6217	69.5	121	3:49
Middle:	6544	71.7	131		5895	68.3	117		5900	68.4	119	
Forward:	5159	69.1	117		5120	68.9	115		5025	68.4	118	

Directions: I-71 to Exit 218 for SR 18 to Medina; left (south) on Wooster Pike (SR 3); right (west) on Wedgewood Rd.; on left 1.5 miles.

Description Nothing wrong with sticking the ol' howitzer in your bag before setting off for this rangy layout of three nines: Blue, Green, and Red. The Red nine was the original when the club started about 40 years ago. Today, tournaments are played on the Blue and Green nines-tournaments played here have included the U.S. Open Qualifier, the Women's State Amateur, and the Ohio Senior Open. One of the rare courses to have a graveyard on the premises.

PRIVATE

Oakwood Club

☎ (216) 291-0679

Area: **East**   City: **Cleveland Hts.**   Difficulty: ● ● ●

Address: 1516 Warrensville Center Rd., Cleveland Hts.   **Pro:** Wink McLaughlan, PGA

Tees	Ydg.	C/r	S/r	Pace
Back:	6709	73.3	128	3:49
Middle:	6289	71.5	125	
Forward:	5609	71.7	122	

Directions: I-271 to Exit 34 for Cedar Rd.; west on Cedar; right (north) on Warrensville Center Rd.; on left.

Description This classic plays long for women players, and it's no pushover for the guys, either.

The Donald Ross design has plenty of hazards, but if golfers are playing well, they won't notice most of them.

The last three holes are Oakwood's version of Amen Corner: the approach on the par 4 No. 16 carries water just in front of the green, the par 3 No. 17 has no bail-out opportunities, and No. 18 plays according to the wind.

Pro Wink McLaughlan hits a driver, then a 4-iron if the wind is in his face. It's a driver, then a wedge if the wind is behind him.

The Oakwood Club has a big bonus at the end: it boasts one of the area's best kitchens.

Oberlin Golf Club

☎ (440) 774-1891

Area: **Far West**   City: **Oberlin**   Difficulty: ● ● ●

Address: 200 Pyle Rd., Oberlin   **Pro:** Cliff Pratello

Tees	Ydg.	C/r	S/r	Pace
Back:	6436	71.0	124	3:45
Middle:	6116	70.0	122	
Forward:	5390	66.5	116	

Directions: SR 2 to exit for SR 58; south on SR 58 for 8 miles; right (west) on Morgan St.; left (west) on Pyle Rd.; on right.

OR, I-480 to Exit 1A for SR 10 west (I-480 ends here); west on SR 10 (merges with US 20) to SR 511; west on SR 511; left (south) on SR 58; right (west) on Morgan St.; left (west) on Pyle Rd.; on right.

Description No debutante balls here. No social memberships, either. Oberlin may be a golf club, but it's a modest one. Modesty notwithstanding, the club has lots of very good players. In the Northern Ohio Golf Association's directory, Oberlin players were winners in the fol-

PRIVATE

lowing categories: stroke play, best ball match play, two-man scramble, and interclub match play.

Is it experience? Could be. The club was formed in 1899.

On the front side, two holes stand out. No. 2 is a great par 4 that begins from an elevated tee. The landing area is framed by a pair of sand traps, and the fairway rises to the green. No. 8, a par 3 that sounds puny at 151 yards, is an elevated tee to an elevated green; wind is a major influence on club selection. On the back, No. 11 is an old-fashioned, gorgeous par 4 of 405 yards with a demanding green.

Pepper Pike Country Club
☎ (216) 831-9400

Area: **East**   City: **Pepper Pike**   Difficulty: ●●●

Address: 2800 SOM Center Rd., Pepper Pike   **Pro:** Carlo Alaqua

Tees	Ydg.	C/r	S/r	Pace
Back:	6658	72.0	129	3:47
Middle:	6261	70.0	125	
Forward:	5555	71.9	120	

Directions: I-271 to Exit 29 for SR 87 (Chagrin Blvd.); east on Chagrin; north on SOM Center Rd. (SR 91); on left.

PRIVATE

Description Ah, Pepper! Last bastion for WASP culture. This would be an ideal club to place in the Smithsonian, reflecting, as it does, the old private club culture. Ver-r-r-r-y exclusive. A backstage pass to a Stones concert is an easier ticket than a membership here.

While the all-male membership is studded with Northeast Ohio's corporate leaders, the membership doesn't care much for golf. Every season Pepper holds the dubious distinction of fewest rounds played.

It is not a long course, but very demanding. Players failing to pay attention to alignment find their scores ballooning. That includes approaches as well as tee shots; many second and third shots must be made from less-than-level lies.

No. 17 is a short par 4, only 338 yards, but it is a dogleg right and plays uphill, which likely adds 40 or 50 yards to club selection. The greens slope from rear to front and are kept at medium speed. If they were to be cut and rolled, the Stimpmeter could go to double digits.

Conditioning here is best described as magnificent. The fairways are so lush, some roll is lost. When he left Cleveland for Baltimore, Art Modell left his clubs here.

Portage Country Club
☎ (330) 836-8565

Area: **Far South**   City: **Akron**   Difficulty: ●●●

Address: 240 N. Portage Path, Akron   **Pro:** Rod Johnston, Master PGA

Tees	Ydg.	C/r	S/r	Pace
Back:	6246	70.5	127	4:00
Middle:	6083	69.7	125	
Forward:	5873	72.4	124	

Directions: I-77 southbound to Exit 138 for Ghent Rd.; right (east) on Ghent Rd.; left (east) on W. Market (SR 18); left (east) on Twin Oaks Rd.; left (north) on N. Portage Path; on left.

OR, I-77 northbound to Exit 132 (White Pond Dr.); right (north) on White Pond; right (east) on Frank Blvd.; right (south) on W. Market St. (SR 18); left (east) on Twin Oaks Rd.; left (north) on N. Portage Path; on left.

Description No secrets on this old and revered course. Get a good night's rest before the match, a good breakfast before teeing it up, and swing easy. Plenty of players, amateurs as well as professionals, have drooled when looking at the yardage figures here, imagining a record round in the near future. Wrong. While getting from tee to green is not difficult, getting into the cup is. The greens are as old as the course: more than 100 years. They are "the claim to fame here . . . very old and very fast," says Master PGA Professional Rod Johnston. "The greens are small, too. And with 78 bunkers, it's a shotmaker's dream."

PRIVATE

Quail Hollow Resort & Country Club
☎ (440) 350-3500

Area: **Far East**   City: **Concord**   Difficulty: ●●●

Address: 11080 Concord Hambden Rd., Concord   **Pro:** Danny Ackerman

Tees	Devlin/Von Hogge				Weiskopf/Morris			
	Ydg.	C/r	S/r	Pace	Ydg.	C/r	S/r	Pace
Back:	6712	72.2	130	4:10	6872	73.9	130	4:20
Middle:	6357	70.6	126		6408	71.4	125	
Forward:	4389	65.7	107		5166	70.0	117	

Directions: I-90 to Exit 200 for SR 44; south on SR 44 to Auburn Rd.; left on Auburn Rd.; right (east) on Concord Hambden Rd.; on right.

Description There are only a few ways to get to play this Bruce Devlin/Robert Von Hogge course: be a member of the club, a guest at the resort, or part of an outing. There is no shortage of qualified players: about 27,000 rounds are played annually between April and October. Regardless of mode of entry, playing here can be memorable.

The terrain pitches and rolls on occasion, and the designers took advantage of that. The course is lined with hardwoods, and during spring and autumn the views and scenery can be breathtaking. Instead of the plain ol' white stake at the 150-yard mark, Quail Hollow uses six yardage markers, from 225 yards down to 100.

The greens are kept in tabletop condition because of the many important tournaments played here: the U.S. Amateur Qualifier, the Ohio Open Championship, the World Championship of Blind Golf, and a slew of Ben Hogan and Nike opens.

The scorecard has two features not seen elsewhere. The first is the Stableford scoring system, best used for outings, and the second is pace measurement. By the time the players leave the first tee, only 15 minutes should have passed. Leaving the No. 6 green, the time spent playing should not exceed 1 hour 24 minutes. By maintaining the pace, players finish a round in 4 hours 9 minutes.

Just after the second course was built, a playing partner who was also a member said he figured that with the outings and tournaments, he was unable to play his own club 24 percent of the time. The new course, the result of the design skills of Tom Weiskopf (the rudest player on the Senior Tour) and Jay Morrish, is open and worthy of the rave reviews.

After Weiskopf's boorish behavior at the U.S. Senior Open at Canterbury GC, it's difficult to remember that the Tour's worst crybaby is one heck of a designer, too. A former pro at the club, speaking of the decision to hire Weiskopf, said, "We were interested in finding the top designer, one who could take the resort to a higher level in the golf world and one to match up the new course to the course we already have." They found the designer they sought. The new Weiskopf-Morrish layout is beautiful and playable. Carved from stands of mature hardwoods, the course has a classic air to it and no shortage of surprises, including the well-planned use of marshland in the fairway.

When Weiskopf was in town to lead reporters, investors, and club members around his latest, he said three elements were necessary for a great course design: water, changes in elevation, and trees. At Quail, he got all three and used them well. Of his latest creation, the winner of the British Open and U.S. Senior Open said, "It's not a long-ball hitters' course at all. In fact, it's just the opposite. It's a finesse course. I would truly regard execution and accuracy from the tee to be more important than length. You'll find a lot of pitching and chipping options around the green."

While there is little to fault hitting it long, accuracy is more important than length here. The fairways are sometimes generous, sometimes more demanding, but putting a ball in the woods here is always costly. The greens are medium–fast and as time marches on will become delightfully frustrating. The course doesn't return at the turn, but club girls in carts keep players stocked with refreshments.

It is an old-fashioned course. And it is a powerful course. No sleeping at the wheel here. Weiskopf said some of his major design influences were the great private layouts in Northeast Ohio, such as The Country Club and Canterbury Golf Club. The greatest compliment, he said, is to hear his designs called classic. That's what he seeks to build: great courses with all the virtues and none of the gimmicks.

Rosemont Country Club   ☎ (330) 666-8109

Area: **Far South**   City: **Fairlawn**   Difficulty: ●●●

Address: 3730 W. Market St., Fairlawn   **Pro:** Bill Rilley, PGA

Tees	Ydg.	C/r	S/r	Pace
Back:	6327	71.8	124	
Middle:	5932	68.8	118	
Forward:	5100	70.3	119	

Directions: I-77 to Exit 137 for SR 18; east on SR 18 (becomes W. Market St.); on right.

Description This wonderful club in Fairlawn was started in 1920. The course was updated by Hurdzan-Fry in recent years, and the clubhouse underwent a renovation as well.

The kitchen is a delight, and the chef's plans are announced a week ahead. If you especially like what he does with roast duckling or rack of veal, scheduling is convenient.

Rosemont has all the amenities a classic club should have, including tennis and swimming. The facilities, for both men and women, include steam, sauna, massage, and fitness room.

Its initiation fee and monthly dues, along with the course and club pro, make it one of the better values in private clubs. Rosemont is tucked away near I-77 and State Route 18, just on the edge of Akron, so it's an easy drive from just about anywhere.

PRIVATE

TIDYMAN'S TIDBITS #22
Eagle-proof par 5s
1) No. 9 Hinckley Hills
2) No. 11 Springvale
3) No. 12 Thunder Hill
4) No. 16 Brandywine
5) No. 17 Seneca B

Rustic Hills Golf Club
☎ (330) 725-4281

Area: **Southwest**   City: **Medina**   Difficulty: ● ● ●

Address: 5399 River Styx Rd., Medina

Tees	Ydg.	C/r	S/r	Pace
Back:	1943	62.5		
Middle:	1778	58.9	91	
Forward:	1599	62.5	98	

Directions: I-71 to Exit 218 for SR 18; west on SR 18; left (south) on River Styx Rd.; on left.

Description What an unusual private club: only nine holes. This layout, put together in the 1960s, is a step above executive length, with four par 3s and five par 4s. Players go around twice, using different tee markers the second time around. No. 7, which often plays about 265 yards, tempts big hitters; the green is surrounded by three ponds, however, so danger lurks. There is a swimming pool, tennis courts, and a large practice green, but no range. The strength of this course is in the greens, which are small, crowned, and fast. Former Ohio Amateur champ Glen Apple is one of about 250 members here. Instead of a pro, club policy has been to hire an aspiring PGA member. Some of these college kids have gone on to positions at Westfield Country Club and Barrington, among others.

PRIVATE

Sand Ridge Golf Club
☎ 440-285-8088

Area: **Far East**   City: **Chardon**   Difficulty: ● ● ●

Address: 12150 Mayfield Rd., Chardon   **Pro:** David Scull

Tees	Ydg.	C/r	S/r	Pace
Back:	7112	75.3	138	
Middle:	6577	72.4	134	
Forward:	5100	64.7	112	

Directions: I-271 to US 322 (Mayfield Rd.); east on US 322 past Bass Lake Rd.; on left.

Description Sand Ridge is the result of the stars being perfectly aligned: a vision and the leadership to carry out the vision; a market anxious for just such a venture and willing to pay for it; a big and rangy piece of property natural for golf; and a designer with the time and energy to take on this project.

The place is pure golf. No debutante balls (no ballroom), no tennis or swimming lessons, no outings. No houses lining fairways. Instead, it offers (and encourages the use of) caddies, and the course itself—

designed by Tom Fazio and spread over 380 acres of Geauga County maple forests so naturally and powerfully beautiful that the emotional dimension of golf is drawn out.

Shaker Heights Country Club   ☎ (216) 991-3324

Area: **East**   City: **Shaker Hts.**   Difficulty: ● ● ●

Address: 3300 Courtland Blvd., Shaker Hts.   **Pro:** Joe Haase, PGA

Tees	Ydg.	C/r	S/r	Pace
Back:	6532	72.6	135	3:50
Middle:	6265	71.4	133	
Forward:	5814	74.3	132	

Directions: I-271 to Exit 29 for Chagrin Blvd.; west on Chagrin; right (north) on Warrensville Center Rd.; left (west) on S. Woodland Rd.; left (south) on Courtland Blvd.

Description Shaker is the Donald Ross course built before World War I as part of the Van Sweringen brothers' development of Shaker Heights. Mr. Ross, the estimable and influential Scotsman, built courses that place a premium on accurate iron play and putting. As it was in 1914, so it is today. Construction costs, however, have risen somewhat in the intervening years; the total bill to build Shaker was $59,233.45. A restoration by architect Brit Stenson took place in 1997.

From the members' tees, the course measures 6,265 yards, but that doesn't mean it plays short. The par 3s and par 5s are short, and the par 4s are long. Even the low handicappers keep the club cover off the driver. Good bunker play here can be worth a stroke or two, and putting, of course, is vital—particularly on No. 5 and No. 7. No. 10 remains Mr. Ross's way of telling us a short par 4 can be tough. Only 252 yards, it calls for a mid-iron and a wedge to a steeply elevated green. Easier to bogey than it looks.

The greens on Nos. 11, 16, and 17 on the back side are the holes the club brags about.

A couple of seasons ago, neurosurgeon Yoshiro Takaoka tested the wind, drew his 5 wood at the elevated 11th tee, and knocked the ball in the hole. The card says the par 3 measures 154 yards, though with pin placement and swirling winds, club selection is a matter of two parts judgment and one part luck.

PRIVATE

Sharon Golf Club

☎ (440) 273-2383

Area: **Far South**   City: **Sharon Center**   Difficulty: ●●●

Address: SR 94, Sharon Center   **Pro:** Dwight Axtell

Tees	Ydg.	C/r	S/r	Pace
Back:	7153	74.0	132	3:57
Middle:	6812	72.5	129	
Forward:	5933	68.8	122	

Directions: I-71 to Exit 218 for SR 18; east on SR 18;
right (south) on SR 94 (N. Ridge Rd.); on left.

Description Sharon Golf Club is private in the truest sense of the word. It seeks no publicity; it doesn't advertise. One member has called it "the best club in the country for casual golf." Built in 1964 and designed by George Cobb of Greenville, South Carolina, it opened in 1966 and was a qualifying site for the U.S. Open. It was here that Arnold Palmer once missed the cut. It is a powerful course with four sets of tees. The longest measures 7,153 yards, par 72 with a course rating of 74 and a slope rating of 132. The next longest route is 6,812 yards, course rating 72.5 and slope of 129. As one member of the management team said, "The strength is that Sharon is strictly a golf club, which affords easy access to members at all times." The number of events here is limited.

PRIVATE

Silver Lake Country Club

☎ (330) 688-6016

Area: **Far South**   City: **Cuyahoga Falls**   Difficulty: ●●●

Address: 1325 Graham Rd., Cuyahoga Falls   **Pro:** Tom Atchison, PGA

Tees	Ydg.	C/r	S/r	Pace
Back:	6646	71.8	128	4:10
Middle:	6344	70.5	125	
Forward:	5483	71.5	118	

Directions: I-271 to Exit 18 for SR 8; south on SR 8;
exit at Graham Rd. in Cuyahoga Falls; left (east) on Graham Rd.; on left.

Description The cover shot on the new scorecard is No. 17, a short par 3 of only 126 yards. What it lacks in length it makes up in glamour, running as it does slightly downhill to a small green nestled among dogwood, azalea, rhododendron, and huge oak trees.

Each hole on this young course (1959) sets up well from the tee. There are no blind shots, and the terrain rolls gently. The greens are big and fast, and the conditioning is excellent. (Grass clippings, for example, are picked up from the fairway). The signature hole on the front side is No. 6, a downhill par 3 of 189 yards with water behind green. While waiting for players in front to putt out, golfers can survey most of the course from the tee, the highest point on the course.

Spring Valley Country Club   ☎ (440) 365-1411

Area: **Far West**   City: **Elyria**   Difficulty: ●●●

Address: 1100 Gulf Rd., Elyria   **Pro:** Michael Caronchi, PGA

Tees	Ydg.	C/r	S/r	Pace
Back:	6555	71.6	128	4:00
Middle:	6293	70.5	126	
Forward:	5440	72.3	121	

Directions: I-90 to Exit 148 for SR 254 (Detroit Rd.); west on SR 254; left (south) on Gulf Rd. for 3 miles; on right.

Description This Lorain County club and course, which features lots of ups and downs, may be the best value in golf. Period.

The initiation fee is low here, and the monthly dues are modest, too. It's a handsome club house and there is no housing around the course to detract from the business at hand.

"It's a finesse course," head golf professional Mike Caronchi said of the 1927 design by Harold Paddock. "And there's nothing more fun than playing well on a finesse course. You don't have to be a low-handicap to enjoy the course, but you have to be good to score well. The course idiosyncrasies as well as the small greens make it a shotmakers' delight."

Lots of redesign has been completed here. Architect Brian Huntley, of Canton, did the work. As the pro tries to explain, "Eleven is now 10. Thirteen is now 11. Fourteen is now 12. Thirteen and 14 are new holes."

PRIVATE

TIDYMAN'S TIDBITS #23
Most likely courses for losing balls:
1) Reserve at Thunder Hill
2) Berkshire Hills
3) The back nine at Brunswick Hills
4) The Pine Valley nine at Emerald Woods

Tanglewood Country Club

☎ (440) 543-3191

Area: **Southeast**   City: **Chagrin Falls**   Difficulty: ●●●

Address: 8745 Tanglewood Trail, Chagrin Falls   **Pro:** Jubal Jerik

Tees	Ydg.	C/r	S/r	Pace
Back:	7029	75.8	144	4:10
Middle:	6313	72.4	137	
Forward:	5320	72.6	125	

Directions: I-271 to Exit 27 for US 422; east on US 422; north on SR 306 (Chillicothe Rd.); right (east) on Tanglewood Trail; on right.

Description Of this young (1967) Chagrin Falls layout, Fuzzy Zoeller once said, "Let the rough grow and you could play the Open there." Water is a factor on only a few holes, but No. 1, the 520-yard (blue tee) par 5, is one of them. From the elevated tee, a drive must be long and accurate. Fading too much will find a lake on the right, and hooking even slightly will mean no shot to the green. The hole bends left less than 100 yards out and crosses a stream before running up to an elevated green. Nothing wrong with an opening par, so a driver-short iron (to the water) approach is a good plan.

This hilly course has a wealth of beautiful tees, and No. 8 is one of them. The fairway on this 457-yard par 4 runs down a steep hill to a stream. The shallow green has sand in front, and pin position can make for big trouble. It looks shorter and easier than it is; it's the number one handicap. On a course with a slope of 144 and a course rating of 75.0, you know you'll be facing a challenge. Likely you're getting a stroke here anyhow, so approach with caution.

On the back side, Nos. 16 and 17 are testers. Most players would score better on No. 16, the 238-yard par 3, by laying up. A severely canted fairway and trees down both sides make it hazardous. No. 17, another elevated tee, is a big dogleg right. Few players can cut the corner, filled as it is with tall hardwoods, so the player who wants to be in the money goes down the middle or just a bit left of the tee.

PRIVATE

Public Relations and Golf Courses

Before this fifth edition rolled off the presses, the publisher sent every course, club, or range in the book a copy of their listing, asking that the information be made current.

When the sixth edition comes out a couple years from now, they'll have to be more specific in their request. They weren't asking for any opinions on the writing style; they were asking for data such as hours of operation, prices, yardages, slopes, and names of owners or golf professionals, or any physical improvements, such as new irrigation, and additional services or programs.

It's hard to pick a favorite from some of the responses, but right now I like the note from one indoor-range operator.

Part of the review I wrote reads, "It's a smoking facility. Who wants to go indoors and inhale cigarette smoke? The staff can be rude and price is getting high—$28 per person per hour. The tee is not adjustable, so everyone has to hit from the same height and the same place. If you're a lefty, you have to pull up the carpet and insert the plastic tee for every tee shot. And remove it as soon as you're done before other players trip on it. The booths are too small to hit longer drivers in."

The manager wrote, "Where did this information come from? If this is someone's idea of a joke, I don't appreciate it. Obviously, this portion [of the review] needs to be omitted."

Like many of the notes penned by owners upset with their reviews, this guy must think this book is for owners and operators. It isn't. It's for players. I don't want someone calling me and saying, "Did you know that place is a smoking joint? And I couldn't hit my extra long driver? And I was better treated when I was inducted into the Army?"

I called twice and left my number. The manager has not yet returned the call. I was going to tell him where the information came from: Me. I played there two or three times, inhaled the smoke, banged the head of my extra long driver on the wall, and was treated rudely by the guy at the desk.

One private club, now in its third century of service to Cleveland's old money, has a brief but positive review in the book. But its general manager wrote on the request, "Do Not Publish." Four times. Double-underlined.

I talked briefly with the manager of a resort course who took offense at my reference to Tom Weiskopf. I don't know why. I called Terrible Tom the rudest man in the PGA, and no one has ever argued. He's more than rude. He's a stuck-up, spoiled brat with a history of behavior that sends most kids to the "time out" room. Be that as it may, Weiskopf did a wonderful job creating one of the two layouts at this course, and the review has high praise for his course as well as the other, older course there, designed by Robert VonHagge.

But the manager insisted the verbiage be changed. When I demurred, he said, "Well, we can't endorse this!" Exactly right.

The manager of one executive-length course insisted his listing be taken out and said it was all lies.

Lies? The last time I was at this course, the starter was yelling at me to tee off . . . while a twosome lingered in the landing area. The first hole has been changed a number of times but never marked. The conditioning and maintenance has been spotty at best, nonexistent at worst. No staff member ever exhibited any friendliness or concern.

And all of that is a shame, because from a design standpoint the course is terrific. If it is going to improve, and I hope it will, now is a good time to start. But it's a bad time to call me a liar.

One course's publicist was kind enough to write a new review for me. He wrote, "With the exception of lengthening and shortening a couple of holes to speed play while maintaining its championship caliber integrity, the golf course remains unchanged from its original layout which dates back to the 20s."

Championship caliber integrity? The first hole is a short par 4 and a severe slice can bounce across the street into a culvert. At least one hole was shortened because players kept knocking balls into the back yards of residents, putting their skulls and other body parts in peril. Also, an ill-conceived housing development was plopped in on the back side. So tell me about all the improvements, but don't tell me about "championship caliber integrity," please.

One manager wrote this piece for me: "The secret is out, and if you haven't played at [our course] lately, do so soon."

In the book, I write that the one of the course's nines is ". . . known to some players as The Nine Holes From Hell. Jungle combat experience provides the best training for this nine . . . the terrain is hilly and best covered by Jeep. The woods get thick enough at times for inexperienced players to need directions to the next tee. Many pack sandwiches and leave a trail of crumbs."

The manager rewrote it for me: "[The course] is tight, with rolling terrain. It requires placement shots as the driver rarely comes out of the bag."

Thanks, but I'll go with what I got after playing there.

The manager of a country club asked, "Do you want one of our pros to write it for you?" He could have been more insulting, but only if he was blowing cigar smoke in my face at the time.

Here's the situation: I try to write a book that will be factual, accurate, and timely. And I write it with a single audience in mind: men and women who play golf. I love it when someone tells me, "you described that course perfectly" That's what I'm supposed to do.

Twin Lakes Country Club   ☎ (330) 673-6665
Area: **Far South**   City: **Kent**   Difficulty: ● ● ●

Address: 1519 Overlook Rd., Kent   **Pro:** Tony Guerreri

Tees	Ydg.	C/r	S/r	Pace
Middle:		70.9	125	
Forward:		73.2	124	

Directions: I-480 to SR 14 east in Streetsboro (I-480 ends here); right (south) on SR 43 (Cleveland-Canton Rd.); left (east) on Overlook Rd.; on right.

Description An invitation to this club means mystery, mystery, mystery! The assistant manager refuses to talk about the club or the course, and swears she can't find a scorecard. That's club life in a college town.

Walden Golf & Tennis Club   ☎ (330) 562-7145
Area: **Southeast**   City: **Aurora**   Difficulty: ● ● ●

Address: 700 Bissell Rd., Aurora   **Pro:** Mitch Camp, PGA

Tees	Ydg.	C/r	S/r	Pace
Back:	6979	74.4	134	3:59
Middle:	6358	71.2	130	
Forward:	5609	72.4	125	

Directions: I-480 to Exit 36 for SR 82; east on SR 82; right (south) on Bissell Rd.; on right.

PRIVATE

Description At Walden, a wonderful course originally designed by William Mitchell (who also did Tanglewood) has been redesigned by Craig Schreiner Co., out of Kansas City, Missouri, and the results are so good many members will think they're playing a magnificent new course.

They are.

Head golf professional Mitch Camp smiles broadly as he brags about his course: "The entire course was redesigned," he said. "All 72 tee boxes—four on every hole, bunkers redone and 60 new bunkers put in, drainage and shaping reworked ..." The list is a long one.

New course records will be shot this season. The old record was shot by Doug Hauenstein, who shot a 64 from the championship tees and a 63 from the member tees. The old championship course measured 6,954 yards. This season, it's 7,192. The member tees used to be 6,390 and are now 6,663.

The work was done, the pro said, because the course was getting old and showing its age. The old course had three sets of tees; the new has four. The irrigation was improved and it will mean a difference in both playability and maintenance.

No. 18, which used to be a blind tee shot, has been reworked. "The fairway was mounded and you couldn't see the ball land," Camp said. "We took four feet off the fairway and moved it back to build up the tee by four or five feet."

Westwood Country Club ☎ (440) 331-3016
Area: **West**   City: **Rocky River**   Difficulty: ●●●

Address: 22625 Detroit Rd., Rocky River   **Pro:** John Sico, PGA

Tees	Ydg.	C/r	S/r	Pace
Back:	6626	73.1	131	3:53
Middle:	6349	71.5	128	
Forward:	5265	66.7	124	

Directions: I-90 westbound to Exit 160 for Clague Rd.; south on Clague; left (east) on Detroit Rd. (SR 254); on right.

OR I-90 eastbound to Exit 161 for Detroit Rd.; right (west) on Detroit; on left.

Description   Who better to advise guests at this West Side club than Gary Eckert, nine-time (and current) champion? The champ never tires of winning, though he says, "Sometimes I feel funny that people might think, 'Is that all he does? Play golf?'" Not at all. He's an accountant.

"Westwood is a fair golf course with no trouble," Mr. Eckert says. "Everyone I know who's played likes it. They think they can tear it up and then can't figure out why they don't score better."

It's not overly long, but it plays a bit longer than rookies think. The adrenaline pump doesn't start until the tee at No. 4. This 183-yard par 3 is moderately long, but it's merciless. "You have to carry the ravine, and if you're going to miss the green, miss on the right," the champ advises. The bottomless pit on the left means almost no shot. When guest Paul Murphy aced the hole a few years ago, he was asked what he used. "Nerves of steel," he said modestly.

TIDYMAN'S TIDBITS #24

Courses with front sides so different from back sides it's hard to believe they're related:

1) Painesville
2) Brandywine
3) Brunswick Hills

PRIVATE

Driving Ranges

Airport Greens Driving Range

Area: **East**   City: **Willoughby Hills**   ☎ **(440) 944-6164**

Address: 28980 White Rd., Willoughby Hills
Tees: 60 **Grass:** 60 **Lighted:** 60 **Covered:** 0
Specials: Plan 1: 10 small $45/reg. $50; Plan 2: 10 large $85/reg. $100; Plan 3: 20 large $165/reg $200
Season: Apr 1–Nov 30 **Hours:** 6 a.m.–10 p.m. **Practice facil:** Range, Putting Green, Chipping Green, Miniature golf **Clubhouse:** Food, Beer, Liquor **Lessons:** Available
Directions: I-90 to Exit 187 for Bishop Rd. in Willoughby Hills; south on Bishop Rd. left (east) on White Rd.; on right.

Azar's New Falls Pro Shop & Golf Range

Area: **Far South**   City: **Cuyahoga Falls**   ☎ **(330) 929-2573**

Address: 3873 Wyoga Lake Rd., Cuyahoga Falls
Tees: 70 **Grass:** 50 **Lighted:** 0 **Covered:** 12
Season: Mar–Sept **Hours:** 11 a.m.–7:30 p.m. **Practice facil:** Range, Chipping Green
Lessons: Available
Directions: I-271 to Exit 18 for SR 8; south on SR 8; west on Steels Corners Rd.; left (south) on Wyoga Lake Rd.; on left. OR SR 8 north to Steels Corners Rd.; west on Steels Corners; left (south) on Wyoga Lake Rd.; on left.

Benko's Driving Range

Area: **Far West**   City: **Elyria**   ☎ **(440) 458-4386**

Address: 10364 Middle Ave., Elyria
Tees: 20 **Grass:** 20 **Lighted:** 0 **Covered:** 0
Specials: Senior specials
Season: Year-round **Hours:** 8:00 a.m.–dark **Practice facil:** Range, Putting Green, Chipping Green, Sand, Club repair available; authorized Ping fitting center.
Clubhouse: Lessons: Available
Directions: I-480 to Exit 1A for SR 10 (I-480 west ends here); west on SR 10 (merges with US 20) to exit for Lagrange Rd.; south on Lagrange; left (east) on Butternut Ridge Rd.; left (north) on Middle Ave.; on left after Elyria Airport.

Brookpark Golf Range

Area: **South**   City: **Parma**   ☎ **(216) 351-2239**

Address: 8707 Brookpark Rd., Parma
Tees: 60 **Grass:** 20 **Lighted:** 60 **Covered:** 6
Season: Year-round **Hours:** 7 a.m.–11 p.m.; call for winter hours
Practice facil: Range, Chipping Green, miniature golf, target on range
is a 30-foot-high golf ball, covered tees are heated
Clubhouse: Food, Beer, Dairy bar, Game room
Lessons: Available **Pro:** Derek Smith
Directions: I-480 to Exit 15 for Ridge Rd. (SR 3); south on Ridge;
right (west) on Brookpark Rd.; 1/2 mile on left.

Buzzard Cove Driving Range

Area: **South**   City: **Hinckley**   ☎ **(330) 278-2384; (216) 831-6650 off season**

Address: 1053 Bellus Rd., Hinckley
Tees: 25 **Grass:** 0 **Lighted:** 25 **Covered:** 12
Season: Apr–Oct (weather permitting) **Hours:** 10 a.m.–8 p.m. spring; 10 a.m.–11
p.m. summer **Practice facil:** Putting Green, Targets on range, 5 elevated greens on
range: 60 yds, 100 yds, 130 yds, 160 yds, 200 yds, with sand traps, 36 hi-tech miniature
golf holes **Clubhouse:** Food**Lessons:** Available **Pro:** Joe Williams
Directions: I-71 to Exit 226 for SR 303; east on SR 303; right (south) on Stony Hill Rd.;
left (east) on Bellus Rd.; at intersection of Bellus Rd. and Hinckley Hills Rd. (SR 606).

Decile's Driving Range

Area: **East**   City: **Highland Hills**   ☎ **(216) 464-9256**

Address: 4201 Green Rd., Highland Hills
Tees: 70 **Grass:** 35 **Lighted:** 0 **Covered:** 0
Season: Mar 12–Nov 15 **Hours:** 8:30 a.m.–10 p.m. **Practice facil:** Range, Putting
Green, Chipping Green, Sand **Clubhouse:** Pavilion, Miniature golf
Lessons: Available **Pro:** Bob Hamrich
Directions: I-271 to Exit 29 for Chagrin Blvd./US 422; west on Chagrin;
left (south) on Green Rd.; on left.

Downview Sports Center

Area: **Far South**   City: **Cuyahoga Falls**   ☎ **(330) 971-8418**

Address: 1617 Bailey Rd., Cuyahoga Falls
Tees: 32 **Grass:** 25 **Lighted:** 15 **Covered:** 15
Specials: Senior specials available
Season: Mar-Dec **Hours:** Memorial Day–Labor Day: 11 a.m.–11 p.m. Mon–Fri,
8 a.m.–11 p.m. Sat, Sun; Sep–Oct 10 a.m.–8 p.m.; Nov–Dec & Mar–May 11 a.m.–7 p.m.
Practice facil: Range, no grass tees (astroturf); 10 heated tees **Clubhouse:** Food,
Pavilion, (refreshments available)**Lessons:** Available **Pro:** Steve Black
Directions: I-271 to Exit 18 for SR 8; south on SR 8; left (east) on Howe Ave.;
"soft" left (north) on Bailey at six-point intersection; on right, after Kennedy Blvd.

RANGES

Firestone Driving Range
Area: **Far South**   City: **Akron**   ☎ **(330) 724-4444**

Address: 600 Swartz Rd., Akron
Tees: 30 **Grass:** 15 **Lighted:** 30 **Covered:** 10
Season: Year-round **Hours:** Summer: 7 a.m.–10 p.m.; winter: 10 a.m.–8 p.m.
Practice facil: Putting Green **Clubhouse:** Food, Beer, Liquor, Dining room, Pavilion,
50-seat grill Lessons: Available **Pro:** Rick Schmidt
Directions: I-277 to Exit 3 for S. Main St.; south on S. Main; east on Swartz Rd.
(Swartz is directly opposite eastbound exit for S. Main); on right.

Forest Hills Golf Center
Area: **Far West**   City: **Elyria**   ☎ **(440) 323-2632**

Address: 41971 Oberlin Rd. (US 20), Elyria
Tees: 20 **Grass:** 20 **Lighted:** 0 **Covered:** 0
Season: Mar 14–Dec 30, weather permitting **Hours:** 7 a.m.–sunset
Practice facil: Range, Putting Green, Chipping Green **Clubhouse:** Food, Beer,
Liquor, Pavilion **Lessons:** Available **Pro:** Thomas S. Porter, PGA
Directions: I-480 west to end; becomes SR 10; west on SR 10 (merges with
US 20 and SR 301) to exit for Lagrange Rd.; right (north) on Lagrange; left (west)
on Butternut Ridge Rd.; right (north) on Oberlin-Elyria Rd.; on right.

Golden Tee Golf Range
Area: **West**   City: **Olmsted Falls**   ☎ **(440) 235-9115**

Address: 27153 Bagley Rd., Olmsted Falls
Tees: 38 **Grass:** 29 **Lighted:** 38 **Covered:** 4
Specials: Senior specials Mon–Fri open–4 p.m.
Season: Mar 1–Oct 31; Nov–Feb weather permitting **Hours:** Summer, 11 a.m.–10
p.m.; spring & fall, noon–dusk **Practice facil:** Range, Putting Green, Chipping Green,
Sand, Target greens **Clubhouse: Lessons:** Available **Pro:** Bob Reid
Directions: I-480 to Exit 3 for Stearns Rd.; south on Stearns to Bagley Rd.;
on southwest corner at Stearns & Bagley.

RANGES

Golf Dome
Area: **Southeast**   City: **Chagrin Falls**   ☎ **(440) 543-1211**

Address: 8198 Washington St., Chagrin Falls
Tees: 34 **Grass:** 0 **Lighted:** 34 **Covered:** 34
Specials: Junior (18 and under) specials Mon–Fri;
Senior specials 9:30 a.m.–5 p.m. Mon–Fri
Season: Year-round **Hours:** 9:30 a.m.–9:30 p.m.; Sat–Sun "prime time" 9:30 a.m.–
9:30 p.m. **Practice facil:** Range, Putting Green, Chipping Green, Sand, Target Greens,
Distance Meters **Clubhouse:** Food, Vending machines Lessons: Available
Pro: Jim Chapman
Directions: I-271 to Exit 27 for US 422; east on US 422 to SR 306; left (north) on SR
306; left (west) on E. Washington St. for 1/2 mile; on right, behind Chagrin Cinemas.

Description There is no snack bar here, but just about everything else golfers need to keep the ol' swing lubed is: clubs, balls, putters, gloves, sweatshirts, wind shirts, towels … and an indoor range of the first order. For $15, your swing can be videotaped and analyzed by one of three teaching professionals. In the middle of a long Northeast Ohio winter, what better treat than to have a golf pro focus on your cut? The video also uses a microwave measuring device that locks in on the spin, direction, and velocity, so you know what the ball would have done had it plowed through the ceiling. Rates are charged by time, not buckets: $6.50 per half hour, an extra buck on weekends. Seniors and juniors can play for $5.25 per half hour, but only until 5 p.m. on weekdays. About 35 percent of the patrons are women. No membership fee, no reservations.

Golfer's Inn

Area: **South**   City: **Hinckley**   ☎ **(330) 225-9933**

> **Address:** 1429 W. 130 St., Hinckley
> **Tees:** 24 **Grass:** 12 **Lighted:** 0 **Covered:** 0
> **Season:** Year-round **Hours:** Sunrise–sunset **Practice facil:** Range **Clubhouse:** Food, Beer, Liquor, Volleyball, Horseshoes Lessons: Available **Pro:** Tim Monroe
> **Directions:** I-71 to Exit 226 for SR 303; east on SR 303;
> right (south) on W. 130 St.; on left.

Highlander Golf & Tennis

Area: **Far South**   City: **Akron**   ☎ **(330) 867-5664**

> **Address:** 2782 Ridgewood Rd., Akron
> **Tees:** 38 **Grass:** 20 **Lighted:** 38 **Covered:** 28
> **Season:** Year-round **Hours:** Summer: 9 a.m.–10 p.m.; winter: 9 a.m.–6 p.m.
> **Practice facil:** Range, 12 heated tees **Clubhouse: Lessons:** Available
> **Directions:** I-77 to Exit 133 for Ridgewood/Miller Rds.; west on Ridgewood; on left.

Hillcrest Golf Range

Area: **Far West**   City: **Avon**   ☎ **(440) 937-6622**

> **Address:** 32575 Detroit Rd. (SR 254), Avon
> **Tees:** 35 **Grass:** 20 **Lighted:** 0 **Covered:** 0
> **Specials:** Weekday specials Mon–Fri 11 a.m.–1 p.m.; Ladies specials Tue
> **Season:** Mar–Oct **Hours:** 9:30 a.m.–sunset **Practice facil:** Putting Green, Chipping Green, Miniature golf **Clubhouse:** Food, Vending machines
> **Lessons:** Available **Pro:** Omar Jonas
> **Directions:** I-90 to Exit 156 for Crocker Rd./Bassett Rd.;
> south on Crocker; right (west) on Detroit Rd. (SR 254); on left.

Description Why they call this Hillcrest is not clear. No hills, ergo, no crest. But for practicing the swing, this old-fashioned range is one of the best. The small shack has a few clubs, a cash register, and a television set.

Mostly grass tees, and greenery all around. It's quiet. No distractions except songbirds. The best value on the West Side. If only the quality of the turf was improved.

Hol-Hi Driving Range

Area: **Far South**   City: **Akron**   ☎ **(330) 644-9815**

Address: 81 Vaughn Rd., Akron
Tees: 27 **Grass:** 10 **Lighted:** 27 **Covered:** 0
Season: Mar–Dec **Hours:** 8 a.m.–9 p.m. **Practice facil:** Range, Putting Green, Chipping Green, Sand **Clubhouse:** Food, Beer, Dining room
Lessons: Free group lesson with large bucket of balls. **Pro:** Mike Kosar
Directions: I-77 to exit for I-277; I-277 to Exit 3 for S. Main St.; south on S. Main; right (west) on Vaughn Rd.; on right.

Lost Nation Sports Park

Area: **East**   City: **Willoughby**   ☎ **(440) 602-4000**

Address: 38630 Jet Center Dr., Willoughby
Tees: 8 **Grass:** 0 **Lighted:** 0 **Covered:** 0
Specials: Senior specials Mon–Fri 8 a.m.–4 p.m.
Season: Year-round **Hours:** Daily 8 a.m.–midnight **Practice facil:** Range
Clubhouse: Food, Beer, Liquor **Lessons:** Available **Pro:** Amy Herrick
Directions: SR 2 to Lost Nation Rd.; north on Lost Nation; right (east) on Jet Center Dr. after Lost Nation Airport.

Mr. Divot's Driving Range

Area: **South**   City: **North Royalton**   ☎ **(440) 237-2226**

Address: 13393 York Rd., North Royalton
Tees: 50 **Grass:** 20 **Lighted:** 30 **Covered:** 0
Specials: Senior specials
Season: Year-round **Hours:** 9 a.m.–11 p.m. in summer; varies with weather **Practice facil:** Range, 18-hole miniature golf, 8 batting cages, sand volleyball **Clubhouse:** Food, Beer, Liquor, Dining room, Patio **Lessons:** Available **Pro:** Corey Brayer
Directions: I-71 to Exit 231 for SR 82 (Royalton Rd.); east on SR 82; left (north) on York Rd.; on right.

RANGES

TIDYMAN'S TIDBITS #25
Cliffside Tee Boxes:
1) Nos. 8 & 18 at Astorhurst
2) No. 15 at Brandywine
3) No. 17 at Tanglewood

The Oaks

Area: **Southwest**   City: **Columbia Station**   ☎ **(440) 236-5060**

> **Address:** 24240 Royalton Rd. (SR 82), Columbia Station
> **Tees:** 80 **Grass:** 50 **Lighted:** 40 **Covered:** 24
> **Specials:** Bucket passes available
> **Season:** Year-round **Hours:** Vary; call ahead **Practice facil:** Range, Putting Green, Chipping Green, Sand, Custom club repair available; Lighted & heated tees
> **Clubhouse:** Food**Lessons:** Available **Pro:** Frank DiSanto, PGA
> **Directions:** I-71 to Exit 231 for SR 82 (Royalton Rd.); west on SR 82; on right.

Description If the temperature is above 30 but still too cold to play, the heated stalls at this range are an acceptable compromise. In each stall is a map detailing the number of yards to the target flags. You can try every stick in the bag here. The quality of the range balls is notably high.

Pine Valley Sports

Area: **Far South**   City: **Akron**   ☎ **(330) 928-2669**

> **Address:** 1870 Akron-Peninsula Rd., Akron
> **Tees:** 65 **Grass:** 40 **Lighted:** 65 **Covered:** 10
> **Specials:** Senior specials available
> **Season:** Mar–Dec **Hours:** 8 a.m.–6 p.m. winter; 6 a.m.–10 p.m. summer
> **Practice facil:** Range, Putting Green, Chipping Green, Sand **Clubhouse:** Food, Beer
> **Lessons:** Available **Pro:** Brian Unk
> **Directions:** I-77 to Exit 138 for Ghent Rd.; west on Ghent; right (east) on Yellow Creek Rd. under I-77; right (east) on W. Bath Rd.; right (south) on Akron-Peninsula Rd.; on right.

The Practice Greens at Bobick's

Area: **East**   City: **Willoughby**   ☎ **(440) 942-4051**

> **Address:** 38882 Mentor Ave., Willoughby
> **Tees:** 80 **Grass:** 50 **Lighted:** 80 **Covered:** 30
> **Season:** Year-round **Hours:** Summer: 9 a.m.–10 p.m.; winter: 9 a.m.–6 p.m.
> **Practice facil:** Range, Putting Green, Chipping Green, Sand, 30 heated tees
> **Clubhouse: Lessons:** Available **Pro:** Joe Whelan
> **Directions:** I-90 to Exit 190 for SR 306; north on SR 306 to Mentor Ave. (US 20); left (west) on US 20 for 3/4 mile; on left.

RANGES

Description The practice range at Bobick's Pro Shop in Willoughby goes where driving ranges have never before gone. On a series of grass tees, players look out to multiple greens, broad fairways, and swaying trees. It looks much more like a golf course than a range.

"I don't even like to call it a driving range, because that brings up the image of somebody just getting up there beating balls," owner George Brown says. Between the multiple tees are practice sand traps. Behind the tee boxes is a grove of tall trees. The trees serve as a buffer against highway noise. For people serious about their games, an annual membership fee of $450 allows unlimited practice on a restricted tee.

The facility was designed by Arthur Hills Associates and built by McCurach Construction—both Florida firms—but it was Brown's idea. He is delighted when equipment reps visit the store, inspect the range, and tell him "I've never seen anything like it."

In addition to the grass tees, Bobick's also has covered mats with natural-gas heaters for year-round practice. Brown has 180,000 golf balls in use there.

Pro Tour Indoor Golf

Area: **Southwest**   City: **Middleburg Hts.**   ☎ **(440) 243-5055**

> **Address:** 18330 Bagley Rd., Middleburg Hts.
> **Tees:** 20 **Grass:** 0 **Lighted:** 0 **Covered:** 0
> **Specials:** Senior specials Mon–Fri 8 a.m.–6 p.m.; Gift certificates available
> **Season:** Year-round **Hours:** 8 a.m.–midnight **Practice facil:** Range
> **Clubhouse:** Food, Beer, Liquor Lessons: Available
> **Directions:** I-71 to exit for Bagley Rd.; west on Bagley; 1/2 mile on right.

Description Thanks to interactive golf, winter's icy grip no longer seems so cruel. Players, bags of clubs clutched to their chests, bow to the wind as they walk from the parking lot to this indoor club. Once inside, the weather becomes a non-issue.

There are six golf simulators at this club, and 20 courses are available, among them Troon North, Banff, Harbour Town, Torrey Pines, and Pebble Beach.

It's a smoking facility. Who wants to go indoors and inhale cigarette smoke? The staff can be rude and the price is getting high—$28 per person per hour. The tee is not adjustable, so everyone has to hit from the same height and the same place. If you're a lefty, you have to pull up the carpet and insert the plastic tee for every tee shot. And remove it as soon as you're done before other players trip on it. The booths are too small to hit longer drivers in.

The Range at Avon

Area: **Far West**   City: **Avon**   ☎ **(440) 937-9464**

> **Address:** 1325 Center Rd. (SR 83), Avon
> **Tees:** 140 **Grass:** 100 **Lighted:** 140 **Covered:** 40
> **Specials:** Frequent player program available: up to 35% discount available for buying balls in advance; Lunch special Mon–Fri 11 a.m.–3 p.m.
> **Season:** Year-round **Hours:** Summer hours: daily 8 a.m.–10 p.m.; winter hours: daily 9 a.m.–9 p.m. **Practice facil:** Range, Putting Green, Chipping Green, Sand, Short game area, fully lit, with 3 bunkers and 4 greens **Clubhouse:** Food, Beer, Liquor, Dining room **Lessons:** Available **Pro:** Mark Weitendorf
> **Directions:** I-90 to Exit 153 for SR 83; north on SR 83 (Center Rd.); on right.

RANGES

Description There's nothing like family. The Range at Avon is the sister of the Range at Boston Hills, where heated stalls, grass tees, and target greens make practice almost as much fun as playing. At both ranges, top-of-the-line irons and woods are available for demo purposes, so if you always wondered if it's possible to buy a game, here's your chance to find out. The West Side facility offers more heated stalls: 40 compared to the East Side's 29. There are 100 grass tees. There is also a chipping green, putting green, and sand. Best of all is the super-duper basket holding 180 balls! Arriving for night practice is fun—from a distance, the lighted greens look like an alien landing.

The Range at Boston Hills Country Club
Area: **South**   City: **Hudson**   ☎ **(330) 463-7888**

Address: 124 E. Hines Hill Rd., Hudson
Tees: 100 **Grass:** 70 **Lighted:** 100 **Covered:** 30
Specials: Frequent-player program: up to 37% discount for buying balls in advance
Season: Year-round; tees are individually heated in winter **Hours:** 7 a.m.–10 p.m. summer; 8 a.m.–9 p.m. winter **Practice facil:** Range, Putting Green, Chipping Green, Sand, Landscaped, laser-measured target greens; Tee markers to each target area; 30 heated tees **Clubhouse:** Food, Beer, Liquor, Dining room, Club repair
Lessons: Available **Pro:** Ron Burke, PGA
Directions: I-271 to Exit 18 for SR 8; south on SR 8; right (west) on E. Hines Hill Rd.; on right. OR, Ohio Turnpike (I-80) to exit 12, 1/4 mile north, turn left at E. Hines Hill Rd.

Description Building a range has traditionally involved shooing the cows away, planting a few colored pennants, and tossing down some mats. As the golf market grows more sophisticated, however, that approach is being left behind. Way behind.

The new practice facility located next to Boston Hills Golf Course is special enough to qualify for proper noun status: The Range. The Range features more than 80 natural grass tees and 30 covered and heated tees. Five target greens lie before players. More than 400 laser measurements went into yardage compilations (yardage is measured to each target and is listed at the tees).

One of many inspirations is the replica of the infamous No. 17 at Sawgrass, the island hole that frustrates Tour players.

The practice greens—there are two totaling 13,000 square feet—can be more difficult than the greens on the nearby course.

The Golfer's Prayer of Forgiveness

Slices...

George R. Plagenz was one of the *Cleveland Press*'s best writers, and his beat, religion, was never covered in such a down-to-earth manner by anyone else. Plagenz, whose degree came from Harvard Divinity School, understood better than any religion writer before or since that God is in the details.

It was Plagenz who set the faithful on their haunches when he began rating church services, giving so many stars for sermon, so many for music, etc. He took heat when he led a service for a dead cat, comforting the late cat's companion, a little girl whose heart was broken.

In the *Press* city room, Plagenz's desk was next to Bus Bergen's, and if ever there was a yin and yang in that place, that was it. Plagenz was quick to smile and fascinated with human nature; when Bergen smiled, it was sardonic, and because he rarely had high hopes for mankind, he was rarely disappointed.

It figures—doesn't it?—that the two men would get along very, very well.

Anyway, I once asked Plagenz to write a prayer for golfers. Here is what he sent:

Forgive me, O Lord, if Sunday morning finds me at the golf course and not in church. Forgive me if I find You not in prayers and hymns but in Your great and glorious outdoors, more magnificent than any cathedral.

My prayers to You on Sunday morning may be unspoken and my hymns to You unsung, but my heart will be always praising You for the beauty of the earth, for spacious skies, for the joys of comradeship, and for this funny little game we play.

Bless my driving and my putting. Direct the ball into the bunker only for my opponent's shots. (If to ask this is unworthy of me, forgive me this, too.)

Amen.

ing Range

☎ (440) 232-7184

d., Bedford
ed: 29 **Covered:** 0
or groups
Hours: Sunrise–10 p.m.; Autumn, sunrise–sunset
utting Green, Chipping Green **Clubhouse:** Food, Beer,
Club repair **Lessons:** Available **Pro:** Jeff Staker
Directions: I-77 to Exit 153 for Pleasant Valley Pkwy.; east on Pleasant Valley (becomes Alexander Rd.); left (north) on Dunham Rd; right (east) on Egbert Rd.; on left.

Silver Tee Driving Range
Area: **West**   City: **Westlake**   ☎ **(440) 871-9225**

Address: 29300 Center Ridge Rd., Westlake
Tees: 70 **Grass:** 30 **Lighted:** 70 **Covered:** 20
Season: Apr 1–Nov 1 **Hours:** 8 a.m.–10 p.m.; Autumn hours: 11:30 a.m.–7 p.m.
Practice facil: Clubhouse: Food, Miniature golf **Lessons:** Available
Directions: I-90 to Exit 156 for Crocker-Bassett Rds.; south on Crocker; left (east) on Center Ridge Rd.; on left, opposite Porter Rd.

Southwest Golf Center
Area: **Southwest**   City: **Berea**   ☎ **(440) 234-3034**

Address: 1005 W. Bagley Rd., Berea
Tees: 60 **Grass:** 32 **Lighted:** 60 **Covered:** 12
Specials: Senior specials
Season: Mar–Oct **Hours:** 9 a.m.–11 p.m. (summer)
Practice facil: Range, 19-hole championship putting course; 3 lighted targets
Clubhouse: Dairy Queen-Brazier **Lessons:** Available **Pro:** John Kennedy
Directions: I-71 to Exit 235 for Bagley Rd.; west on Bagley (becomes W. Bagley); on left.

Description You can get a lot of golf in at this pro shop/driving range/ custard stand/miniature golf/teaching facility. Lessons are offered by PGA members and go for $25 per half hour. Speaking of lessons, owner Dick Straub says, "Women students are on the increase, and juniors, too, both boys and girls." The driving range here has a unique feature: lighted target greens.

RANGES

Sports Haven
Area: **Far East**   City: **Novelty**   ☎ **(440) 338-5301**

Address: 9887 Kinsman Rd. (SR 87), Novelty
Tees: 45 **Grass:** 30 **Lighted:** 45 **Covered:** 0
Season: Apr–Nov **Hours:** 8 a.m.–dark **Practice facil:**
Lessons: Not available
Directions: I-271 to Exit 29 for SR 87 (Chagrin Blvd.); east on SR 87
(becomes Kinsman Rd.); 3 miles of SR 306, on left.

Strongsville Golf Center
Area: **Southwest**   City: **Strongsville**   ☎ **(440) 238-6443**

Address: 15919 Pearl Rd. (US 42), Strongsville
Tees: 60 **Grass:** 40 **Lighted:** 60 **Covered:** 10
Specials: Senior discount with Buckeye card
Season: Year-round **Hours:** Summer: 9 a.m.–11 p.m.; Winter: noon–8 p.m. Mon–Fri, 10
a.m.–8 p.m. Sat, Sun **Practice facil:** Range, Sand, Target greens **Clubhouse:** 18-hole
miniature golf, 2 indoor simulators Lessons: Available **Pro:** Brad Ruminski
Directions: I-71 to Exit 231 for SR 82/Royalton Rd.; west on SR 82;
south on Pearl Rd. (US 42); on left.

Tiny Pines Golf Center
Area: **Far West**   City: **Elyria**   ☎ **(440) 324-4052**

Address: 6604 Lake Ave., Elyria
Tees: 17 **Grass:** 10 **Lighted:** 0 **Covered:** 0
Specials: Senior specials
Season: Mar–Dec **Hours:** 10 a.m.-dusk **Practice facil:** Range, Putting Green,
Chipping Green, Miniature golf **Clubhouse: Lessons:** Available **Pro:** Kevin Lukz
Directions: I-90 to Exit 145 for SR 57 (Lorain Blvd.); south on SR 57;
right (west) on Griswold Rd.; right (north) on Lake Ave.; on left.

Description A Mom-and-Pop place: a place for lessons, practice, and
custom clubs. Nothing fancy. The Elyria range has 17 stalls, some adjacent grass tees, and a pitching and chipping green.

RANGES

Valley View Dome & Golf Center
Area: **South**   City: **Valley View**   ☎ **(216) 573-4990**

Address: 6060 West Canal Rd., Valley View
Tees: 176 **Grass:** **Lighted:** 176 **Covered:** 176
Season: Year-round **Hours:** Daily 9 a.m.–10 p.m. **Practice facil:** Range,
Putting Green, Chipping Green, Sand, Both outside and inside the dome.
Clubhouse: Lessons: Available **Pro:** Jeff Hogge
Directions: I-77 to Exit 155 for Rockside Rd.; east on Rockside;
left (north) on Canal Rd.; on left.

Description From the nearby I-480 bridge, it looks like a moon-sized golf ball from outer space plugged in the rough near the Ohio Canal. This unique training facility has a fiber roof supported by air, 80 feet high in the center of the round structure, 320 feet in diameter.

Inside are almost five dozen hitting stations on two levels, a sand hazard, and a putting green. For players who want lessons, a wide selection is available.

Hitting a ball under the dome feels strange at first, but once a few balls have been driven into the fabric wall—a hundred yards away—the dome's value as a practice facility becomes evident. There is just enough space between tee and wall to see where the ball is going.

The facility is for players of all abilities.

At various times 80 lighted outdoor tees can be used for practice. A two-tiered deck has 40 hitting stations below featuring mats and synthetic grass and 40 upper-level stations with individual mats. Inside the dome, 57 lighted tee stations, with mats, are available.

West Pines Golf Range

Area: **Far West**   City: **Avon**   ☎ **(440) 871-1414**

Address: 34455 Chester Rd., Avon
Tees: 116 **Grass:** 70 **Lighted:** 20 **Covered:** 20
Specials: Lunchtime special Mon–Fri until 2 p.m.
Season: Mar 1–Nov 1 **Hours:** 8 a.m.–10 p.m. **Practice facil:** Range,
Putting Green **Clubhouse:** Custom club fitting and repair
Lessons: Available **Pro:** Bob Barto and Jerry Boykin
Directions: I-90 to Exit 153 for SR 83; north on SR 83 (Center Rd.); SR 83 will turn right, then left; instead of turning left, go straight on Chester Rd.; on right.

Westlawn Golf Range

Area: **Far South**   City: **Akron**   ☎ **(330) 836-0011**

Address: 1423 Collier Rd., Akron
Tees: 50 **Grass:** 40 **Lighted:** 0 **Covered:** 8
Specials: Summer & winter specials
Season: Year-round **Hours:** 9:00 a.m.–sunset **Practice facil:** Range, Putting Green,
Chipping Green, Sand, 2 heated tees **Clubhouse: Lessons:** Available
Directions: I-77 to Exit 131 for Copley Rd.; west on Copley; left (south) on Collier Rd.; on right.

RANGES

Golf Organizations

Blue Tee Golfer
8304 Dogwood Ln., Cleveland • Phone: (440) 779-5311

Blue Tee Golfer helps companies, charities, and other groups plan golf outings and fundraisers. They also sponsor the Blue Tee Classic, one of the larger public golf tournaments in Northern Ohio. (It is held from June through the end of September, rotating among various courses.) A newsletter that goes out to members contains updates on tournaments, golf resort and travel package information, and golf discount advertising. The services of Blue Tee Golfer are also available to individuals.

Executive Women's Golf League
P.O. Box 31704, Independence • Phone: (216) 999-9664

The Executive Women's Golf League (EWG) was formed to help women take up the game of golf, network with other female executives, and learn how to make the game an effective tool for business and personal success.

The Cleveland chapter, formed in 1992 with 80 members playing at Sweetbriar Golf Club, was the first chapter formed outside of Florida, where the league was established in 1991. Now, the EWG has more than 500 Northeast Ohio members, with chapters in Cleveland, Akron, Canton, and Youngstown. Cleveland members tee it up at Pine Hills, Pine Ridge, The Links, and Highland; Akron members play at Boston Hills and Mayfair; Canton members play at Clearview and Tam O'Shanter.

Regular league season membership ($100) includes local and national membership in the EWG, weekly handicap calculations, monthly events, and prizes during the season. Off-season activities include golf-related networking events and educational programs. The membership fee does not include weekly greens or cart fees.

League members are expected to attend regularly scheduled play for the entire season. National members receive EWG's national newsletter, *From Tee to Green*; all members receive Northeast Ohio EWG's newsletter, *The Clubhouse*.

Trying to get through to the organization, however, is not as easy as it should be. Numerous messages left for the executive director and other officers are ignored and left unanswered.

Inter-Club Public Golf Association
3959 Walter Rd., North Olmsted • Phone: (440) 779-1923

The Inter-Club Public Golf Association (ICPGA) serves public golfers and golf groups by sponsoring a regular series of tournaments at public and private courses throughout the season.

All golfers 18 years of age or older are welcome to participate. Events use both gross and net scores by class. A nominal entry fee covers prizes and an optional skin game. Greens fees are collected on the day of play; cart fees vary from course to course. For dates, advance tee time reservations, and general information, call the "Reservation Hotline" at (440) 954-4069.

ICPGA annual membership is $5. Handicap service and a monthly newsletter are also available for $5 and $7, respectively. To request information and a membership application, or to obtain a free sample copy of the newsletter, send a self-addressed, stamped envelope to the above address.

Northern Ohio Golf Association
10210 Brecksville Rd., Brecksville • Phone: (440) 838-8733

The Northern Ohio Golf Association (NOGA), founded in 1917, provides administrative support to its members, 50 private golf clubs around the area. It is also the area liaison for several national golf-related associations, including the United States Golf Association. As the USGA designee for Northeast Ohio, NOGA maintains unified handicapping, course, slope, and pace ratings, and oversees the rules and officiating for USGA tournaments. It also sponsors a variety of special tournaments and events, in addition to hosting seminars for golf course managers and pros. It publishes *NOGA Fairways*, a quarterly magazine. Information about NOGA is available on the Internet at www.noga.org, or via email at noga@usga.org.

Northern Ohio PGA
38121 Euclid Ave., Willoughby • Phone: (440) 951-4546

The Northern Ohio PGA (NOPGA) organizes and sponsors tournaments for PGA professionals from area country clubs and public courses. The series of tournaments runs from mid-April through October. Play is scheduled for every Monday and rotates among area courses. The NOPGA provides no services to other golfers except an invitation to watch the area pros.

Ohio Golf Association
4701 Olentangy River Rd. #200-A, Columbus • Phone: (614) 457-8169

The Ohio Golf Association sponsors and promotes five tournaments each year for the 157 private golf clubs in its membership. The premier

OTHER

event is their Amateur Championship, scheduled every July. In June, there is a junior tournament; the seniors' championship is held in September. Inaugurated in 1997 is the Senior Amateur Championship for golfers over 55 with handicaps under 7.

Ohio Golf Course Owners Association

6478 Fiesta Dr., Columbus • Phone: (800) 761-4394

The Ohio Golf Course Owners Association serves more than 275 member courses throughout the state by helping course owners and managers improve their golf operations. It recently affiliated with the National Golf Course Owners Association and offers dual membership.

Director Allan Whaling and his staff travel extensively to courses across the country in search of new ideas and innovative solutions to common problems. They share them with members at regular round-table meetings.

OGCOA sponsors two statewide junior golf events annually for young men and women. The events are open to players who have not reached their 20th birthday on or before the end of August during the tournament year.

The OGCOA maintains a website: www.ohio-golf.com. It also offers a Workers Compensation Savings Group for club owners and discounts for member courses from over 90 major golf course suppliers. It sponsors a three-day general membership meeting and trade show in March for both members and nonmembers interested in joining up.

Ohio Women's Golf Association

4813 Rean Meadow Dr., Kettering • Phone: (937) 435-9311

The Ohio Women's Golf Association (OWGA) sponsors one tournament a year, a 36-stroke amateur championship for women residents of the state of Ohio. Players are handicapped according to flight. The championship is held on the first Monday and Tuesday after Labor Day every September and rotates among Ohio state park courses. More than 100 women take part each year. There is also a senior division for women 50 years and older. In 1997 the "Jane Climer Super Seniors" division will be inaugurated. Entry applications are available in June from the OWGA. They are also available at local public courses. Entry deadline is mid-August.

Women's Ohio State Golf Association

4221 High Point Dr., Medina • Phone: (330) 723-0598

The Women's Ohio State Golf Association (WOSGA) sponsors the Women's Ohio State Golf Invitational Championship. This event is open to members of private clubs that belong to WOSGA, but low-handicap (0–8) public links golfers are also invited to participate. The

OTHER

field is limited to 96 golfers. The Championship is held every July; the location rotates among courses throughout the state.

WOSGA recently inaugurated a state seniors' championship. Golfers over the age of 50 by June of the tournament year are eligible. There's also the Ohio State Juniors Championship held at the Marion Country Club each July. Any young woman under the age of 18 may participate.

TIDYMAN'S TIDBITS #26

Courses that look easy but ain't. Sneaky-Tough awards go to:

1) B Side at Seneca
2) Sweetbriar
3) Good Park

Indexes

ALPHABETICAL INDEX

INDEXES

INDEXES

GEOGRAPHICAL INDEX

Cleveland Guides & Gifts
More good books from Gray & Company ...

If you enjoyed this book, try one of these other great books about Cleveland ...

Golf Getaways from Cleveland / 50 easy weekend golf trips just a short drive away. Where to play, where to stay, and other things to do nearby. *John H. Tidyman* / $14.95 softcover

Cleveland Fishing Guide / Best public fishing spots in Northeast Ohio, what kind of fish you'll find, and how to catch them. Directory of fishing resources. *John Barbo* / $13.95 softcover

Bed & Breakfast Getaways from Cleveland / 80 charming small inns perfect for an easy weekend or evening away from home. *Doris Larson* / $13.95 softcover

Neil Zurcher's Favorite One Tank Trips (Book 1)
More of Neil Zurcher's One Tank Trips (Book 2)
One Tank Trips Road Food (Book 3)
Hundreds of unusual nearby getaway ideas in three books by Northeast Ohio's favorite TV travel reporter. / $13.95 softcover (each)

Ohio Oddities / This armchair guide describes the offbeat, way out, wacky, oddball, and otherwise curious roadside attractions of the Buckeye State. *Neil Zurcher* / $13.95 softcover

Dick Goddard's Weather Guide for Northeast Ohio / Seasonal facts, folklore, storm tips, and weather wit from Cleveland's top meteorologist. / $13.95 softcover

Dick Goddard's Almanac for Northeast Ohio / A fun mix of monthly weather data, fun facts, cartoons, and entertaining essays by Dick Goddard and friends. / $9.95 softcover

Cleveland Ethnic Eats / Discover hundreds of *authentic* ethnic restaurants and markets, and taste the flavors of the world without leaving town! *Laura Taxel* / $13.95 softcover

52 Romantic Outings in Greater Cleveland / Easy-to-follow "recipes" for romance, for a lunch hour, an evening, or a full day together. *Miriam Carey* / $13.95 softcover

365 Ways to Meet People in Cleveland / Friendship, romance, and networking ideas for singles, couples, and families. *Miriam Carey* / $8.95 softcover

Cleveland Family Fun / Great ideas for places to go and things to do with kids of all ages. Written by parents, for parents. *Jennifer Stoffel* / $13.95 softcover

Cleveland Cemeteries / Meet Cleveland's most interesting "permanent" residents in these 61 outdoor history parks. *Vicki Blum Vigil* / $13.95 softcover

Cleveland On Foot
Beyond Cleveland On Foot / Two books of self-guided walking tours: first, through Greater Cleveland's neighborhoods, suburbs, and metroparks; then, through parks and small towns of 7 neighboring counties. *Patience Cameron Hoskins* / $14.95 softcover

What's So Big About Cleveland, Ohio? / What does a well-traveled 10-year-old think about her first visit to Cleveland? "B-o-o-o-ring". Until, that is, she discovers a very special little secret ... *Sara Holbrook & Ennis McNulty* / $17.95 hardcover

Continued ...

Photo from *Cleveland: A Portrait of the City*, by Jonathan Wayne

Cleveland: A Portrait / 105 color photographs capture Greater Cleveland's landmarks and hidden details in all seasons. *Jonathan Wayne* / $35.00 hardcover *(Photo above is from this book.)*

Ghoulardi / The behind-the-scenes story of Cleveland's wildest TV legend. Rare photos, interviews, show transcripts, and Ghoulardi trivia. *Tom Feran & R. D. Heldenfels* / $17.95 softcover

The Ghoul Scrapbook / Rare photos, show transcripts, and video captures from "The Main Maniac" of Cleveland late-night TV. *Ron Sweed & Mike Olszewski* / $17.95 softcover

Feagler's Cleveland / The best from three decades of commentary by Cleveland's top columnist, Dick Feagler. Witty, insightful, opinionated, thoughtful. / $13.95 softcover

"Did You Read Feagler Today?" / The most talked about recent columns by Cleveland's most outspoken columnist. / $13.95 softcover

On Being Brown / Thoughtful essays and interviews exploring what it means to be a true fan of the Cleveland Browns. *Scott Huler* / $18.95 hardcover, $10.95 softcover

Omar! / Cleveland Indians star shortstop Omar Vizquel retells his life story on and off the field in this candid baseball memoir. Includes 41 color photos. *with Bob Dyer* / $24.95 hardcover

Indians on the Game / Quotations from favorite Cleveland ballplayers give an insider's look at the game of baseball. *Wayne Stewart* / $9.95 softcover

Barnaby and Me / Linn Sheldon, a Cleveland TV legend as "Barnaby", tells the fascinating story of his own extraordinary life. / $20.00 hardcover

The Great Indoors / The first decade of Eric Broder's hilarious weekly "Great Indoors" column. Reread favorites, or get caught up with the ongoing saga. / $13.95 softcover

Cleveland Sports Trivia Quiz / Test your knowledge with these 500 brain-teasing questions and answers on all kinds of Cleveland sports. *Tim Long* / $6.95 softcover

They Died Crawling and Other Tales
The Maniac in the Bushes
The Corpse in the Cellar / Three collections of gripping true tales about Cleveland crimes and disasters. Include spine-chilling photos. *John Stark Bellamy* / $13.95 softcover (each)

The Cleveland Orchestra Story / How a midwestern orchestra became a titan in the world of classical music. With 102 rare photographs. *Donald Rosenberg* / $40.00 hardcover

Cleveland TV Memories / Remember when TV was local? A nostalgic collection of 365 favorite local shows, hosts, jingles, bloopers, stunts, and more. *Feran & Heldenfels* / $6.95 softcover

Available at your local bookstore.

These books are stocked at Northeast Ohio bookstores, are available from most online book retailers, and can be ordered at any bookstore in the U.S.

Need help finding a retailer near you? Call us toll-free: **1-800-915-3609**.

Gray & Company, Publishers

1588 E. 40th St., Cleveland, OH 44103 / 216-431-2665
for more information at **www.grayco.com**